Strategic
Pokes

Strategic
Pokes
The Business Jalebi

Shombit Sengupta

www.sagepublications.com

Los Angeles • London • New Delhi • Singapore • Washington DC

First published in 2014 by

SAGE Response
B1/I-1 Mohan Cooperative Industrial Area
Mathura Road, New Delhi 110 044, India

SAGE Publications Inc
2455 Teller Road
Thousand Oaks, California 91320, USA

SAGE Publications Ltd
1 Oliver's Yard, 55 City Road
London EC1Y 1SP, United Kingdom

SAGE Publications Asia-Pacific Pte Ltd
3 Church Street
#10-04 Samsung Hub
Singapore 049483

Published by Vivek Mehra for SAGE Publications India Pvt Ltd, typeset in 11/14 ITC Century Book by RECTO Graphics, Delhi, and printed at Saurabh Printers Pvt Ltd, New Delhi.

Library of Congress Cataloging-in-Publication Data

Sengupta, Shombit.
  Strategic pokes : the business jalebi / Shombit Sengupta.
    pages cm.
  1. Management. 2. Strategic planning. I. Title.
  HD31.S3844   658.4'012—dc23   2013   2013030460

ISBN: 978-81-321-1163-4 (PB)

The SAGE Team: Sachin Sharma, Shreya Chakraborti, Rajib Chatterjee and Anju Saxena

For my parents,
Lila and Apurba Sengupta

Also my profuse thanks to Prahalada Rao,
Shikha Mukherjee, Hardik Mehta, Robin Raj,
Vibhu Hajela, and Renee Jhala.

Thank you for choosing a SAGE product! If you have any comment,
observation or feedback, I would like to personally hear from you.
Please write to me at <u>contactceo@sagepub.in</u>

—Vivek Mehra, Managing Director and CEO,
SAGE Publications India Pvt Ltd, New Delhi

Bulk Sales

SAGE India offers special discounts for purchase of books in bulk.
We also make available special imprints and excerpts from our
books on demand.

For orders and enquiries, write to us at

Marketing Department
SAGE Publications India Pvt Ltd
B1/I-1, Mohan Cooperative Industrial Area
Mathura Road, Post Bag 7
New Delhi 110044, India
E-mail us at <u>marketing@sagepub.in</u>

Get to know more about SAGE, be invited to SAGE events, get on
our mailing list. Write today to <u>marketing@sagepub.in</u>

This book is also available as an e-book.

Contents

Prologue

Incredible quality of customer understanding will take you to the summit of business. A customer's purchase ecosystem is totally unstructured. My perspective in this book is on how different customers prioritize their day's activities, including any purchase they make. He/she can buy a toothpaste in the morning, noon, or evening, there's no process driving him/her, unlike the discipline you have to follow in business, no matter from which industry you are, in providing him/her a product or service. In the world external to an enterprise, the social system gives you many unexpected pokes. Although this book follows that logic of the customer's unstructured ways, here's a structure that follows the idea of that poke.

Chapter 1
Biz in an Uneven Society
Enterprises Have to Define and Deal with India's Billion+ Pokes

Chapter 2
Visual Art for Business
Resources to Deal with Pokes

Chapter 3
Quality Customers Want
Quality Required to Poke with

Chapter 4
Human Ingenuity for Business
Poke to Bring Organizational Change

Chapter 5
Disruptive Platform in Business
Shock-of-the-poke for the New

Epilogue
Action Surpassmark
Pokes for Your To-Do List

Foreword

To describe Shombit Sengupta as a maverick would do great injustice to him in two ways. One, the description is judgmental for a mind as brilliantly unusual as Shombit's. And, two, it would sound too lazy and simplistic as if we had borrowed our vocabulary from the geniuses who write "breaking news" headlines on our TV screens for someone so alert and unconventional. Perhaps, a more suitable description for Shombit would be an original, one of a kind. But that is also so unoriginal and prosaic that it is probably better to stop searching for a label to fit him.

That is precisely why his writing, mind, and personality are so interesting and stimulating. As a professional, his incredible ability is to look at the picture from somewhere else, altogether.

Shombit's creative talent is drawn from an ideation process that effortlessly transcends business strategy, marketing, design, and technology with popular culture. That's the reason why his column in the *Sunday Express* Opinion page, which has always boasted a marquee cast of writers, is impossible to put in a box. It is not political, corporate, cultural, and philosophical. It is possibly all of these. That is why, almost like a precocious child learning to speak sometimes confects a vocabulary uniquely his own, Shombit invents his own gems.

My favorite is "This is a zap generation." And as you read along, you will discover eternally quotable favorites of your own.

This is Shombit's book, and I am flattered to bask in his halo, so let me not try and expend more ink talking about it. You must discover Shombit on your own. For that, you have to engage with his mind. And you will never be disappointed. Of course, his fame has spread far and wide, all over the world. But he has almost never repeated a successful formula again. Each of his successes has been sui generis. The only thing I can guarantee, therefore, is that if you do engage with him, you cannot go home without a delightful and, often, useful takeaway.

In one of our earlier conversations, I was wrestling with the challenge of positioning the *Indian Express* in this market crowded by heavyweights that all competed for the newspaper-of-record status. What should the *Express* be telling its readers that makes it different and worthy of their consideration? Shombit simply said, "Cut all crap."

"Just sell the essence, Shekhar, just sell the essence," he said making that brilliant gesture with his thumb rubbing his forefingers, starting at his nose, as he pretended to sniff hard at a fragrance that was almost reaching me across the coffee table. The essence of your paper, he said, is credibility and trust. Just stick to that and you will be smiling. No wonder the *Indian Express* has been smiling in the marketplace since and has been proudly giving Shombit a home in it every Sunday morning.

Over to the essence.

Shekhar Gupta
Editor-in-Chief
The Indian Express Limited
New Delhi

Preface

Variegated Ideas in Doses

Sitting on an office chair of nails? Ouch! Even *sadhubaba*s meditating on beds of nails do not take such strategic pokes. Like the *jalebi*'s connotation of being not so straight, you may have to take many indirect detours to come to your selling point in business. At the end of the day, the jalebi is sweet, just as business benefits should be for the seller and the buyer.

My first book in the *Jalebi* trilogy, *Jalebi Management*, was about how Indian industry can compete globally by creating seamless interconnections like a jalebi among different business aspects to enjoy delicious and profitable bites.

The opposite character of the jalebi, its unpredictable twists and turns that give it a dicey connotation is *Strategic Pokes: The Business Jalebi*. It tells you about why the poor with potential remain trapped and, more importantly, what can be done to facilitate their escape from poverty. Without underestimating the difficulties, it looks at how to unleash the immense potential and productivity of India's billion plus people. How aware is India about its own demands when it is schooled to mimic the West in framing its aspirations and expectations?

Strategic Pokes de-schools the conventional and inspires and entices the unorthodox. This smorgasbord of ideas covers business strategies in product development, manufacturing, marketing, and retailing and why soft skill training is essential for India's information technology (IT), retail, and manufacturing and service industries. The examples from the US, Europe, Japan, South Korea, and China give a macro perspective, a bird's eye view of global business and the worm's eye view of operating a business as well.

The jalebi's negative aspects reflect on Indian industry and business. The educated young are going after good marks and good degrees to get a good job with a good salary and play in the share market and become rich. On the other hand, the working class, earning ₹6,000 to ₹30,000, are far superior as entrepreneurs, but they are highly neglected. This class of society is the backbone and future of the country. Yet they get no recognition from society for being entrepreneurs, and no support from industry in terms of modern tools and machinery for work.

The manufacturing sector is the most critical for tomorrow's India, but it is mired in the jalebi's twirl. This second book in the *Jalebi* trilogy is about how to extricate Indian business from this negative part. Up to now, Indian brands have always got low recognition and sell at a lower price vis-à-vis global successful brands in India. In foreign countries Indian brands do not perform at all. *Strategic Pokes: The Business Jalebi* is about creatively disentangling Indian industry from a mired jalebi.

Poke doses: Today's generation is always short on time and patience. *Strategic Pokes* responds to readers with an unusual organization of the content, with ideas in poke doses. Divided into five major chapters, each chapter has several subsection subjects expressed in chunks. Each chunk is a poke dose. So use the book as a companion to snatch disruptive pokes on different business subjects when time is at a premium.

Introduction

The second book of Shombit Sengupta's trilogy, *Strategic Pokes—The Business Jalebi*, offers a very clear answer to the question of how to unleash the potential of Indian companies. Certainly not by imitating the West, but on the contrary by developing creative strategies based on Indian-specific character, skills, and entrepreneurial talent!

Strategy experts say that you can compete either on cost or on differentiation, but that if you try to do both at the same time, you might miss the target. To create value, one has to build on its own strengths and distinctive competences. Shombit Sengupta's book is the opposite of a dogmatic lesson. It is opening new avenues for sensing market opportunities and thinking about our companies' future.

The book is about entrepreneurship, innovation, creative solutions, and the art of building or renewing the brand image of the firm and its corporate identity. This process has to do with the CEO's vision of the firm, but also with the development of human capital: the skills, the commitment, the loyalty of the personnel sharing this vision, and the values of the company.

Shombit Sengupta gives us the example of French luxury brand Hermes which has launched a limited edition of Indian saris in 2011. The president of Hermes India said that it was part of the firm's "effort to connect to India's culture and to the tradition of elegance of Indian women." Hermes, which entered India only five years ago, has since moved a step further by opening a flagship store at Horniman Circle in Mumbai.

Hermes, which was founded in 1837, is even today an independent family business. Its competitive advantage is not based only on creativity in craftsmanship; the success of the company is based too on management rigor, long-term investment, entrepreneurial spirit, commitment to international development, and greater attention to brand and corporate identity building. What Hermes is undertaking in India could be done by an Indian firm in Europe: building on one's corporate culture, the skills of the employees, and strong Indian trading capabilities.

The Indian government is step-by-step opening the door of the Indian market to foreign companies, which is a good thing for the Indian economy and Indian customer. It does not mean that Indian companies should imitate foreign multinationals. To serve the needs of the new generation of Indian customers, Indian companies can forge their own route with unconventional business models and disruptive strategies.

And the door will be opened both ways. The lowering of trade barriers creates new growth opportunities not only for large Indian business groups and leading companies in the IT or pharma business, but also for small and medium Indian companies, which can build on their specific advantages to sell successfully on international markets.

Shombit Sengupta's new book will give you hundreds of fresh ideas on how to develop your business and stronger confidence in how to tap the potential of your organization to develop new strategies and business models.

Jean-Paul Larçon
Professor of International Business,
HEC Paris School of Management
(Senior Associate Dean for International
Development, HEC Paris)

1

Biz in an Uneven Society

Enterprises Have to Define and Deal with India's Billion+ Pokes

No two jalebis can ever be the same. When you are doing business in an uneven society, you are mired into jalebi-economics that is totally unpredictable. Enterprises in India, whether family-run or otherwise, have to consider their license-raj heritage in the light of today's digi-techno-savvy customers they sell to.

Catering to a highly demand-led market, Indian business houses have little initiative to transform. They need to inject substance that is perceptible in the demand-led market to stand out and encash premium earnings. In fact, we are still far from creating a new demand for the greenfield market. Nor is the disruptive impact of digital technology being exploited for driving business in global markets.

The very inventive developed Western countries, creator of breakthroughs and benefit-led solutions, have suffered recessionary trends since 2008. This economic crisis will continue to aggravate until they bring back the manufacturing and service bases they had shifted to the East. Japan started the trend of outstanding execution excellence in the digital paradigm in end-user interface, but the cost of living has become so exorbitant that they are in a tight economic situation. Korea, followed by China, is driving a similar digital superiority through price competitiveness.

Though, for how long they will drive their leadership in the West is questionable as developed countries, realizing that they are left with no other choice, are now beginning to bring manufacturing back into their countries. So everyone is caught in the global jalebi web. Only those who rid themselves of the jalebi's unstructured interweave and provide exceptionally beneficial end-user interface with competitive pricing will ride the global market.

As out-of-the-mould as a jalebi's form can be, in the business domain India lacks in finesse of craftsmanship, enduring quality, sense of aesthetics, and excellence of functionality. To match up to global benchmarks with a holistic, disciplined approach, we need to hone technical skill sets. Setting up A-schools (activation school for go-to-market excellence), such as B-schools, is one route. A-schools will produce outstanding skilled professional floor staff for manufacturing and customer interface for mass services to retail industry. Read on for poke doses in an uneven business environment. In India's uneven society, shouldn't enterprises drill capability into employees to drive customer behavior with stringent self-discipline to address global competitiveness?

How viable are family-name corporations?

A corporate name with aspirational evocation is timeless. New generation global business leaders such as Bill Gates,

Steve Jobs, John Chambers, and Philip Knight, among others, have figured that out in the last 40 years. Instead of anointing their companies with their own names, they chose to ignite end-customer imagination and coined Microsoft, Apple, Cisco (from San Francisco), and Nike (Greek goddess of victory). There's absolutely no problem if the founder with his family is the company's owner, but the business does not need to carry the family name. Except for creative businesses such as fashion or jewelry that cannot avoid the creator's authenticity, so designers such as Louis Vuitton, Jean-Paul Gaultier endorse their brands.

Ford

For a recognized inventor, giving his company his name can work, for example, Henry Ford. The inventor becomes the world's icon, his family name and brand become synonymous with an invention. Sometimes though, even such a corporate brand can carry a risk. When Henry Ford's picture was found in Adolf Hitler's desk, a crisis erupted. It proved that Ford was aligned to a Jew-killing regime.

Actually Ford's anti-Semitic outlook emerged earlier in 1920 when he wrote in his newspaper, *Dearborn Independent*: "If fans need to know the trouble with American baseball, they have it in 3 words—too much Jew." His book, *The International Jew, the World's Foremost Problem*, inspired young Nazis. On Hitler's birthday, Ford would gift him US$50,000. In the US, he managed his surname as his company's brand because he commanded immense power with superior business acumen and invention. But would not his hobnobbing with Hitler negatively impact a customer or employee of Ford, especially a Jewish one?

Renault

On the other hand, Louis Renault could not manage his aura in spite of having invented the automobile's drum brake, hydraulic shock absorbers, and compressed gas ignition. During German occupation of France in World War II, he supplied 34,232 vehicles to Hitler. Liberated France imprisoned him for betrayal. He died in Fresnes Prison near Paris awaiting trial. His family was denied his company; the French government nationalized Renault's management and has since avoided the mention of Louis Renault. Renault's grandchildren were ignored in the Renault Centenary Celebrations 1999.

L'Oreal

Another Frenchman with a Nazi association saved his family business and his daughter, Madame Liliane Bettencourt, became the world's richest woman. Her father Eugene Schueller invented hair-dye formula, *Aureale*, in 1907. He had actively supported the violent Fascist organization, *La Cagoule*, yet his company L'Oreal became successful for creating groundbreaking products that understood women's desire for beauty. This innovative power overshadows his reputation, taking L'Oreal to global heights. What portrait would L'Oreal carry today if it were named Schueller?

American companies

Breakthrough 19th-century inventor, Thomas Alva Edison, did not foist his name on his company, General Electric (GE). His many inventions inherently find meaning in "GE Imagination at Work," where history and contemporariness fit the company's authenticity like a glove. Another American, Sam Walton, founded Walton's 5 & 10 in March 1951. Changing it to Wal-Mart in 1962 to start his retail chain, he corporatized it to Walmart in 2008. Global image takes a different dimension when a company does not bear a family name.

Japanese companies

Japan's Toyoda family were loom specialists, but entering the customer-connect business of automobiles they changed to Toyota in 1939. Apart from Honda and Mitsui, most Japanese companies have gone global without using family names. In their urge to become international and universal, companies such as Mitsubishi, Hitachi, Toshiba, Nissan, Sony, Canon, and Shiseido have company names not related to the founder's name.

In footwear

Let us compare performance and global image using family and non-family names in the footwear industry. Bill Bowerman and Philip Knight founded Blue Ribbon Sports in 1964. In 1978, they had the guts to change their fully operational footwear business to Nike, taking it global without using their own names. Family-owned Bata, founded by Tomas Bata in Czechoslovakia in 1894, retails in 50 countries, having sold 14+ billion shoes. Yet Bata could not create the global culture that revolutionized the footwear business as Nike did.

Handicaps of family-named companies

The first handicap is security for family members. Next, if any family member gets discredited for external reasons, it reflects on the business. Others who carry the same surname can use it inappropriately, making the original business vulnerable. There's no telling if the founder's heirs will continue the business as passionately. When digital technology is bringing fortnightly advancements, it is difficult to change a perception about a company if it is associated with a person in the past. The founder's value system may not make it credible to contemporary times.

For an employee at any level, it connotes working for the owner. Unnecessary problems can be created by activists too who see nothing beyond the founder's wealth. Aspiration is another problem. "Knight just do it" may be construed as Philip Knight's diktat, but when Goddess Nike says "just do it," you are totally enamored.

Indian companies

Without passing judgment on Indian founder's family-named companies, my perspective here is to imagine their future in the global field. In the license-raj era, Indian companies, with heritage family names as the corporate brand, have induced trust as being bona fide for end-customers. Now that global competition is already here, end-customers have the choice to compare differences. Several Indian companies are already taking a beating in benchmarking against global biggies. Indian companies, being not yet associated with fundamental invention, are likely to continue to operate with available adopted technology.

India reflects more as a trading society rather than being inventive. This is the time to transform the family name to a more mystic brand before global companies overwhelm and entice end-customers away. A well-researched company name should evoke its product and service greater than its basic substance so that multiple market usage can never make it look tired or boring. It should never reflect the generic of a category.

The company's future is more prospective when it has an added value name with universal appeal rather than a family name. When combined with quality products and services, incredible communication, and point-of-purchase experience, it should give differentiated perspective and benefit to end users.

Fractured technical skill set

Go-to-market is easier for brands with names that add value to the product or service. You, of course, have to understand your customers' needs but, before that, technical skills will help monetize your big business idea.

Distinguish with technical skills

Idea generation, supported by advanced technical skill sets, creates distinction for a product or service. This provides tremendous returns to an industry and its future, and the company gets recognized, sustains, and acquires brand worth. Only when technical skill sets are highly efficient can idea generation and breakthrough differentiation happen.

Devoid of distinction, a product or service easily gets imitated or falls into the commodity zone. A simple example is the UK, renowned as the pioneer of the Industrial Revolution. From about 1980s, the UK lost its monopoly in the generation of ideas and technical skill sets when it chose to de-link from manufacturing industries and enter the financial engineering domain. Here the British concentrated on evolving further as a nerve center for finance. The country consequently suffered tremendous economic downturn with negligible industrial manufacturing to fall back upon.

In contrast, Germany retained its industrial strength and sprang back after its total destruction in World War II. Continuity in honing technical skill sets has allowed Germany to maintain high-quality manufacturing, even as it went through the 21st century's recessionary times with the rest of the world.

India lost its industrial base in political turmoil

Ancient and medieval India, China, and Japan had multifaceted technical skill sets in different technology streams. In subsequent political turmoil, many of these were lost. China and Japan have since then developed contemporary technical skill sets, whereas India is yet to manifest how to regain its legendary technical skill sets.

Let us go back to the 10th century. Exceptionally high technical and artistic skill sets were displayed at Khajuraho, among others. In every square foot of creating and replicating a theme, you can see meticulously crafted design, elaborately executed with passion and harmony. Where has that generation's incomparable gene of technical skills gone? Irrespective of their domain knowledge being mechanical, electronics, or electrical engineering, the majority of technical graduates today dream only of joining the IT industry. So industries such as automobiles and electronics are suffering a technical skills shortfall.

Japan bounced back

Since the nuclear implosion of World War II, Japan bounced back from the defeat and obliteration of its economy, landscape, and self-esteem after the War. Japan may not have generated exceptional fundamental new ideas in industrial products the way Western Europe or North America has done, but exceptional technical skill set makes Japan among the world's most recognized in terms of quality and user-friendly miniaturization of industrial products.

China's superb technical skill sets for production

China's superb technical skill sets for production have been unquestionably proven since the 6th-century Tang dynasty. China is currently the world's biggest manufacturing hub in spite of setbacks after its political switchover to establishing Communist ideology. When I visited a state-of-the-art factory for bringing an industrial design into production, I enquired why China had a reputation for bad quality.

The factory manager explained that to get faster return on investment (ROI), China maintains a four-pronged quality and price system for the same product. Everyone goes to China for cost reduction, so China delivers on price as per customer demand. He cited the example of iPod having "Made in

China" imprinted on the back. If quality deficiency was really there, neither Apple nor customers would have accepted it. Reverting to their superior technical skill set from ancient times to today's digital era, China is fast overcoming quality scarcity even for low-priced products.

Indian industry does not prize technical skill sets

Indian industry does not prize technical skill sets, so in turn, society does not glorify the techno-savvy professional. Actually, technical skill excellence is the foremost value that leads an enterprise to idea generation and capability for differentiation. I have seen when nonresident Indians (NRIs) who are techno-skilled professionals return to India, they abandon their superior technical skill set area to get into management and business. The system compels them to bypass their technical stream. So dismally, these techno-professionals do not rise in reputation nor do they become recognized leaders in their technical skill set.

Work involving technical skill set per se is not perceived to be high category jobs in India. The reason is the caste system. In India, the techno-savvy were traditionally artisans who were always from the lower castes. Unless they become business managers with financial targets, techno-professionals do not get high remuneration either. Society judges career advancement by the large number of people that a manager supervises over. The technical professional with fewer reportees and subordinates loses out here as well. Climbing the technical ladder brings him no reverence, only stagnation. So he willynilly acquires managerial skill. This is the way we kill our technical skill set; subsequently, idea generation and creating distinction are lost.

The combined mentality of the Indian employer, employee, and society is responsible for killing this technical skill set. I have heard of an IT engineer who was being paid significantly more to stay on in the technical stream but he pleaded to be shifted to a managerial role. He said his parents were about to arrange his marriage, but his marriageable value was crumbling as he was not managing too many people, which amounts to not being recognized as holding a top-notch position.

Most Indian IT companies neglect developing technical skills

This hampers their going up the value chain to develop products, productized services, or provide high-end technology consultancy to clients. Engineers in the IT business want to enter the business area or are sent for body shopping. Consequently, the Western world does not experience the technology prowess of young techno-savvy Indians, and India is considered only good for very basic IT coding for routine customer requirements. Indian IT engineers may have quickly got rich, but there will always remain a gap in their technical skill set competency and capability.

Footballer analogy

An industry's technical skill set is exactly like that of a football player. You cannot be a famous footballer or opinion leader of football if your score in 5,390 sq. m within 90 minutes is not very high. This is the skill set. People can handle football clubs or football merchandise, but without the skill set of football players on the ground, football tournaments cannot exist. Absorbing this football metaphor, India needs to have the passion to invest in and build technical skill sets in every domain.

Every industry has its specific technical skill set that needs to be sharpened and encouraged with high rewards, elevated designations, and better social recognition. It is about time Indian industries paid attention to developing their employees' technical skill set at every level so that individual "football players," in whatever position they are playing in, are able to excel at the company job.

Instead of migrating technical people to business areas, raising technical skill set excellence will lead the enterprise to superior idea generation and distinction. That will help to command the global market and be sustainable there.

Who is influencing your shopping?

Honing technical skills is important for the young generation that is about to enter the workplace. But much before that stage, youngsters are already swaying every purchase decision made in every home today.

In childhood, for those of us born before 1980, we had experienced our fathers, sometimes mothers, doing the family's shopping. Our parents were the influencers, buyers, and customers for all home requirement purchases. We accepted everything without questioning, be it food, clothing, or pocket money for fear of a reprimand. Showing good results in school was license to negotiate hard with our mother for extra pocket money. We even managed a small *Lakshmi bhandar* (terracotta piggy bank) in the hope that the Hindu goddess of wealth will always protect our savings.

Up to 1990, every father's pocket was sealed, but today, it has all become topsy-turvy. Lakshmi bhandar potters may have lost their business because the Zap generation does not save, they just love to spend.

Digital Zap: Born in 1986 or after; the span can go back to 1980 to all those below 30 years

Compromise generation: Born after 1965 up to 1980; 30–45 years

Retro generation: Born before 1965; 45+ years

Busy parents compensate guilt at denying quality time to children by becoming indulgent. The buyer, influencer, and customer are not the same person anymore. People of the age of 5 to 22 years make choices for all types of products for the family. From savings and frugal spending, the trend is to shop, shop, and shop to overcome situations such as boredom, depression, or excitement at festivities.

Different living conditions

Tracking the impact of 1991 economic reforms, we have found India's traditional joint family has broken into nine living structures, especially in urban areas:

(1 & 2) *Young working boy or working girl living independently when far from home.*
(3) *Nuclear family where only the husband works.*
(4) *Nuclear families where both husband and wife work*: They pander to children's demands. For

Double Income No Kids (DINKS), the spend is of a different kind, on travel or high-end gear.

(5)   *Married couple*

(6)   *Unmarried boy and girl living together:* Acceptance of this relationship is an inverted situation for Compromise and Retro parents. Those who cannot accept, pretend not to know anything.

(7)   *Joint family:* Inside which are self-indulging goodies such as expensive chocolates not shared outside the nuclear unit. According to the income or family size, there could be different refrigerators in a joint family. But cooking happens in one kitchen only.

(8)   *Neo-joint family:* All married brothers living under the same roof with separate kitchens adhere to the great SAM principle: *solpa adjust madi* meaning "just adjust a bit" in the South Indian language, Kannada. This reflects the accommodating and tolerant character of Indians. Family members meet periodically for lunch or dinner in the parents' kitchen.

In customer homes I visited in Ludhiana during a research for a real estate company, a neo-joint family member was elucidating the boons and dilemmas of family bonding. He wanted to buy a Mercedes, but his elder brother drove a Maruti. Socially the elder had to own a car of similar or higher status, so the younger brother felt constrained. Although his elder brother did not mind, what would his parents think, or society say? Not to disturb family hierarchy, he resorted to family PR to get everyone's green signal. He convinced his mother to speak to his elder brother, and then held his breath at what would transpire. Total relief overtook him when the elder brother announced the happy event of a Mercedes entering the family precincts.

(9)   *Retired couples*: In a research trip to Andhra Pradesh and Bihar, I was taken aback talking with retired couples living in B-class towns. Their vocabulary was "buck" driven, about exchange rate fluctuation with the dollar. The fact was that their children working in the IT sector in the US would send them monthly allowances with bonus on Mother's Day and Father's Day. These were not yesteryear's old-fashioned retired couples, bankers were lining up to woo them to get a bit of their "greenback" savings.

Business gains

Why is it necessary to know how people live? For customer-market business, it is among the most important opportunities to enlarge their offer. This multi-complexity arising from India's diverse culture, religion, and language does not exist anywhere else in the world. The family size cues product quantity or size, and clarifies different packet sizes to be handled for efficient supply chain management. It indicates the price band, sharpens the inventory, and gives an idea of what products to bundle as special offers.

If manufacturers know family living conditions, they can provide high proximity to different family-size buyers through retailers. A retailer's neighborhood catchment also rationalizes the store's space accordingly. Without addressing this fundamental business source, marketers often bring Western marketing culture, which undoubtedly is innovative, but it must adapt to Indian situations. Only localized application can bring success.

Influencer, buyer, and customer

Purchase behavior radically changes even 60 km from metros. A 35-year-old mother with ₹25,000 per month household income says her 11-year-old daughter decides the lipstick she should wear. Even the father of a 15-year-old bemoans his child's interference in his dressing. Clearly, Zappers are influencing every family purchase today. Sometimes they become buyers and customers too. Compromise and Retro buy as per commanding Zapper influence. For instance, parents depend on Zapper recommendation for styling, technology, and trend in buying a car although the father is the more frequent user.

In contrast, the older Zappers just below 30 years who enter the corporate world feel a kind of discord. They cannot influence decision-making as Compromise and Retro do not value their knowledge of society and trend. So they often switch off and flirt with jobs outside to enrich their resumes.

To win their loyalty, work passion, and reduce attrition industries need to drastically change their traditional outlook and contemporize corporate culture. Zap influence will more easily connect products and services to the external world because at the end of the day, Zappers are society's influencers.

Serpentine avenue of trends

India with 6.9 percent growth rate in 2009, second highest in the world after China's 8.9 percent, was exhibiting extraordinary miscellany. However unacceptable our unemployment rates are compared to developing countries, and gross domestic product (GDP) having come down to 5 percent for India and 7.8 percent for China in 2012, somehow growth is happening, especially for Zappers who comprise almost half our 1.2 billion population.

Happenings in the air

The gradual shift of economic power from West to East is becoming evident when you hear of growth, 1.6 percent, 1.5 percent, 1.4 percent, 0.8 percent, and minus 1 percent in the US, Germany, France, UK, and Japan, respectively. Developed nations are grappling with recession and steep unemployment. Something positive is in the air in India, you almost would not believe the entrepreneurship among the young working class. They are not waiting for the government to give them jobs.

In my nonstop research interactions with people from different social layers, I find their differences are becoming spectacular and really juicy. The mobile phone and motorbike have become most valuable in moneymaking for 20- to 30-year-olds in macro-rural areas (70–100 km from cities). Young professionals such as electricians, TV repairmen, plumbers, mechanics, and masons in macro-rurals are crisscrossing a large circumference to service their customers. They are working hard, earning more, and setting enjoyment as an agenda to be fulfilled.

Acquiring an experimental mindset, their caste prejudices are quickly dissolving. A low-caste barber's job is viewed as a lucrative business. The simple haircut for men has become serpentine. You can charge a different amount for full hair color, streaked look, gel finish, curly effect, especially in macro-rural "beauty parlors" for men and women. The post-cut massage has segregated costs too for only head or neck-shoulder-arms, or extended-to-back massage. Differentiation and packaging is clearly the name of the game.

Digital livelihood

The stolid *kirana* shop, those about 12 million mom-and-pop (sometimes pop and his sons or pop and his brothers) grocery stores dotting the length and breadth of India selling daily needs, is changing when handled by the young. Following digital trends, young *kiranawala*s are proving that virtual power provides better livelihood with services that were nonexistent before. In a macro-rural they can buy a computer at ₹18,000 to download all types of music and cinema, from Bollywood to Hollywood.

They even have a global collection of pornography. Their open sales talk with knowledge about different kinds of sex acts and exciting virtual fare will make porn-watching Karnataka legislators, caught in the act at the Assembly house, look innocent. For ₹30 the kiranawala will fill 2 GB space to the brim with porno, movies, and songs. If you only have ₹10, do not fret. That is worth one movie or three songs. Their customers are the local Zap generation below 30 years.

Most striking in this new trend is India's 360-degree shift from a hoarding society to a consumption-oriented one. When I asked how they store what they buy in the ₹2,500 Nokia mobile phone which supports 32 GB only, or even cheaper Chinese mobiles that support 16 GB space, they replied they delete everything after two-to-three-times usage. This delete action means throwing money into the dustbin.

This is a real change. It reminds me of a story a Bengali friend had narrated about how a license-raj banker, after his return from England post his higher education, was given a director's position, and he eulogized bank automation through computer usage. Employees felt happy when he said everybody could now discard their huge piles of paper. The director ended his speech, saying, "Before throwing away all old documents, keep a photocopy at least." From such a savings mentality to today's throw-away outlook, it has certainly been a long journey.

Lipstick is like wall paint

In 1996, when I modernized the Lakme brand, 25-to-30-year-old Indian women customers had said during research that Lakme is the only brand that understands Indian skin and beauty. They would attend research sessions wearing bright lipstick, but this generation has become old fashioned now. As per current research, today's urban young girls below 30 years loathe lipstick. They say it is sticky, overpainted, theatrical, vanishes when you eat, reminds them of mother's generation, and does not match their attire. They prefer lip gloss only. This new trend is exclusively Indian, not happening anywhere else in the world.

Just to give an idea, Western Europe generates US$6 billion per year from lipstick alone, whereas India sells only US$81 million lipsticks, of which 20 percent is lip gloss. This breakthrough trend does not mean Indian women are not alert about looking good. From the language of their body hugging and revealing apparel you can observe how conscious they are of a sexy representation. About 15–20 years ago when the prevalent sari covered everything, you could not gauge a girl's figure. Today her dressing style demarcates her body shape. Of course, there was an exception even 30 years ago. Westernized and fashionable women had begun revealing their contours by wearing hipster saris; blouses went up, sari petticoat went down. But that was a niche, urban phenomenon.

Gold is only yellow metal

Today's young urban women have created another disruption in beauty. Earlier, possessing gold jewelry was the biggest factor to show-off, to indicate status, wealth, and family tradition. This trend has disappeared among the young as per our research. They call it yellow metal, and find it monotonous, traditional, the older woman's fashion, and not for them. Just to satisfy parents at family gatherings and weddings, they wear it, but are uncomfortable.

Artificial jewelry is trendy for the urban young. It is far superior to mix-n-match with their dress. Enormous choice in artificial jewelry helps them change their mood, fantasize, and surprise everyone around them. If you look at their dressing drawer, you would be pleasantly surprised. They continuously buy artificial jewelry. In the West, I have heard women use artificial jewelry for the cost factor, but they still admire gold. Traditionally, through the ages, Indian women have also adorned themselves with fabulous glass and lac bangles and other affordable accessories such as the Punjabi *parandi*, the ribbon, or else flowers.

Quantity versus economy

This young generation is not only changing trends but changing usage patterns too. Their consumption, in terms of both quantity and variety, of face and body lotion or cream is very high compared to their mothers. A pot of cream the mother uses for three months, the daughter will finish in a fortnight. They rationalized this during our research by saying they are working girls exposed to pollution outside, so they have to protect their skin's smoothness. The manufacturer, of course, is joyous as the per capita growth is unlimited in future.

In the West, organized industry's business model has been collective trend forecast. Business houses in India are yet to develop this practice. Like a serpentine avenue when the snake glides in twists and turns in fast motion, many things are happening in different societal layers. If as a manufacturer you are not curious, you do not look out for that latent trend, you may lose out.

Global consumerism trauma

Compromise (30 to 45 years) and Retro (above 45) generations continue to drive 20th century culture in the 21st century through business decisions that they take. That switches off the below 30 Digital Zap generation. Nor do last century's advertisement style and many brands connect to them.

Zappers skeptical of ads

In fact Zappers just do not like advertisements, they like symbolic provocation. Using new media does not make much sense if the content is not relevant to them. Repetition with the same advertising message based on the classic advertising architecture irritates them. They would rather see one theme with changing messages that provoke.

Unchanged messages lack contemporariness

The century gap is a real, tremendous, and visible phenomenon. But it seems to have totally passed certain mass daily usage global brands by, such as Heinz Ketchup, Coca-Cola, Cadbury's, Mr Clean, Colgate, Evian, and Laughing Cow, among others. These companies may have very good quarter-to-quarter results, but do they keep up with the breakthrough trends the 21st century's Digital Zap is dazzling us with? The brands can argue that they are sustaining some old value, but do the disruptive Digital Zappers connect to them? Digital Zap may require these products by necessity, but their aspirational attachment to these products is questionable.

Cherishing tradition is a different matter altogether and is always good. There are certain brands and products such as olive oil, whiskey, camembert cheese, or preserves that have better value when they are steeped in deep-rooted, traditional authenticity. People will always be nostalgic for gourmet or connoisseur items; I am not questioning that at all.

Eight socio-behavioral clusters

Historically, social stratification from feudal agrarian to socio-economic classification followed an evolutionary process. In our consulting practice, we have now identified that socio-behavioral clusters apply today as they defy all predictable segmentation parameters. We have created a revolutionary way of researching to measure people's attitudes, behavior, motivation, and aspiration in the 21st century. In a master research methodology, we have studied socio-behavioral phenomenon every year for the last 10 years and have found that they are common to the three generations.

The eight behavioral clusters with their characteristics in parenthesis are given below:

(1) Low key (simple living with quality life)

(2) Value seeker (gets involved only when a worthwhile payoff is seen)
(3) Sober (goes in for calm efficiency)
(4) Flamboyant (exhibitionist to grab attention)
(5) Critical (perfectionist, not easy to satisfy)
(6) Novelty seeker (curious for the new)
(7) Techy (goes for the digital mode of life)
(8) Gizmo lover (likes gadgets and goes for differentiation)

These eight behavioral clusters exist in all the three generational groups. Digital Zappers supremely influence everything, so connecting to them is critical for the future. The Compromise generation tries hard to follow Zappers to be trendy and "with it," but do not quite get there as they are a bit "stuffy." They also feel compelled to satisfy their seniors, so they are truly compromising in their attitude.

The Retro generation is generally quite "stiff." Their complaint is that their grandchildren have lost the human touch, they are always equipped with earphones, in front of computers, and do not even talk on the mobile phone, choosing just to send text messages. The open-minded among the Retro would love to co-opt some influence of the Digital Zap, but this number is very low. You may not find many Retros in the flamboyant, gizmo lover, and techy socio-behavioral clusters.

Is income still a factor for customer segmentation?

For any business, if you follow the traditional socioeconomic stratification of customers, you will not go far today. That is because the eight socio-behavioral clusters are prevalent across all age groups and generations, all income groups, and across all countries and cultural systems. Income is no longer a key factor for purchase of value added products.

The world is moving toward a situation where, at any price point, there has to be a combined surge of cost, quality, and aspiration in the selling proposition. Today in the West, even low-cost products have trendy aspects. Expensive luxury brands that low-income groups cannot afford should not be advertised in mass areas. In fact, when luxury brands advertise like mass products, they lose their coveted worth.

Every brand cannot attract every socio-behavioral cluster. For a brand to address all eight socio-behavioral clusters, it requires a huge magnifying glass. It has to very clearly unearth the customer behavioral clusters and drive strategic planning accordingly. There will be immense pressure from low-cost, trendy brands that are affordable for everybody. Zara, for example, would connect to the critical, flamboyant, novelty seeker, techy, and gizmo lovers. On the other hand, Nivea and Nokia would address the sober, low key, and value-seeker clusters.

But the strategy that Swatch watch has created in the West has been so brilliant that it enviably touches all behavioral clusters. I am sure Swatch will follow the same path in developing countries too.

Bulldozing per capita consumption

In developed countries, the consuming base is small, so marketers bulldoze customers to increase their per capita consumption. In the food industry, for example, just look at how many types of product benefits are being offered, from functional food to low salt, low fat, organic, no salt added, value to luxury food, and sugar free, among many others. Does this not confuse the customer?

It is amazing that technology's rapid changes have not sparkled creative ideation in the same measure. Digitalization is commoditizing every aspect of business. If you take flat television sets, all the brands look more or less the same; so do DVD players and microwave ovens. These industries are suffering from a lack of distinction also because the manufacturer ideation process of Compromise and Retro is not connected to Zapper mentality.

Nightmare of how to penetrate

The overriding phenomenon in developing countries is how to achieve penetration for a product or service. As population is huge in these countries but infrastructure readiness is generally poor, the nightmare is how to reach the billions in remote places. Another challenge is understanding and catering to the vast cultural differences of customers at large.

An experiential product or service study that delves into the psycho-socio-behavioral context gives the socio-behavioral dimension. In India, we have seen that the joint family structure has more or less been broken now into nine different living conditions to cope with mobility while pursuing careers. Family compositions determine multiple things that are very significant for business growth.

I have often seen researchers go to market for validation with structured preparation. So before customers talk, they already establish what they want to find. This is not right. With a global mind frame we need to achieve local proximity to deliver extra benefit. Research cannot be like the wheat pasta dough that you can put in a machine to get a variety of different shapes of pasta or noodles as per your expectation.

Trauma in activation

The buzz: "India has high growth potential." Question: How to unleash it? Answer: It is not only looking at market penetration issues. We need large numbers of skilled working-class people who are sensitive craftsman, almost like connoisseurs. We need to hone the country's technical skill sets.

Frontline, hands-on workers are the real delivery persons in manufacturing or service industries. They are the artillery for activation. I can never think of any strategy for my clients if I cannot visualize its effect in activation. From my practical working and learning in the field I can confidently say that every business in India is poised to achieve 40 percent additional growth right away if frontline activation is effective. These people need to be trained in discipline, ownership, passion at work, craftsmanship, and communication skills as appropriate to the industry they are working in.

A personal aside

Here is what passion in one's work can achieve. Gourango Kaku (uncle), a neighbor in the refugee colony I spent my childhood in, was a carpenter in the British railway workshop nearby. The British work culture had three skill classifications: high-skilled, medium-skilled, and low-skilled workers. Using his high carpentry skills he made me a hand-push toy that worked on the mechanical principles of the steam railway wheel movement. He crafted a wheel system on two joints, one to hold the long handle to the wheel and the other a moving mechanism in another part of the hand. This was my most valuable plaything, and more ingenious in functioning than the sophisticated toys my parents had no means to buy.

My grandmother told me an inspiring story of my great grandfather who had basic education and became an eminent activation professional. He had literally absconded from our zamindar family home in Dhaka to build his career in Burma in early 20th century. My great grandfather returned home with fame and the prestigious title of "Rai Saheb" awarded by the British Crown for his excellent activation craftsmanship. He had helped the British army make and execute the master plan of the strategic Stilwell (Burma) Road. This proved invaluable for sending supplies to beleaguered China to resist Japanese invasion during World War II.

By coincidence, over 50 years later, I too adventured into Paris at the age 19 with just US$8 to spend and without knowing a soul in France. In my profession, I have always prioritized activation as the most vital aspect to step into the future.

Activation school

Corporate houses employ engineers-management graduates, so everyone aspires for a Master of Business Administration (MBA) degree. Hundreds of B-schools, copying Western formulae, have sprung up, but the industry's big pain area is lack of skilled frontline business-activation professionals. No postgraduate course trains practically for activation in India's specific market conditions, nor is there any benchmark of this competence.

India's dire need is for A-schools (A = Activation). In a flourishing liberalized economy, businesses in private, public, or multinational companies (MNCs) sectors require huge number of activation professionals to interface with the market and customers. Three prominent areas: basic human resources (HR), marketing-sales, and retail face a dearth in quality and number of such professionals.

Activation in basic HR

The last-mile connect to the end-customer always lies with the floor staff that put the product together. Delivery from an engineering manufacturing factory could have scratches on the product or defects in the production assembly line convoy in spite of the factory being state of the art. But the staff remains untrained in customer expectation from that product.

HR professionals need to create passion for their industry among shop floor employees. They may have imparted training on end-customer sensitivity, shop floor discipline, high-level hygiene and civic sense, and stringent adherence to corporate processes, values, vision, and goals, but post the training how much of the content has been absorbed or internalized by the floor staff has to be verified. Rushing headlong into implementation before the content has been absorbed is ineffective.

Activation in marketing–sales

In India, 70 to 80 percent of the market has not been scanned by market-research companies so such market data is not available. The wholesaler decides on the brands and sells them to small traditional retail outlets. Large companies that believe in rural penetration apply no science to exploit this potential. Only theoretical boardroom marketing cannot run businesses. Marketing activation staff has to reach unscanned markets to understand that these areas are not homogenous.

Business transactions are cost-centric and pragmatic, cultural nuances are high and emotive factors not expressed. There are plenty of infrastructure problems and the brand's visibility, proximity, and availability, vital at the point of purchase, must be physically ascertained and corrected. Sophisticated engineers-management graduates are averse to this type of hands-on action. Activation graduates with practical marketing–sales training are required.

Activation at the point of purchase

Everything starts from the shopper's focus. Front-end sales persons must be trained to befriend shoppers, understand their body language, and customize to increase their purchase decision. On the other hand, the back-end personnel should emphasize on stringent sourcing and quality control in manufacturing and supply chain to deliver and sustain the value of the merchandise.

Dealing with defects

Often sales people at sophisticated fashion retails do not have the skill to address high, medium, or low-value customers, and get intimidated by them. If the merchandise price is not written, they do not know what the price is.

If you are drooling over a high-tech futuristic car, the showroom salesman will rarely have the knowledge or vocabulary to explain its tech functions. Servicing such a car can be a nightmare; your perfectly functioning music speaker may not work after the garage run.

The mobile-phone market is booming, but do frontline sales people keep up with the rapidly changing next version technology? So service after sales can be disastrous, obliging you to buy a new handset as they cannot estimate the time required to repair your old one.

White and brown goods very often turn out defective after home delivery. Worse still, service inferiority makes you question why you took on this unnecessary tension of purchase.

How many times have insurance or banking telemarketing persons disturbed you, either changing your gender or calling you by another name? Without basic activation training, these companies are merely negating their goodwill with potential customers.

Defects come from untrained frontline people. Billion-peopled India needs thousands of high-caliber, two-year residential A-schools. Simple graduates can be trained to become high-skilled activation professionals for interacting with the market's unpredictability.

A-schools can increase the skill of the masses. Training this level of people will make our country's base very solid as they can contribute tremendously to high, sustaining GDP growth.

Digi not physi?

Financial cut-and-paste executed with sophisticated financial cutlery made the share market in developed countries a virtual valuation casino. The West threw out manufacturing industries and suffered economic recession as the backlash. In this scenario, India has to find ways of unleashing the capacity of her young people to improvise and discipline this capacity and then put it to work.

The digi-mania

Everything changed with advances in digital technology in the last 20 years. Nobody assessed what danger could lurk behind it for fulfilling basic human needs in future, somewhat like suddenly discovering the Y2K bug at the turn of the millennium. Nobody bothered to tread the serpentine avenue of trends.

This virtual digi-viagra is marvelous for eye and mind enjoyment anytime, anywhere. It can reduce distances, overload information in your pocket, allow you to acquire huge knowledge with little effort, give you innumerable social network addresses to connect to people, but you cannot smell any of them. The titillating digital circus cannot gratify human physical need and desire. Just imagine, digi-world has no solution for your empty stomach, roof over your head, garments, medical necessities, transportation, and sex. These are irreplaceable fundamental physical requirements. I'm reminded of scientist Albert Einstein's words, "I fear the day when the technology overlaps with our humanity. The world will only have a generation of idiots."

Low-cost, high-efficient, digitally engineered machines for India's poor

Overcoming tremendous day-to-day life hardships are those in the ₹3,000–10,000 per month income bracket within the 600 million population range. These people are surprisingly quick to respond to entrepreneurial challenges. They want to earn more by working harder. But they desperately need mech + digi help. A variety of more productive livelihood generation tools and machines can reduce unnecessary physical sweat and speed up efficiency. To enhance living quality while working in their current professions, they could certainly use easy, affordable, and individual transportation.

Unfortunately there is no research, and subsequently scant industrialization of specific mech + digi low-cost, high-efficient, digitally engineered machines that such working class professionals require. Only when this working class flourishes, can India Vision 2020 to become a developed country be realized.

Raison d'être for Western society's digital space

Digi-space had a different purpose for the West, that of making life for their society always easy. Their invention platform invariably looked for better ways to reduce effort while increasing people's comfort. Colonization served the purpose of getting new sources for inputs to ensure predictability of everyday need supplies. Exoticism from foreign shores made colonizers experience a life that is better than what they already had.

More importantly, they acquired slaves for manual labor to reduce their own physical exertion. Industrialization was the elemental drive which then led from mechanical to electronic to digital inventions. This helped create the mass market where low-income, US$1,200–1,500 per month, earners could pay for and enjoy life's everyday essentials of food, housing, clothing, travel, and health care.

The spin-off from their slavery mindset was to displace manufacturing units so that people from other countries can undertake the physical part of work. They wanted to be rid of pollution and trade-union problems, enjoy unpolluted air, and not suffer bodily hard work. What was the result? All basic jobs were packed off to poor and developing countries.

Even digital junk gets deported as hardware scrap; the favorite dustbin of developed countries being India, China, and some African countries. The US is world leader in e-waste, annually rubbishing three million tons, while Europe discards 100 million phones every year. Although they have understood that virtual dreams cannot fulfill life's essentials, digital technology has enabled them to win the slavery game from afar. Today it is called globalization and outsourcing.

Dissonance of Western digi with India's poor people requirement

Satisfying the outsourcing needs of developed countries through digital technology opens up merely a few jobs, pubs, and cafes; chic foreign cars and motorbikes become visible. If India concentrates only on global service business, the ₹3,000–10,000 per month income band will never see a better life. There is a sub-₹3,000 per month class below them too. In sophisticated coffee-table discussion or by government, they are designated below poverty line (BPL).

The traditional rich and nouveau riche talk glibly in TV interviews about their donations to charities and NGOs. They quote progress of the poor by throwing big-size statistics of mobile phone and TV-set penetration in rural areas. But can virtual entertainment or information solve the livelihood and basic needs of poor people?

Can digital technology shape Indian rubbish?

Let us not talk only of Western e-waste affecting India's poor. The rubbish that society discards here is collected and sorted by poor people who display high entrepreneurship even with such ad hoc means of livelihood. We have irregular consumption and trashing patterns, with almost no mechanical or modernization of waste collection and disposal systems. Most developed countries have five to six types of organized dustbins. The public follow the ritual of throwing different kinds of waste into designated bins such as paper, metal, and plastic, among others. For industrial waste disposal there is a controlled procedure. Littering is a national Indian pastime of rich and poor alike. Is digital-technology intervention to change this paradigm possible? Resourceful BPLers, totally neglected and living in unhygienic surroundings, however, perform a well-processed sorting job to earn a few rupees so that society at large can enjoy better hygiene.

Global disaster

Natural digi-mutation is creating version after version to rationalize its worldly existence. Such restless virtual developments are signs pointing to another imminent global disaster such as financial engineering that led to global recession. Every industry's marketing purpose may require some trendy digi-imagery to connect to youth. But can digi, so easily drumming up complex world poverty statistics, get basic enough to quell hunger pangs? We must, always, value the physical aspect.

You do not need any effort to see Leonardo da Vinci's Mona Lisa painting as your mobile phone can download it. Yet last year nine million people from different countries of the world visited Mona Lisa in the Louvre Museum, Paris.

Digital engineering's unquestionable positives are here to stay. Its inventors sitting somewhere in the West will never think of how to apply its benefits to rid India of poverty. It is time for Indian digi-designers and industries to start catering to the physical professional requirements of ₹3,000–10,000 per month earners who need low-cost, high-efficiency, and digitally engineered machines.

Let us achieve the developed country tag by 2020. Otherwise poor people will continue to sort and clean rich people's consumption leftovers in the dustbin as that grows into more and more of a mountain.

Demand-led market is a disease

Business across the world operates in the paradigm of either catering to demand or leading the market with value. A demand-led market is akin to trading, supplying to fill an order. But crafting value to lead the market requires ample use of brain ware. For the value-led market you need both physi + digi.

Easy to cater to the demand-led market

When huge market demand exists for a product or service, it would mean the requirement is basic and useful. This market flourishes with high user demand, and it is the easiest situation for business houses to deal with. There is 100 percent certainty of big revenue generation with sizable investment in infrastructure and standard, average people. The only problem here is how to improve the bottom line and sustain it because competition is rife. There is always the temptation to increase volume, irrespective of the quality of the product, service, or people behind it.

Because every competitor can deliver more or less similarly in demand-led markets, and the hunger for increased business is so high, there is negligible scope to create differentiation. Willy-nilly, this situation compels an enterprise to reduce profitability year after year. The demand-led market is extremely vulnerable as anybody with money, infrastructure, people, and good trading skills can enter it. In this space, you do not have to worry about competency, skill set, distinction, quality standard, or outstanding collective capability. You can also forget about high profit after tax. You are generating revenue on big volume alone.

Moneymaking opportunity in the value-led market

Conversely, in the value-led market, you can actually get sizable margins. Take the simple banana that has high demand in world markets. How can you create a distinction with a banana?

A talented chef can take two ripe bananas that cost 50 cents, dramatically change their value by using crème, chocolate sauce, nuts for another dollar, and then with appetizing food styling he can make and sell a banana desert for US$15 in his restaurant. A four-star restaurant can even sell it at US$50. Doing that, the basic banana has been transformed to enter the value-led market.

Sophisticated developed countries have displayed tremendous flair in creating the value-led market. Value here does not always mean bringing in fundamental invention. It requires guts and willingness to learn from others' best practices. Shared passion between the leader and team is essential for market study, forward planning, stringent execution and go-to-market with excellence of execution.

My favorite value-led market example

My favorite value-led market example is the innovative success of Swatch. If we look back at the Swatch adventure under cofounder Nicholas Hayek, who unfortunately expired in 2010, it happened when digital watches from Japan threatened the Swiss-watch industry in the 1970s. Swiss entry-level watches with manual craftsmanship were losing market share. Swatch not only innovated through high technology, but reduced parts in the watch from over 91 to 51, and with aggressive marketing, daring designs, and unfailing quality made Swatch into a fashion category beyond timekeeping. Swatch means both Swiss watch and second watch. This low priced US$30 "change your dress, change your Swatch" was cheeky and good fun; girls even wore it as ponytail bands. Swatch proved that you can drive aspirational value even with low pricing.

The company has become so successful since its 1983 launch that Swatch has acquired some of the world's most sophisticated watch brands, including Breguet, Blancpain, Jaquet Droz, Glashütte Original, Léon Hatot, Omega, Tiffany & Co., Rado, Longines, Union Glashütte, Tissot, Calvin Klein, Certina, Mido, Pierre Balmain, Hamilton, Flik Flak, and Endura. All-time trendy Swatch is the first individual brand in the watch category to bring out a business model through a retail chain.

Walking along New York's Times Square on some work five years ago, I suddenly crossed a very funky painting gallery. Intrigued, I walked in and discovered the Swatch retail. Just imagine the guts of the low-cost watch Swatch team; spending a veritable bomb per square feet money to hypnotize passersby with fascinating art. Inside there were very few watches interspersed with cult images and trendy gear. When an enterprise ideates like that in the demand-led watch market, it gives you the learning of how to radically transfer from demand–supply to lead with value and win customers and profit.

How to fill a market gap

By 1970s, fast-food outlets, McDonald's, KFC, and Pizza Hut, among others, had established their brands. But a gap existed in fast-food chains. They somehow made you feel pressurized: eat quickly and leave so somebody else can occupy your chair. This is the way their revenues went up. There were those who looked at this gap of how to create fast-food chains that would give people a relaxed ambience so they can linger as long as they want.

Latin societies such as Italy and France have a cafe culture where with a glass of beer or coffee, you sit in individually owned cafes for hours enjoying street fun such as couples romancing. Europeans have never imagined that their cafe heritage can be made into a global chain. But three Americans, by founding Starbucks, have successfully commercialized this space, given it value, and transported the concept to

55 countries. This is the value-led market approach with lateral ideation; Starbucks easily created a new benchmark without copying other fast-food chains. Americans undoubtedly have incredible scaling capability, perhaps because of their heritage of being a large geography and having the largest single-language speaking population in Western society.

India performed well in fulfilling demand

In the 20 years since economic liberalization, India has responded extremely well to the demand-led market in most industries and amassed critical mass. It sounds very good that we have big size, billion dollar Indian companies with a global footprint, but while benchmarking with global competitors, we have a great deal of catching up to do. In a demand-led situation, Indian companies can certainly grow in revenue. But they will be under huge profit pressure in the coming years unless they can change gear to move in the direction of the value-led market.

The more companies drive toward value, attrition will come down as people will work with pride to grow the company they want to be a part of. When people work with passion, quality sensitivity becomes exceptional, and they can create distinct, perceptible quality in products or services. Such a company's brand gets magnified when it becomes a topic of conversation in society, which automatically would lead to increased profitability, or even becoming the industry benchmark.

India's vision in the next 20 years should be to climb up the value-led market. It requires only guts and brain ware to get there.

US$200 billion virgin market of branded food

Want to see pure exhibitionist tendencies in a value-led market? Here it is: Once upon a time a hundred years ago, the wealthy developed a craze to cross the Atlantic in the lap of luxury. Boarding RMS Titanic, the world's first most luxurious, avant-garde, first-class ocean liner sailing from Britain's Southampton to New York, they were not going on a cruise, but just displaying affluence.

Creating the Titanic fissure term

Publicized as invincible against natural calamities and piloting mistakes, Titanic was tom-tommed as unsinkable. Yet the way crewmembers misused their every moment operating discipline (EMOD) took passengers to a watery grave. If vigilance with binoculars was delayed due to not finding them easily, it seemed like rat-like negligence in the ship's elephantine preparations.

Overconfidence was so high that for 2,229 passengers just 20 lifeboats were provided, which saved 710 lives only when suddenly mid-Atlantic, mid-April 1912, Titanic hit an iceberg. As per the ship's size and much touted fantastic engineering, it was inconceivable that an iceberg hit could sink it. In sum, being high-tech, gigantic, accident-proof, pilot-mistake-proof, and offering overwhelming experience all went for a toss for a lack of 360-degree foresight, poor contingency planning, and cocksure arrogance. This is the Titanic fissure.

Guard against the Titanic fissure

Before creating a value-led market, let us be alert that your business can suffer a Titanic fissure too at any time, irrespective of size. Unless you are watchful, any size of hole in your enterprise ship can destabilize it. Growth mantra in business can have Titanic fissure symptoms resulting in inevitable disaster. Business requires a boundary fence, beyond which lurk these Titanic fissures.

In emerging countries, jumping this fence for growth has become a religion. As demand is high, corporate culture fulfills it with vanilla supply. This syndrome of delivering on demand without caring about delivering real distinction has seen company bottom lines plummet to 1–3 percent when global trend in the same industry is 8–10 percent. What is the point of making a billion dollars in revenue but only minuscule profits? Even a bank-fixed deposit gives you 9.25 percent; when you go for high-risk venture capital investment you can achieve up to 25 percent or even more.

To win in business, provide extra benefit visibly

Indian companies need to concentrate on the inner meaning of perceptible distinction. If two soup-makers vary their soup in color, advertising story, or packaging design, is there a difference beyond the pictorial? If customers perceive no functional benefit, tongue enjoyment, and health benefit among the competing soups, they are all similar.

Real differentiation comes when extra benefit is provided to improve customer's quality of life. With the proliferation of global brands in India today, customers understand this difference. So brands offering no perceptible distinction cannot charge a premium. With all brands in a category aligned to the basic, the result can only be depressing profitability for the companies.

Let us take the food category

The critical area to satisfy is uplifting what is perceptible to customers. Tongue enjoyment, functional health benefit, and perceived distinction are reasons for customers to readily pay premium for branded food. Has the food industry debated upon or tried to understand the score or deeper meaning of the customer's organoleptic sensation? They merely seem to highlight supply chain issues, downscaling production or input cost, contracting temporary labor to shrink cost, and creating entertaining Bollywood-style advertising.

Look at how young Indians are changing their food habit with American burgers, pizzas, and fried chicken. You may say global companies are attracting them with big ad spends. But look objectively at their business model; with less than 10 varieties they are delivering a totally different taste to Indian food. It is not the fast-food chain ambience people are returning to, they are being offered a haunting taste which is stomach filling and compelling. Food, after all, is about memory; you remember taste more than any other sensory experience.

The French love food

With 63 million people, France's food market is worth €200 billion. Branded food accounts for 30 percent; 50 percent is driven by the retail industry's private labels while 20 percent comprises unbranded categories. The dominance of private labels reveals how brand companies conceitedly stopped distinguishing product delivery since 1980s. They figured brand awareness and advertising would allow them to charge premium. But private labels challenged with equivalent quality and up to 30 percent lower price. So brands became vulnerable and private labels picked up market share.

Indians love food too

At least 200 million people in India can afford branded food, which can translate to a US$200 billion market tomorrow compared to approximately US$15 billion today. But lack of vision and execution capacity of India's food industry has blocked profitable market growth.

Companies need to invest to understand the customer's social environment and culture, from enjoyment delivered to taste buds to health benefit. Only from research can a platform emerge for a food brand that customers will devour. Marketing can sell the product but cannot design the product proposition of customer organoleptics-driven food. Nor can research and development (R&D) professionals technically develop it. An analysis of customer organoleptics using the world's finest industrial chefs who have total knowledge about the customer's taste buds can define and deliver the platform.

Food is a very sensitive category

Up to now, people in India cooked their food or enjoyed it in restaurants, taking responsibility for their health. But a food company's fundamental duty is to take total responsibility of the customer, from indulging taste to digestion to providing health benefit. A food manufacturer need not develop a diverse product portfolio or jump from one category to another with no core relationship among products. As India's food market is vast, saturation will take place only after 15–20 years.

So food companies have immense possibility to grow within a predetermined boundary as per their know-how competence.

A food company should design a limited number of categories that kowtow to the customer's taste preference up to digestion and health benefit, and not get blinkered by the manufacturing backend. The more specialized the company is, the better its chances of making multibillion dollar revenue and double-digit profit.

A viable retail model draws in shoppers

To continue with the food business, organized grocery retails in India are not driven by traditional social and shopping habits. Is that why, in spite of hypermarkets and supermarkets erupting in urban areas, you can forget about quick ROI? High rentals and heavy discounting culture cannot run a grocery retail in metros without distinctive, unparalleled merchandise.

What shoppers want

As shoppers, what do we love in organized grocery retails? Good ambience, hygienic packaging and displays, AC-cooling, self-help, and everything under one roof. Offers are galore and you get the right bill. But what we hate are long billing counter queues, no bargaining, no credit, inconsistency of merchandise availability, especially when you expect that corn you buy to be of the same size and color every time. Also, you are forced to buy more as groceries are prepacked.

Compare that with shopping at your local kirana (the so-called "mom and pop") store. The shopkeeper knows you, your household members, and makes home deliveries on a phone call. Greeting you with a smile, he gives you credit and you can bargain. When the exact merchandise you need is not available, his advice on where to find it is genuine, or he offers a substitute with his assurance. You choose any small amount you want to buy, he will even oblige with a single piece from an offer pack.

Of course there is downside too. The loose merchandise is open to the elements, so hygiene is doubtful. Small stores do not stock dairy and fresh vegetables and you have to wait for the retailer to serve you.

Three never-do things

If you are an organized retailer, your store will never be successful if you do three things: imitate successful Western model without localization, hire fast-moving consumer goods (FMCG) professionals to run the business (of course exceptions are always there), and not make the shop indispensible to shoppers. Here are the reasons why:

(1) *FMCG professionals are not cut out to run the organized retail's catchment, multi-category sourcing, and footfall to conversion*: FMCG professionals neither have the merchant's mentality, nor the capacity

to manage ultra-diverse product categories. That is because their expertise is different. It is on raw materials' purchase, how to innovate new product lines, sales and marketing of focused product segments and line extensions, and sometimes the manufacturing process, if it is not outsourced.

Taking management graduates is a big mistake too; they dream of joining big corporations to do desk jobs. Grocery retail is an everyday, nitty-gritty, painstaking, and hard working job. People perfect for grocery development is the huge graduate population waiting to prove its competency. You may require senior procurement and supply-chain professionals, and a few management graduates to help understand the shopper's psycho-socioeconomic and family conditions and anticipate their needs and desires as part of a retail-marketing process.

Converting kirana store people into organized retail salespersons is the real answer. They have real experience in supply chain, stocks, off take, and naturally manage relationships with shoppers because that is culturally authentic and socially prescribed. It creates ownership.

(2) *Benchmarking Western organized retail model is hara-kiri*: The logic in the West was that all product categories are already branded so retails can give self-experience to shoppers. To increase income, retailers started the private-label concept that mirrors national brands but gives shoppers about 30 percent discount. In developed countries, as organized retailers are the only outlet for manufacturer brands, they command a 30 percent margin, allowing the retailer flexibility on mark up.

In contrast, Indian organized retailers have no power as they represent only 5 to 6 percent of the manufacturer brands' business. So they barely get 15 percent margin with only a small window for offering discounts.

(3) *Misinterpretation of private label*: Private labels that Western retailers created get 50 percent margin. Fresh counters selling non-packaged fruits, vegetables, meat, fish, and seafood fetch about 50 percent margin. In Europe, fresh products are not available on streets as they are in India even today.

Misinterpreting its meaning, Indian organized retails sell commodities as private label that have no brand significance in the market. In every area, from private label to manufacturer's brands and fresh counter, their margins are very low. Without solving these issues, it is a grave mistake for organized retail to spend on high-cost real estate and expensive foreign and Indian professionals.

In such immature markets, those who invested in retail were betting that a Bollywood film would turn into a box-office hit within five weeks. They could never bring in ROI. Applications like these in emerging markets create no business model. It is unclear whether their business is genuine or merely to create valuation to sell to global biggies in future.

Commodity products cannot drive organized retail

The first disconnect is competing with unbranded commodities that do not justify the earning per square foot value. Are organized retailers providing extra benefit to shoppers here?

Can they prove added value in their brinjals and potatoes beyond vegetables sold by the cart-seller just outside the multilevel retail store? How many of the majority of urban shoppers below ₹25,000 income per month know or consume that rare avocado or broccoli you introduced?

Kirana stores are shopper-sensitive

Retail business is very different from running a manufacturing or service industry. Retail requires understanding of the catchment area, procurement of multiple categories and brands, techniques of acquiring shopper footfall, and the alchemy of conversion in the store by frequently creating eye-catching activities.

Kirana store owners are the genuine retail merchants that shoppers return to because of the familiarity aspect. So it is a waste of money for retail owners to hire highly educated professionals when only an intelligent merchant mentality is required.

New model for a viable retail model

The requirement is to seriously reduce real-estate cost by creating a hypermarket outside the city and arranging transportation for shoppers. The low cost will benefit shoppers, inviting them to come regularly. Divide the store in one floor as under:

(1) Sell commodity through high-tech dispensers like those used for boiled candy where the product is

visible but not touchable. A touch-and-feel sample can be exposed separately to fulfill Indian habits.

(2) Surround three walls with fresh fruits, vegetables, and bakery. An aromatic bakery is big income to compensate the loss from wastage of fruits and vegetables.

(3) In the center, put FMCG branded category products with general merchandise.

(4) Put the hypermarket's cheeky fashion lifestyle products, from garments to customer electronics and entertainment, in another part of the store. These require huge marketing of the quality factor. So it would be better to market need-based rather than exhibitionist lifestyle and customer electronics products.

(5) Divide the store-named private label into three layers: basic, superior, and premium, and do marketing that is credible to shoppers. Sell national brand alternatives without copying them.

(6) Promote the retail brand and private label as a value proposition that is aspirational. This will avoid making the store appear as a discount store. Any discount offer should reflect as the store's transaction for the customer's benefit.

(7) Create outstanding retail marketing, with fast movement of national brands so your margin from them can increase from 15 to 30 percent.

(8) Organize the merchandise into a planogram that excites the shopper to hop in when he/she sees an entry, mid, and premium price.

If you are a retailer, ask your shoppers what they think of these points. You will definitely get "this is the way to go" as the answer.

Will 100 percent foreign direct investment (FDI) blast away Indian fashion retailers?

Shoppers at fashion retails are looking for something more than what a hypermarket offers. They want the intangible.

Fashion means exuberance

Fashion means exuberance, also, newness, getting away from boredom, making customers dream, and shocking society. Shock-of-the-new is a trigger in society and in the mind of customers who drive society. It has to be seen, become a buzz, and incite a craze in people to know more. Developed countries have mastered it, maintained it. So their 21st century fashion communication is not only provocative, it stimulates the desires and fantasies hidden deep in the customer's mind.

100 percent FDI will create shock-of-the-new

With FDI opening up for multi-brand retailing in India, international multi-brand stores will create shock-of-the-new, sustain, and change the color of fashion retailing here. To avoid getting blasted away, Indian multi-brand retailers will have to market the intangibles of fashion in retailing and branding.

Anybody can do apparel business with five basic elements: fabric, texture, color, cut, and stitch, but a fashion brand is created only when fabric transforms into an imagination metaphor with the infusion of visual art effects. International mass fashion brands such as FCUK and Zara, among others, have no designer name. They compensate that at every customer touch point with regular changing fashionable merchandise at the retail through visual merchandising, façade, shelf, and fixtures interwoven with visual art.

India allows up to 100 percent FDI in single brand retailing today, and 100 percent in the cash and carry business. A few shock-of-the-new examples: From 1991 to 2004, customer electronics brands arrived from developed countries and almost knocked Indian brands out of the market. World Trade Organization (WTO) regulations in 2004 resulted in foreign automobile brands almost fully marginalizing Indian sedans, such that they have become taxis. A brand sustains an idea by bringing in change and at the same time retaining, year after year, the core that creates the shock-of-the-new.

Take Apple, the brand that has sustained an element of shock-of-the-new in all its products from the first Apple machine in 1976 to Mac computers, iPods, iPhones, and iPads today. On August 9, 2011, Apple nudged past Exxon Mobil to be crowned the world's most valuable company with a market capitalization of US$337.2 billion.

Indian versus international brands

Living in a truly liberalized atmosphere with access to worldwide media, Western marketing tactics have proliferated here making Indians more brand conscious. In a recent study, we found that Zappers below 30 years believe international brands to be trendy, fashionable, with new designs, and better quality styling. The 31–45 years Compromise generation sees wider options in international brands. They are ready to spend in economy categories of international products.

The 45+ Rétro generation prefers to buy Indian, but, for upliftment of status, can shift to international brands.

Shock-of-the-new has a positive impact on society's drivers
comprising socio-behavioral clusters of flamboyant, novelty
seeker, critical, techy, and gizmo lovers. The trends they set
spread to society's followers, the low key, sober, and value
seekers. As driver-behavioral characteristics are growing in
India, we can expect drastic changes in fashion retailing with
100 percent FDI in multi-brand retailing.

Localization cannot be ignored

Individual modern retail stores are multiplying like mushrooms
in India. They do not follow fashion's diktat. Localization is
always required, but you cannot localize something that is not
part of your culture and competence without first learning its
function in depth. Take the case of French Galleries Lafayette
opening a store in New York's Trump Tower with US$8 million
yearly rent in 1991. They failed to localize according to
American customers, and had to close shop within three years.

Every fashion category requires the association of imagination. It is like looking at a single image created from multiple
mirror images. In India, we do not learn any established fashion code but invent fashion in a sporadic way. For example,
putting a skin cosmetic product in a sophisticated container
with a model wearing a Bollywood-style expression on it
cannot create hedonism. The two are not complementary.
Bollywood is an ephemeral world while a skin cosmetics
brand requires some tangible benefit first.

Provoke-understand-buy (PUB)

With FDI opening up to 100 percent for single brand retails, global lifestyle brands with huge brand pull will enter and indoctrinate the retailing system in India. If allowed to source freely, they will offer multiple international brands at aggressive, multi-layer price points. They can crash the price very low as they know volumes will be very high in India.

To ride the shock-of-the-new wave, Indian multi-brand retailer must ignite the PUB Reflex, a framework I created. PUB *provokes* the customer to *understand* so he/she *buys*. It is certainly possible to compete and sustain as is evident when China opened 100 percent FDI. Chinese brand Li-Ning managed to dislodge all international brands in sportswear in 2004 and became second only to Nike (16.7 percent market share). Li-Ning's 14.2 percent market share came from leveraging subtle nuances of Chinese heritage to build a brand globally.

Fashion advertising driven by visual art

Fashion marketing is very different from FMCG marketing, which is more tangible with a price boundary that requires rational and functional superiority. Fashion marketing is driven by visual art and continuously empowered from backstage. Pierre Berger, cofounding manager-partner of haute couture designer Yves Saint Laurent (YSL) says, "I've always watched what Yves would do, and never interfered with his actions. From backstage, I would collect the nuances of his creativity to highlight for marketing and to strengthen the brand YSL we created."

Fashion highlights intangibles

Fashion marketing's real job is to magnify visual art so the merchandise becomes larger than reality. Fashion reflects desire, self-seduction, projection, and high spirits, not customer need. Manufacturing, supply chain, or production cannot replace the lack of visual art in the marketing of intangible: fashion. Mass fashion started in the West since the 1980s while challenging the impact and doctrine of haute couture.

The latest retail-marketing innovation is the totally new departure made by H&M. Being a mono-brand retail, H&M is co-branding with reputed designer brands, such as Lanvin and Versace, among others, to give customers a multi-brand experience. Even Walmart's private label Metro 7 induces fashion intangibles. The more fashion associates with visual art, it becomes more intangible, and so can command its price.

A cowboy triggers big business

Irrespective of India opening up FDI in multi-brand retailing, politicians can do business, as did this American cowboy in November 2010.

Lassoing in the loot

He swaggered in on Air Force One, while keeping a watchful eye on the herds in wide-open ranges back home. The cowboy was riding center stage. Taxpayers were looking askance at his millions-of-dollars trip, his Indian hosts had big expectations, and neighboring Pakistan and China were flinching over his terse references to them. Skillfully swinging his lasso over Indian businessmen, he reined in US$10–15 billion worth of contracts for American firms.

President Barack Obama proved that, like the modern-day cowboy in a rodeo, he could still sit atop his bucking bull bronco electorate to emerge victorious. His lasso boasted a kill of 54,000 jobs for his countrymen, from India. That too, without repeating his first presidential election words of preferring Buffalo, in New Jersey, to Bangalore for outsourcing. Nor did he expose a possible future trend that Ohio Governor Ted Strickland started in September 2010 to ban outsourcing.

Deal-making is part-and-parcel of American capitalist society. They can grab an opportunity and align it to a national-level strategic decision. When visiting Michigan in 2010, I heard their governor say that the US should export, not import. GE's super-boss announced GE's five-year ambition to sell American products of US$10 billion in India. And President Obama demonstrated how to execute this strategy.

This coherent drive of a nation stems from a powerful political opposition that compels even the president of the world's superpower to travel to different countries with a business collection box.

Lessons on opportunity grabbing

What are India's learnings from this cultural discipline on how to drive opportunity and strengthen future directions?

(1) *Need a strong opposition*: Without a strong political opposition that reflects mass sentiments, our democratic government gets no back-pressure to drive for people's benefit. Coffeehouse, table-talk protest of

Leftist parties is not challenge enough. Having run the liberalized economy for two decades, it is time India became shrewd and intelligent to extract the best for the common man.

Even China has relooked at economic reforms without changing their political system. Does a Left protest against the US president's visit have any meaning when everyone knows India exports over US$69 billion IT services to the US every year? Only a vigilant opposition bench can be a threat to the ruling party to defend the country's economy, society, and people.

(2) *Concentrate on manufacturing*: The US is beginning to understand that vacating the manufacturing space was another cause of their downturn. In trying to repair this mistake, they are peddling products now. India tom-toms its US$69 billion IT exports in 2010, but that comprises basic, non-innovative work, somewhat similar to commodity services such as electricity and water. Of course two million IT-related jobs were created, but that has drained engineering talent for mere coding.

Even mechanical and electrical engineers opt for IT jobs that pay better, so our manufacturing industries remain deprived. India's manufacturing quality and high-skill precision are far behind those of China, Korea, and Japan, but without manufacturing, our economy cannot be robust in future. Over that manufacturing cake, IT services can be only the top layer of cream to raise the taste.

(3) *Opening local companies overseas is a start*: India's cost-advantage IT service is a fragile business with body shopping by Western societies. Can the jobless in an economic drought tolerate what they perceive as jobs escaping to foreigners? Such situations breed

monsters like extreme-right pseudo-Nazis who wait in shallow stupor to erupt when instigated. IT professionals claim American corporations cannot run without outsourcing to India. That may be true, but the requirements of American companies and American society are not the same.

If India was the inventor of products such as SAP, Oracle, Microsoft then adding services behind them could have been interesting. Unfortunately, Indian IT service does not reflect any innovative streak, just large-scale people supply. We need to add value beyond meeting physical numbers to avoid the "been Bangalored" slogan. In the US that means "jobs gone to India." How come American IT connotes Silicon Valley, evokes invention and innovation, whereas India's IT reference reeks of basic jobs scuttled away to foreign shores? These are jobs that the Americans would not do because they are low paid, low skilled, and monotonous.

Companies such as Accenture and IBM employ more Indian engineers in India than in their US operations. They serve Western clients too, but are they facing this political bogeyman that Indian companies have to put up with? Perhaps not, because their local interface and value addition to their customers' business are so high that they can easily hide everything else. Opening local companies may not solve the negativity toward outsourcing if the economic crisis continues, but at least it can temper the conflict situation.

Secretly setting up India development centers: What is already happening is Western IT service companies employ Indian engineers en masse in India. They try to keep this under wraps to avoid the wrath of their country's unemployed. To stop being badgered as job snatchers, Indian companies can take the bold step of localization. People in Europe, America, or any other country in the world should consider that they are dealing with a local company. Whether its back-office is offshore does not disturb anyone when customer interface is highly localized in a foreign country.

(4) *Innovate*: Even as the US president is marketing India, Indian companies should not expect that American technology know-how will easily transfer to India even if we are paying for it. Do not mix India up with Israel. Americans are ready to fork out largesse to Israel because of their strategic interest in controlling Middle East Arab states that are floating on petroleum reserves. Israel and American Jewish communities share a high-pitched brotherhood bonding. The "greenback" is plentifully invested in Israel to fund high-tech research and invention. This kind of open-pocket support can never come India's way.

Traditionally India has been a trading society, so breakthrough invention as in US garages has not happened here. The finest example is Bill Gates who went on to become the world's richest man. Garage inventions are encouraged, given "Popular Science Awards" every year. Our societal gene for invention is not developed, nor is there any precedent of a new departure from Indian invention.

Industries in India follow the American capital market system of quarter-to-quarter results to satisfy shareholders. Where is the inclination for investment in invention? Without getting into hardcore manufacturing, export of manufactured products with high-quality image, the Indian economy will not be robust tomorrow.

Developed countries are targeting India's huge customer base that manages a good lifestyle with proportionately lower income than Western counterparts. That is enough for country presidents and CEOs to come for encashing business here to raise their country's economy. Cannot our ministers and CEOs become business cowboys for India too?

2

Visual Art for Business

Resources to Deal with Pokes

A symbiosis between visual art and a selling proposition can bring multiple business returns beyond expectation. It is like dipping a jalebi in milk or eating a hot jalebi with ice cream. When visual-art effects play out the imagination metaphor, lengths of fabric get transformed into fashion. Similarly, strong visual art at every customer touch point makes the product proposition elusive, engaging the end-user's mindshare, resulting in grabbing his/her wallet share. If the jalebi looks good outside but its dough quality and fermentation are not perfect, your tongue will immediately throw it out. In the same way, if the intrinsic quality and functional benefits of the selling proposition are compromised, the customer will reject it.

Visual art existed even before civilization began, it is intangible and has unlimited value. A corporation's restricted boundaries may not allow ideas beyond the obvious, yet to differentiate in business, CEOs expect leaders and their teams to ideate out-of-the-box.

The more intangible the selling proposition, premium earning becomes obvious and without boundary.

In the perspective of this out-of-the-box dimension, I created, for the first time in the world, an initiative called Painter CEO in 2010. I went to CEOs and invited them to paint their vision without constraints. CEOs have proved through their paintings that they have an interesting creative bent of mind to successfully manage their businesses against all odds. Forty-eight CEOs have painted already. In this chapter you will find how famous CEOs, who have never painted before, were inspired to express themselves in a new medium, that of visual art.

Such intangibles comprise a seny rauxa *allure of two opposites on a foundation of believable quality. Seny means rational and rauxa amounts to crazy energy in Spanish art. Remember jalebis also have two sides, the deliciously sweet and the connotation of being a googly. The fascinating seny rauxa combine has unleashed new schools of art. Artistic poke doses here may even propel you crunch into an uneven jalebi, even as you take paint on a brush and approach a canvas. In this market banality, how can you distinguish business delivery from competitors without art, expression, and intangibles?*

The fabulous art–business combine

Art was a human inclination in the cave age.

World's first communication medium was art

The earliest cave painters at Lascaux, France, dating back 30,000 years, drew animals. The San people in South Africa drew people in 27,000-year-old caves. Ancient Indian cave art 20,000 years ago in Bhimbetka, Madhya Pradesh, had both animals and people, often fighting wars.

Several civilizations have been lost over centuries, buried under the soil with volcanic or earthquake eruptions, or vanished due to human destruction or negligence. But in all discoveries made to date, testimony has always come from cave paintings, stone engraving, or sculptures with figurative or nature expressions. Art was the first medium of communication in human society. The era of petroglyphs faded to pictograms before logographic writing gave way to the alphabet.

Five fundamentals of art and business

My questioning was, if art is so elemental for expression, why is it not better meshed into business? There is great symbiosis between art and business. They share the same five fundamentals of imagination, subtlety, elegance, loudness, and sustainability. In art, imagination translates to a unique idea beyond time, subtlety is subliminal, and elegance is being always displayed in a sophisticated place, whereas loudness in art is the shock of the new expression of an artist. Art is sustainable as its monetary value rises with time and because the artist bears testimony to his/her times.

Similarly in business, you need to ideate on how to strategize to expand the market with uniqueness. Subtlety is engraving the product or service into the customer's top-of-mind recall, while elegance is being aspirational. Business needs loudness to have distinction all the time in the market while sustainability is business growth with high net worth.

World's first exhibition of CEO paintings

In the last 35 years I have been privileged to spend time with several CEOs, managing directors (MDs), and chairmen in different countries across four continents on business transactions for their companies' growth and increased net worth. Our discussions invariably took place at a strategic and creative level followed by execution excellence as I am always finicky to get high-quality action. I found creativity in their ideas while interacting with me. I found the enterprise itself was a canvas with all possibilities to create distinguishing perspective. This inspired me to consider how their businesses can gain end-customer connect on a sustained basis. From such interactions I have long been convinced that CEOs are successful in business because they have a high value artist's hidden palette in their minds, similar to the management palette. So I have strongly believed that a CEO's performance on canvas would definitely be brilliant.

In an attempt to execute this idea, a unique venture has emerged. We inaugurated in Mumbai in March 2010 the world's first exhibition of paintings done by CEOs. For the first time in their lives, CEOs took the brush in hand and boldly put colors on canvas. You can view their out-of-the-box art at www.painterceo.com.

CEOs have something extra

Art helped me to see end-customers in a very creative way. It has made my approach disruptive, so my strategic delivery to my clients is slanted toward benefitting their end-customers. In fact, we use this perspective in all areas of our consulting work, be it in branding, retail design, industrial design, or delivering transformation through the corporate business identity. Selling my disquieting ideas to different CEOs worldwide, I understood their extreme creativity. Otherwise they would not have so liberally accepted my radical outside-in, from-the-public-park-bench ideas that invariably turned their companies around toward high growth.

That CEOs orchestrate different kinds of people, employees, investors, customers, and suppliers who have different qualities, aspirations, and needs as well as bring high financial results is an art by itself. Working with global CEOs gave me the insight that unfurling the creativity hidden inside them would be extremely fascinating.

This is how the saga started

I would write asking CEOs to spend a crazy, creative session with me without divulging anything more. The beauty of this initiative was that my sudden proposition for them to paint was like an enigma. My fine arts career and that I still paint is generally known. Perhaps that was why most CEOs spontaneously agreed and immediately became engrossed in painting.

I met them either in office or at home. They could have avoided the painting session, but they seemed to have a hidden urge for expression. They chose their colors. Confidence would soar when I mentioned, "You are at total liberty here. There's no shareholder, promoter, employee, or competitor scrutinizing you!" It was just as well that I discreetly captured them with my movie camera as they painted, because people ask me now if I had helped them. This just goes to show how appealing their paintings are. The spontaneity of CEOs in idea generation and application was indeed a lesson for me.

Beyond the boundary of numbers

Business always runs with rationality and the glamour of numbers. But the tragedy is that business crunched with numbers alone confines you to mere logic in some predetermined locked system. Shareholders always expect to encash unlimited multiplication of their investment. Only an empty canvas can inspire you to paint with unrestrained idea for business.

A vision with numbers can be foggy and hypothetical, so the next step for CEOs is to go beyond that boundary. When you can paint your vision on canvas, imagination gets concretized and unlimited possibilities morph into those visuals. That can be discussed, analyzed, and acted upon. Once art that is executed is understood, application is mere technicality.

Art circles always critique the craftsmanship and quality of an artist's painting. Painter CEOs can be considered a new art movement because they took up the challenge at a moment's notice, made no trial, yet their boldness, confidence, and passion on the canvas were outstanding. Asking them to sing or write would not have taken me anywhere. But this adventurous act has proved that the expression of art is an inherent human inclination that demystifies an idiom. In fact, a few CEOs became so absorbed they took the initiative to paint on a second canvas.

Everybody in business talks about creating differentiation. My prime objective of inspiring CEOs to pull out their creativity was to prove that differentiation is not the buzzword it has become in business today. In this uniform, digital world, distinction that is tangible in a product or service will bring business success.

A new art movement

Western art has had several collective movements after prehistoric cave paintings: from the medieval period's religious art to the masters' painted realistic portraits that reproduced real life around 1506. When photography was invented in 1826, it shocked the art world as realism was no longer required. So artists had to ideate out-of-the-box and express images in their mind. Art movements have since then given a boost to the world to ideate differently. These movements were expressionism (1888), impressionism (1897), cubism (1910), surrealism (1929), abstract (1940), pop (1960), and graphic art (1965) to street graffiti (1969), vanishing art (1994), and extrapolated art (2006).

As no globally renowned contemporary movement of painting has emerged in India so far, Painter CEOs can represent a new, collective, first-time effort and movement that can be taken forward to become part of global art history of the 21st century.

The backdrop is the humdrum of business news

After the 1991 economic reforms, we have heard many different stories on new India's corporate battlefield. Everyday's news up to 1997 was of one corporate tie-up after another; then tie breaks with mismatch of cultures and business intent comprised the news. Most dramatic was the IT industry growth. Next, family businesses were breaking up as professionalism was taking over. Corporate houses were making visible their big size by inventing organized retail without much experience. Most lost money like crazy, many have folded, others are waiting to sell and earn huge valuations with multi-brand FDI opening in India.

Among these activities, the corporate world was seeing no adventure in the artistic domain, even though the word differentiation was tirelessly emerging in business. But as distinction is an art, I was propelled into my quest for discovering art amongst business leaders.

Aligning artistically to CEOs in the West

I have to admit my experience with Western society CEOs who have always been inspired by my artistic background. In many cases they would want to have meetings in my painting studio instead of the office. Or just drop by to look at my paintings as their personal involvement with art is quite deep. One such visit was from Romain Nouffert, the chief of Lu Biscuits. After we finished the work connected with the strategic platform for a new category of biscuits, he came to unwind in my studio in Paris. As he looked around, one of my paintings caught his attention and he asked, "Why aren't you testing this one with the new concept?" So finally the product came out with my painting.

Victor Scherrer, CEO of Grand Metropolitan, once invited me to a restaurant when we were working on a pan-European project. He had brought along some textured sketch paper, brush, and black ink. While eating, he suddenly displayed everything on the table and said, "Don't hesitate to sketch whenever you want." Sitting at Le Doyen, one of Paris' oldest since 1791, and most renowned restaurants in Champs Elysees, he knew exactly how to tempt me to create.

Later, visiting his beautiful chateau I found that Victor is a great collector of art, but at that time he wanted to experience an instant art session on the dining table. I had gone to the restaurant with a corporate mindset, but he turned it around to become totally creative. Our discussion on the project thereafter took on quite a new and lateral angle, all because we both went into a tangent, spellbound with art over dinner. My Christmas gift to my client CEOs one year was a sketch book and a set of sketch pens. My message was, "Design yourself." You cannot believe the response I got. Many of them expressed how positive and different they felt after drawing sketches, and most of them sent me their striking creations. These instances of interfacing Western world CEOs with art culminated in my strong belief that CEOs would surely have some painting talent. That started my Painter CEO journey (www.painterceo.com) with Keshub Mahindra, chairman of Mahindra & Mahindra.

Start of the Painter CEO link with Keshub Mahindra

CEOs who participated in an adventure to discover their creative expressions were initially quite anxious, but their wonderful artistic output validates my belief about their creative abilities. Let me share a painting session with a doyen of Indian industry so you can imagine him beyond the corporate world.

Arriving in Mahindra Towers, Mumbai, pulling my big trolley suitcase got me bemused looks. Upon reaching Keshub Mahindra's office, I had to convince all who wanted to help take the suitcase away for safekeeping while I met the chairman, that I absolutely wanted it in his room. They indulged me. Mr Mahindra, totally surprised to see the big suitcase, joked in his genial way about bringing in the holiday spirit. When I spoke of a painting session, he thought I had come to show him how I painted. I proceeded to his table, cleared it up to accommodate the canvas, colors, and brushes.

"You want me to paint?" he asked incredulously. When I smiled in the affirmative, he continued looking at me, at a loss for words. Then slowly, very deliberately, he took up the brush, started with colors, and was lost in high engagement in his painting session. He created a human attitude with multiple layers of soft colors. He left a lot of white space at the edges, concentrating on the subject that looked quite dreamlike. I captured his absorption with my movie camera, moving from here to there.

Mr Mahindra was so engrossed that he was not looking anywhere else. He did exactly what we artists do in the atelier, he even wiped his face with the small towel I had given him to wipe the brushes. At the end he said, "I've never done this before in my life." The whole painting reflects his generosity, his focus, and the incredible humane behavior of Keshub Mahindra. Take a look at him in this link (http://www.painter-ceo.com/participants/2010/Keshub-Mahindra.php).

Exclusive Painter CEO Club of 2012

Professional CEO careers are limited within a boundary, and then retirement happens. But paintings of the same CEOs are timeless. They never become old or a thing of the past. Dauntless when orchestrating diverse corporate functions, from nitty-gritty internal happenings to juggling the multifaceted outside environment, CEOs have something invincible. That is ingenious imagination.

To capture that lasting value beyond corporate work, we have created the exclusive club for sensitive Painter CEOs (www.painterceo.com). Up to 2013, 48 CEOs have spontaneously held color in a brush to let their mind's eye take over a canvas. Let us look at how the 2012 Painter CEO Club entrants painted their thoughts.

Priya Paul

Reaching Delhi's office-cum-residence of Priya Paul, chairperson of Apeejay Surrendra Park Hotels, I had started arranging brushes, colors, and palette when suddenly a big dog breezed in, pounced at a tube of paint, and strode off challengingly like a lion king who has got what he had wanted. "Don't bother with him," Priya said walking in. "He just wants to attract attention."

Watching a tree in her garden, Priya displayed her fabulous perspective of colors, "Painting today made me happy, fulfilled and excited to do more." Soon enough the dog quietly returned the paint in exactly the place he had taken it from.

Hari Bhartia

"Seeing these beautiful colors and your colorful shirt Shombit, I feel compelled to paint you," smiled Hari Bhartia, Jubilant Group's cochairman. His brother, Chairman Shyam Bhartia walked in and looked appreciatively at Hari engrossed in painting. "Business is also creativity," said Hari. "You need to create something all the time, make it work, make it sustainable."

Aniruddha Deshmukh

Traveling next to Thane, I found Aniruddha Deshmukh, president, textiles of Raymond, reflecting on his travels:

"While I cannot put actual shape to thought, as I was painting I could visualize the outdoors I love, the sea, the forests. I've never done this, but I really felt it is one of my most pleasurable moments."

Rajesh Jejurikar

Rajesh Jejurikar, chief executive of Mahindra Tractor and Farm Mechanisation, literally devoured the paints, giving life to nature and corporate promise, Mahindra RISE. "Our vehicles go through multiple terrains, greenery, water, dust and mud, to a destination close to the sun which enables people to rise." Rajesh said he had enjoyed "expressing the spirit of freedom, energy and upliftment."

Gunender Kapur

"I want to capture the radiance of Om," said Gunender Kapur, CEO, TPG Wholesale. "The beginning of everything is Om. I had just these two letters in mind. It's been a fantastic experience."

Sambhu Sivalenka

Sambhu Sivalenka, chief managing director (CMD), Amrutanjan Health Care, said "Painting is a primeval urge in human evolution. Heck, the caveman did it!" He reminiscences:

> Connecting brush to canvas, some old memories came rushing back.
> Just like life, these involutes I'm making have a beginning and end.

Painting challenges you to lose the security that comes with definition and rote, the finite numbers and cash flow statements CEOs spend time with.

Guy Goves

"Shombit I know you could be up to something crazy, but I didn't think you'd go to this length to get me to paint," laughed Guy Goves, president of Agri Business, Deepak Fertilizers and Petrochemicals. "My painting is an expression of finding yourself in nature's beauty, a great gift to mankind. You learn from it, gain from it, share it. To keep nature intact for our children to enjoy is of paramount importance to me today."

Bijou Kurien

Geometric light is what Bijou Kurien, president, Lifestyle, Reliance Retail drew.

> This is a huge learning experience to use brushes, contrasting geometrical shapes, experiment with flowers, put paint on paint. Having never dabbled with paints, once you figure it out, you feel a sense of satisfaction of doing something original. There's a parallel with the way you build companies and start businesses.

Vivek Mehra

"There's always a storm brewing," said Vivek Mehra, MD/CEO, SAGE Publications, India. "One goes away, another is waiting to happen. The question is about knowing you have

the courage to ride it." Deftly painting a mysterious purple
storm he said, "I've not held a brush since 8th standard. It's
surprisingly like riding a bicycle, you really don't lose touch."

Ashish Dikshit

Ashish Dikshit, president, Madura Fashion & Lifestyle, tried
escaping this painting session for a year. As luck would have
it, I had a meeting with Anuradha Narasimhan, category
director, Britannia, and discovered in our conversation that
she is married to Ashish. Anuradha sportingly collaborated
with me, accepted my dinner invitation at home. Ashish was
spellbound when I put colors before him, he painted wonderfully. "My expression was all about freshness, vibrancy,
beautiful things, young and exciting. The experience was like
any normal meeting with Shombit, unexpected, surprising, full
of challenges, creativity into areas I've never ventured into."

Dileep Ranjekar

"Question mark is my favourite symbol. It's the ovum in
the womb here," said Dileep Ranjekar, CEO, Azim Premji
Foundation. He marveled at how easily paints rolled out creativity from his fingers. His wife Nandini said his circle was
imperfect. While still painting Dileep explained that learning
comes only when we interrogate, so the non-idyllic circle.
Their husband–wife love and affection were coming through
like a painting. "More inquisitive people should be born, rebel-
ling against the establishment, current fundamentals, seeking
knowledge, change. The black spot here is like a mistake that
happens and you live with," said Dileep.

D.P. Singh

D.P. Singh, CMD, Punjab & Sind Bank, said this was his first attempt at painting, "I had carpentry classes in school." His memories returned to Giverny, France, "Remember that arched bridge? I'm interpreting where Monet lived, where nature grows its own way, giving you a feeling of freedom unlike organized gardens anywhere in the world."

Every painting of the 48 Painter CEO Club members is priceless. It arrests the CEO's state of being in the most productive time of his/her professional life. Freezing these unique pieces of art into corporate memorabilia, future generations can appreciate how each CEO handled this complex, heady, and industrious period. The Painter CEO Club is helping CEOs expose their embedded creative streak, so they can lead their companies toward differentiation to meet the challenges of global competition.

Art sustains beyond a distinguished corporate career

Among Painter CEOs who spontaneously painted on my subtle nudge, let me present Jacques Vincent. He is the key transformer of US$26.6 billion Groupe Danone where I have strategized about 200 brands since 1984.

First meeting at my atelier

One day in 1988, I got a call that Jacques, who had just been posted back to France, wanted to meet me, but at my atelier, not my office. He arrived and talked about the liberty of expression I had created in the hardcore strategy of corporate requirement. I later asked what made him come to my studio. Familiar with all the work I had done for Danone, he knew I was a painter, so was curious to find my source of creativity. Looking around my personal painting studio, he commented that the freshness in the work I had delivered to Danone now falls into place in his mind.

Art's cultural association with food

He was not finished exploring the creative aspect, he said. Jacques always wanted my perspective on marketing through art. He asked me to present him how art is culturally associated with food, the parallel between the evolution of classic and contemporary art, and the last 100 years' pattern of human consumption. I organized our next meeting in Foundation Cartier, at Jouy en Josas, an artistic seminar place in Paris' outskirts.

That he agreed to spend the whole day away from his corporate world to view business through art's fresh perspective proves that Jacques' business success comes from lateral imagination. I gave him my take on the trajectory of art, food, and how they mesh in Western society's culture, adding that marketing ought to be sociocultural rather than statistically driven in future. This subject snowballed in my subsequent meetings with Jacques over the years.

It is important to append here how luxury brand Cartier promotes various artists in a large gallery of collections in this sophisticated contemporary art museum. Foundation Cartier shows how business can go beyond industry to support art that is timeless.

A creative father-of-the-bride suit

Another sudden call from Jacques in Brazil that I will never forget is him asking me if I could design the dress "with your type of colors" that he would wear for his daughter's wedding. I was nonplussed. Was this hardcore Western corporate gentleman joking? I made my wonderful assistant Caroline check with Jacques' secretary. Yes! That was exactly what he had requested! Some other work was bringing me to Bangalore then, so I picked up violet raw-silk material and had his suit custom-tailored in Paris. I hand-painted his necktie, silk handkerchief for the jacket pocket, and socks. He accepted everything exactly the way I had designed them.

Can you imagine Jacques, whom everybody had seen in corporate formal dark colors only, wearing this violet suit? People at the wedding were wide-eyed in admiration. All I can say is that it clearly exposed Jacques' creative and daring mind, the quality that allowed him to turn around BSN, a holding company of 14 verticals, into Danone, world leader in dairy products today. Jacques asking me to design his dress the way I do my paintings was an incredible demand from the vice chairman of a global company.

I will always treasure this memory. Pinned up in my office is a photograph of a violet-suited Jacques hugging his beautiful daughter wearing a white wedding gown. This poignant father–daughter relationship really looks like a piece of my painting.

Joining the Painter CEO Club

So when in 2010 Jacques revisited India, and I had helped him find some direction for Danone's expansion here, our first year's Painter CEO calendar was already out. Sitting in

Jacques' chamber at Shining Consulting, Bangalore, where we have allocated him a regular office as he prefers to conduct business from here whenever he is in India, I invited him to join the Painter CEO Club. "What's that?" he asked. I explained my belief that CEOs are perforce creative as they magnificently manage diverse situations and people while striving for that bloated bottom line. He connected to this creed and readily agreed to paint in my Bangalore studio this time. I videotaped him (http://www.painterceo.com/ participants/2011/ Jacques-Vincent.php) as he carefully chose brushes, colors, and concentrated on painting.

His attentive stance reminded me of our many meetings in Danone when he would listen intently as I spoke on customer value and social trends. In fact, in 1995, when Jacques asked me to work for Britannia where Danone had a share then, it was the first time I was coming to work in India. From Charles de Gaulle airport to Mumbai he made me talk continuously on cultural aspects of different societies I had worked with across the globe, and took specific notes with multiple geometric shapes. Our discussions always veered on how art and culture can influence marketing.

The freshness of art

After painting he said it was tough, very unlike his 40 management years. "You get inspiration when you put the brush in water, the colours you see and don't see. It's exciting the first 15 minutes, then there's anxiety, and creativity rises again." Jacques' outstanding determination came through in seamless strokes he confidently made, leaving white space at the bottom, and converging power at the top. Twenty-two years after he had visited my atelier for the origin of freshness, his painting revealed he was still carrying freshness, as also unique focus with which he had made Danone deliver healthy dairy products and water globally.

Wait, Jacques' artistic inclination does not end there. After painting, Jacques told me that his retirement plan was to start an art gallery. I was there when his Art for Smile Gallery on 28 Quai du Louvre (www.artforsmile.com) was getting its interiors done. This incredible gallery is just behind Louvre Museum on River Seine, Paris, opposite to my art college Ecole de Beaux-Arts. It has many fascinating styles from artists around the globe. When people buy a painting, part of the proceeds go to CARE France, an NGO.

Different CEOs often ask how I generated the Painter CEO idea. I have spent a lot of time with Jacques Vincent; this incredible story of a high-level corporate leader retiring into the brightness of colors and milieu of artists is an inspiration among others that I have inherited from French society since my early career. Painter CEO is a truthful manifestation of CEO creativity which has immense value in society, much beyond their professional lives.

Emotion of a billionaire businessman

Corporate idea tanks spawn strategies on paperboards exactly the way a painter's brush downloads ideas. Similarities between art and business gave credence to the Painter CEO adventure. Colors, the artists' ammunition, can be compared to industry's raw material procurement system for producing finished products. Liken industry's manufacturing machine to the canvas, the transformer podium between brush–colors and artist's mind.

Art is unique, business is reproduction

But the big difference is that the canvas holds one piece of art, whereas industry is mechanized to produce unlimited duplications with one mold. The art of idea generation to create distinction is prevalent in the industrial parameter even if it is reproduced.

Studying in Paris' 350-year-old Ecole Nationale des Beaux-Arts, the legacy of European art, I stepped into the art sphere. But let me submit that art's uncertainty of take-home pay drove me into the corporate world as I had to earn to support my family. I have always carried my corporate strategy work into my atelier but with one difference: as artists we work alone, in corporations we work collectively.

Never having abandoned art, I could instil the entrepreneurial spirit when working together with large teams. The consultative approach of delivering big creativity at all customer touch points for the client's business growth convinced global corporations that art pays. This artistic corporate challenge often took me from country to country.

Discovering Azim Premji

A case in point is a call from Azim Premji's office in 1996. Nobody knew me in India then as my first consulting work with Britannia hit the market only in 1997. Mr Premji is known as that hardcore businessman who only loves his company's growth, growth, and growth. But since he found me in 1996, I have experienced a certain corner of emotion in my relationship with him.

In flashback, I marvel at this creative-minded person who was so convinced with the work we delivered that he turned his company upside-down to implement the rainbow flower corporate symbol with "Applying Thought." He changed the corporate credo from beliefs to a promise system with a set of four values as enterprise drive.

Wipro's repositioning work

Wipro's repositioning work took me two years before its 1998 launch. When we recommended different platforms after researching and diagnosing the company, the management team chose the "Caring" proposal with a mother-and-child symbol. I had explained then that IT is the engine driving Wipro's future, but the image of all IT companies was boring, very backend industrial blue centric, whereas Wipro stood for "Essential to Intelligent" for human society. To get the whole team's buy-in for my recommended "Rainbow Flower" Performing Biz Identity was proving difficult.

Mr Premji was the first to totally see its colorful logic from day one. But in the umpteen meetings with his management team, his comments stood among other employee versions, not as the promoter's influence. He never imposed his preference, instead made everyone fight it out.

And how they all fought! Even the multicolored gay flag from San Francisco's Castro District was thrown into the rainbow flower comparison fray. The team did extensive research with different stakeholders on the caring and rainbow-flower symbols, where the emotional connect and reasoning behind the rainbow flower proved perfect.

When everybody finally converged in acceptance, to those residual dissenting voices during its international roll-out,

Mr Premji said, "You may like it, you may not like it, but you will never forget it." That showed me Mr Premji's excellence of emotional balance and his extraordinary understanding of art through the business window.

Warming Premji to painting

So in November 2009, as the Painter CEO initiative was germinating, I zeroed in on Mr Premji. He was traveling, so I waited. Then arriving with painting materials, I readied his corporate dining table for painting. He breezed in jovially, the perfect luncheon host; then stopped in his tracks. Like a child, he immediately threw a tantrum saying he cannot paint. But in time, in-between our usual banter on different subjects, glancing oftentimes in a friendly way at the colors, canvas, and brushes I had laid out, his fretfulness was melting away.

With a smile he halfheartedly attempted negotiating, when I asked him what colors he would like. He boldly replied, "Give me green, white, blue and black." And then I got to enjoy his self-indulgent innocence as I have always done in our rapport. It may be a hidden treasure between him and me. If you look at how he looked at me just after starting to paint (I have captured him on video http://www.painterceo. com/participants/2011/Azim-Premji.php), this is the real Azim Premji I know. His eyes were telling me, "Shombit, you are asking me to do a crazy job." I can never forget that instant.

Nobody can imagine Azim Premji this way. He looked very differently intent as he picked up paint, made intrepid application on the canvas. I was the only person devouring his solid brush strokes against a beautiful January afternoon light dappling through bright pink bougainvillea outside the window. Another picture layer was getting crafted, like a painting, with Mr Premji busy at artistic creation against that flowery backdrop.

He finished one painting, it was perfect. On his own initiative he took another canvas and started painting again. Now he was fully engrossed. He left well-balanced white space around as he very precisely painted a coconut tree in a breezy atmosphere. Not overpainted, very limited strokes, graceful nature clearly emerging. His movements were emotional, indicating where to start, where to finish. Twelve years after we had repositioned Wipro, I found in Mr Premji's painting the pictorial depiction of the same spirit of continuity of the rainbow flower he had so spontaneously chosen above all else.

In today's digital world, homogeneity is so strong that business requires huge differentiation to get better net worth in future. Visual art always contributes toward differentiation. In this parallel I am making between art and business, irrespective of him being a hardcore global billionaire-club businessman, Azim Premji's emotion in art will, in my eyes, always raise his value as a man beyond business.

Visual art transforms fabrics to fashion

Visual art that inspires CEOs is the only tool that changes the character of fabrics. An apparel brand has to command premium price so as to gain the customers' high pride of ownership. They have to return to it and influence others in society.

Visual art embellishes the shopper's mind with bigger-than-life images to create the lifestyle trend. Most Indian apparel brands suffer as they miss out on the visual-art effect.

Genesis of dressing style

Fashion as we know it today originated from European monarchy's obsession with visual art. Royalty patronized art and desired distinction from their subjects. France's 18th century Queen Marie Antoinette wore strikingly different dresses with daily advice from designer Rose Bertin, known as minister of fashion. The Queen's radical, often disturbing, fashion gave her visible force and autonomy outside tradition. Her provocative *robe a la polonaise* had a bosom-enhancing bodice, billowy, ankle-baring skirts, a three-foot powdered hair "pouf" decked with plumes and veils.

Even when she rode to her death by guillotine, Marie Antoinette wore a brand-new white chemise she had secretly saved, a white fichu around her shoulders, and a pleated white cap to dazzle the thousands of citizens who watched in stunned silence. Her exquisite sense of visual art made her apparel sophisticated and visually distinguished from the masses and this left a grand memoir of fashion.

Democratization of fashion

In Paris in 1846, Englishman Charles Frederick Worth democratized the individualism that royalty kept to themselves. He started haute couture, the ultimate in high fashion for the rich, which royals also patronized. The haute couture label belongs to France, possibly because it was invented from French monarchic heritage.

Today, haute couture dresses have been known to take up to 900 hours (100 days) to create, with multiple interventions by artistic craftsmen working with the principal designer, that single dress on the fashion ramp for just 120 seconds. Visual art is exposed in every square inch of such a dress, with beads, sequins, different textured embroidery, and blend of colors. Visual art then takes that garment into another sphere for public presentation to create an impact beyond imagination. Haute couture is always presented as a piece of visual art on a model doing the catwalk. To make a statement about the intellectual-artistic construction of a particular idea, the designer plans the order in which each model walks out wearing a specific outfit in the collection. It is then left to the audience to visually deconstruct each outfit, appreciate its detail and craftsmanship, and understand the designer's ideas.

Contemporary designers produce their shows as theatrical productions using elaborate sets of artistic technology components with live music to make the garment totally hallucinating on the fashion ramp. You may say the dress is just a single element in the show, but this is not true. Represented with visual art, the dress on the model becomes so powerful that it stays on in people's mind even if they cannot afford it.

Sketchy visual art for fashion

Dressmaking was not fashion in the 19th century. It was considered low class, just a matter of cut and fit. In the 1920s, when European fine art was booming, visual art brought fashion onto the drawing board. Designers such as Gabrielle Coco Chanel made drawings and sketches of garments for selective society. Her 1931 sketch "White Satin" shows how she generated fashion through visual art. YSL was inspired by Pablo Picasso's paintings and Coco Channel's designs among other contemporary art influences. His 1976 collection is based on the 1920s abstract costumes created for Ballet Russe by painter Leon Bakst. The illustrative drawings of Chanel,

Dior, and YSL transported fashion from royal individualism to a larger clientele.

Industrialization of fashion through visual art

Everybody cannot afford haute couture, which is fashion's window to just build a brand's image. Prominently using visual art, these styles are made into prêt-a-porter (ready-to- wear) through industrial production systems for mainstream markets. In 1971, the first St. Laurent Rive Gauche (left bank of Paris) showroom opened to woo less affluent customers. In today's huge market of mass fashion, even low-cost brands are injecting high aspiration by creating outstanding trendy looks with visual art.

Visual art for mass fashion

Mass fashion brands, such as FCUK, Zara, and H&M, among others, do not have a designer's name. To compensate that, every customer touch point at the retail store such as visual merchandising, façade, shelf, and fixtures are interwoven with visual art. In New York's Fifth Avenue, a jewelry store in a high-rise building has colorful balloons and huge metal cones, atop which are finger rings that sparkle in laser lighting. Shoppers cannot see the rings from 200 m, but the display looking like a modern art painting, attracts them.

From Marie Antoinette to haute couture, prêt-a-porter to mass fashion, it all happened with visual art, that is, drawings and sketches that have nothing to do with measuring and fitting. Visual art conceptualized fashion, translated fabrics to style, made a grand spectacle with models catwalking the ramp against the backdrop of technology, music, and mood. Even at the retail, from in-store ambience, lighting, character of mannequins, and the bag shoppers will carry the garments home in, all comprise visual art that defines the brand's personality.

A shopper pays a higher price, particularly in men's apparel, from the visual art impact of the brand he carries in his mind as pride of ownership. A fashion brand that is associated with regularly changing visual art makes the shopper feel he is wearing this unlimited creative sense on his body. This is what transforms fabrics into a fashion brand.

Should not Indian apparel brands incorporate visual art as part of their strategy too? They need to exit the vicious cycle of improving backend management with fabrics, texture, color, cut, and stitch to price engineer the product for hard discount sales. Instead they can enter the unlimited avenue of visual art in fashion.

Visual art to transform engineering products

There is a difference between visual art and aesthetics. Aesthetics is very difficult to define as it exists in nature and the human form. Visual art is the composition of human intelligence that adapts different things in people's mind and expresses them in collage form. Visual art is human expression with any kind of material in the form of art.

Visual art drives the economy through industrial design

Since ever so long, engineering products have improved human life, initially providing superior functionality that brings comfort into life as the prime factor. In today's competitive scenario, distinction through industrial design is what breaks the benchmark.

Industrial design, a combination of applied art and applied science that improves marketability and production by incorporating visual art, ergonomics, and product usability drives a developed country's economy. From automobiles, two-wheelers, mobile phones, home appliances, office furniture, electronics, medical equipment, tools, machinery, and transportation, among others, it is all empowered by visual art. Originating in Europe, established manufacturers have tremendously prioritized creating distinction in industrial design through visual art aesthetics. Later the US, Japan, and Korea followed suit.

Visual art at all design touch points

When people reach a certain economic height in personal life, they get involved with different engineered design products as extensions of life, either at home or in office. So strong visual art in every touch point counts and it makes them feel they are surrounded with unique things in daily living. The collage of different materials and textures in multiple elements play as visual art in such a product's visible areas of design.

Visual art starts from nonvisible areas

Every industrial design has a form, shape, and a few prime areas of customer or professional touch points. It is not enough to address the overall visible aspect of a product with external visual aesthetics. When a customer opens a car's bonnet or looks under its floor carpet to find that its hidden mechanical engineering components, digital technology circuit board, or electrical wiring lines are not well designed with visual art, he/she can lose consideration in the vehicle and its aspiration.

When your mobile phone falls from your hand and opens up, that is the time you can experience outstanding visual art if you discover your phone's inner circuitry to have exquisitely neat design. Should your washing machine require repair, and the technician comes and opens its panel and you find the chamber inside looks untidy, exposing no visual art, you will never consider the brand to be aspirational. Psychologically, in your next purchase, you will not buy the same brand. That is because washing itself is a chore, and this product's inner functionality corroborates that tedious task. So the washing machine did not aesthetically elevate itself to reveal its efficiency during its repair state.

Visual art is so powerful that no engineer with an aesthetic sense will leave nonvisible industrial design areas devoid of it. French sculptor César proved that even scraps of metal can have visual art. He astonished art lovers by showing three crushed cars at a Paris exhibition. César selected particular elements for crushing and mixing from differently colored vehicles to control the surface pattern and color scheme of his works. He became renowned for his "Compressions" Sculpture art.

Visual art in industrial product retails

The retail outlets of even sophisticated industrial design such as automobiles or washing machines are left very archaic, just walls, floor, and lighting. Visual-art effort is required to make their façade and interiors hallucinating by using engineering components from the product design under sale. Customer experience in the store should take the product beyond its mere functional aspect to become an extension of customer lives.

Calling it Reezig, Reebok ingeniously used the yellow corrugated, zigzag shoe sole of their latest design to decorate the entire store and façade. This gave the shoe a dimension larger than life. It demonstrated how a single touch point can be magnified to mesmerize customers. This is the way visual art can change the retail character of industrial products.

Free from user manuals

The 21st century's digital technology era has created another phase where the experience of functionality in industrial design is implicit. This means a product's look and touch should be so compelling that customers can figure it out instantly without the help of user manuals. As digital technology is commoditizing most products, the importance of distinction through engineering design is becoming a prime factor where visual art plays the central role. At any price point, if the industrial design does not have high quality and aspiration, customers or professionals will not be inclined to buy the product nor talk about it in social networking.

The partly slanted mud table

In designing industrial products, I strongly respect engineering rationalities, even as I deploy my palette of colors in different types of forms and shapes, always co-opting visual art. The inspiration probably comes from my mother who, in our Shahidnagar refugee colony near Kolkata, made me an 18 inch, partly slanted reading table with mud. I could sit on the floor, keep my books there to read and write on. Saying poverty is no excuse for ugliness, she would obsessively keep everything very aesthetically, particularly swabbing my table with cow dung and water every day.

The monsoon season invariably broke everything. When water lashed into our bamboo-wall, thatched-roof mud house, her priority was always on how quickly she can remake my slanting table. Thereafter, as I attended my gorgeous British-architecture art college in Kolkata and went on to become a designer in Paris, I realized my mother's sense of visual art in design in that slanted mud table. My childhood training has grown in me as I breathe visual art in my way of life today.

Beyond 2 + 2 = 4

An engineering product design that is associated with visual art has high and unlimited appeal, beyond the $2 + 2 = 4$ equation. India requires massive numbers of engineering designers with the capacity to transform an engineering design to a selling proposition that is driven by visual art. There is great potential for such careers that command attractive remuneration. But the product's quality, functionality, and performance can never be compromised for the duration of its lifespan in customer or professional usage as per its industry standard. In mass production, visual art is a very decisive factor for business success.

Seny rauxa pull for business

When digital technology is commoditizing the world, the only way for a brand or corporation to survive is with the pull of seny rauxa. That is visual art too.

The combine of opposites

While working in the Spanish market with my business associate, I understood the content of two opposites embedded in Spanish art; on one side is *seny* which means rational and on the other is *rauxa* which amounts to crazy energy. This fascinating seny rauxa culture is alive in Spain's incredible 20th century paintings, architecture, music, and films. It is this combine that has unleashed new schools of art from a troubled Spanish society.

From growing political instability, Spain was plunged into a bloody civil war in 1936. The war ended in a nationalist dictatorship led by General Francisco Franco with the support of Nazi Germany and Fascist Italy. Over 500,000 lives were lost and half a million citizens fled the country, mainly to Latin America. Franco remained neutral but sympathetic to the Axis powers in World War II and controlled Spain until his death in 1975.

Distinction in Spanish art

Among those fleeing Spain were artists Pablo Picasso (1881–1973), Joan Miró (1893–1983), and Salvador Dalí (1904–1989). Their revolt against the Spanish political situation was so strong a friction that it let loose very high rauxa (crazy energy) from them. That rauxa created a phenomenal pull factor in the world, raising high both their name and their branding as painters. At the same time, the command they had over their craftsmanship and the cause they espoused were extremely seny (rational).

Picasso, among history's most prolific artists, worked in France. His most famous painting, Guernica, was inspired by his revulsion at the bombing of the Basque town in Spain's Civil War. Versatile Miró created a distinctive, witty style, blending surrealism and abstraction. Salvador Dalí, a flamboyant painter, sculptor, and experimental filmmaker, is probably the greatest surrealist artist who worked from France and the US. He used bizarre rauxa dream imagery to create unforgettable landscapes of his inner world. The unmistakable seny rauxa balance in these Spanish artists' works was so powerful that they continue to create waves across cultures, helping people see things differently even today.

Spaniard Antonio Gaudi's architecture was totally rauxa. He translated human flesh into brick and mortar, but his architectural plan was seeped in seny. The fanatical virtuoso Spanish flamenco guitarist Paco de Lucía brought rauxa in his guitar stroke and sound, but was totally seny in Western music's scientific grammar.

Surrealism in films

Spanish filmmaker Luis Bunuel founded surrealism in films with totally rauxa attitude based on seny film techniques. In his famous 1967 film, *Belle de Jour* (Daytime Beauty), he illustrated rauxa in France's sophisticated but incestuous high society. It was the story of a woman who does not sleep with her husband as she feels frigid and sexually unfulfilled. One day she overhears a friend talking about a chic Parisian brothel. This triggers her, quite uncharacteristically, to want to experience prostitution to satisfy different kinds of people with sex. She decides to spend her midweek afternoons as a prostitute, so she was *Belle de Jour*. The film depicts how the brothel's well-to-do middle-aged clients do not like her amateur street-whore-acting stunts, and how she fell in love with an ugly young underground crook with artificial teeth.

The film exposed the power of women much ahead of its time as the first Women's Liberation Conference was held later in 1969 at Ruskin College, UK. It can be argued that *Belle de Jour*, totally disturbing the society, was the departure for the women's liberation movement, but it certainly represented surrealism in films.

This seny rauxa paradox from artists, cinema, music, or architecture was highly recognized by the masses. In their day-to-day social context, the public may only have seny without the occasion to express rauxa, but the seny rauxa contradiction provokes and stimulates them, creating a huge pull factor. Digital technology is making today's world seny, that is, logical. So you may miss the blend of seny rauxa in business areas such as building leaders, how you treat your brand, or how end-customers look at your organization. If they are indifferent to your brand, it means your market value will

be very low. So you can imagine how this impact can drain
your bottom line.

Five sensorial facets

Brands of any category, or corporations in any industry, are
totally framed around the end-customer's five sensorial fac-
ets of seeing, smelling, tasting, hearing, and touching. These
five senses ignite purchase behavior and bring business to
all companies. But these senses touch every end-customer's
mental chord differently. If you are only seny you will not be
perceived, being only rauxa, people will consider you mad.
But your seny rauxa blend can create the pull that converts
to the act of purchase.

Take Apple's devices, their look and application procedure
are totally seny. But Apple encourages customers to experience their own rauxa by what is inside the product or service.
That is why Apple's brand pull, admiration, bottom line, and
market cap are all so seny today.

McDonald's is another seny rauxa balance

In the heart of the world's most expensive, classy boulevard,
Champs Elysses in Paris, McDonald's mesmerizes masses
who cannot afford any other restaurant in this up-market
place to enjoy dinner or celebrate a birthday at Euro 5 per
person. Crossing Nashik, Maharashtra, five years ago, I found
McDonald's here too. The outlet's young public relations
(PR) person from a nearby village took me on a tour of their
backend.

He said the first thing employees are required to do every morning is clean their hands up to their armpits with soap and water in a separate sink in the kitchen. He explained how they do not mix vegetarian and nonvegetarian food. He then opened a dustbin with fresh-looking hamburgers. These were fried but not consumed within a certain period of time, so McDonald's required that they be trashed. Such processes are all part of seny, including selling a ₹25 hamburger in a sophisticated McDonald's in India.

Customers anywhere in the world visit an American McDonald's to experience oversize rauxa energy. They feel crazily rauxa clicking photographs with Roland McDonald statue sitting on a bench outside. This crazy energy (rauxa) is Mc Donald's familiarity.

India's below-30 Zapper generation is wrapped up in seny rauxa; they love its bad, ugly, and good combine. In their psychology, good is the seny, and bad and ugly the rauxa. If you are not in tune with the seny rauxa balance from the end-customer's perspective, stagnancy may prevent your way forward. So bring in the seny rauxa pull into your corporation and brand.

Intangibles extend every human moment

Whenever I speak of intangibles having unlimited value, I am often met with silence in India. Intangibles comprise that seny rauxa combine of allure on a foundation of believable quality.

Never a readymade formula

In our consulting practice, we need to constantly create intangibles for our clients' deliverables. We work to sustainably connect them to their end-customers in today's banal market. Intangibles always come from a strong, tangible craftsmanship platform. Anything tangible has to have logic, science, and is materialistic, but these are technicalities. When elevated to a certain point they become elusive, making them intangible.

The boundary-less, elusive substance that is the intangible is absolutely nonintellectual; it is never a readymade formula. What is intangible for you may not be for me. So creating intangibles in a subject for mass consumption requires passion and a multi-angle approach beyond the obvious. In business, intangibles are invaluable, the basis of an organization's goodwill. Only when customers first appreciate this intangible, will they pay a premium for it, and return for repeat purchase. Better profitability, better share price, and better market capitalization are all related to intangibles (see Figure 2.1).

Figure 2.1   The Trajectory of Intangible Creation

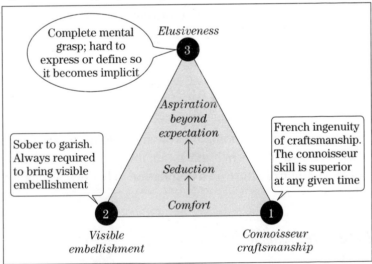

Source: Author's own.

Being nurtured with intangibles

Learning of, admiring, and ingraining intangibles in my body and mind may have roots in the milieu of artists I was associated with at the start of my life in France. As part of my sweeper's job in a lithography print shop, I had to deliver packets of 175 lithography proofs to the painter's car. When the painter would offer me a service tip, I would refuse and instead ask for a chance to spend time in his atelier.

Maitre Arte

When I met Maitre (Master) Arte, Russian-born Parisian artist and designer, at his atelier, he told me of his obsession with the *encadreure* (framer) of his paintings. It took me time to understand that Arte found a framer to be unique because he understood the artistic value of Arte's paintings.

Yves Brayer

Another famous French landscape painter, Yves Brayer, used to sit me down in his atelier and narrate his imagination of the south of France, the primary subject of his paintings. I have since then been to the south of France many times, but I have always seen its reality overshadowed through Brayer's paintings.

My fixation on the intangible went through several artistes. I became good friends with celebrated mime Marcel Marceau, illustrious photographer Marc Riboud, and feted writer-singer

Francis Lemarque; they all showed me the tangible base of the intangible.

Daniel Prevost

Renowned theater-TV-film actor Daniel Prevost, of the famous film *The Dinner Game* where he acted as an income tax officer, told me about professionalism. He recounted how he drops his persona when on stage. He recounted how, on the day he lost his loved one, he had to playact comic absurdity to create the intangible so that his theater audience could connect and be mesmerized. "People don't see Daniel Prevost when I play a role, they see what I represent. So I detach myself on stage to create the intangible of the character."

Francis Lemarque

Francis Lemarque eulogized the beauty of Paris in a song that traveled across the globe. One day he described to me his sad childhood, how his Lithuanian Jewish mother was suddenly transported off to the Auschwitz Nazi gas chamber, and he had to overcome this mental stress. He said he looked up at the Paris skyline to write the song that intangibly made the world dream about Paris, but his own ground reality was very cruel.

Marcel Marceau

After watching Marcel Marceau's mime artistry in Le Theatre des Champs-Elysees I asked him how, through his "art of silence," he could transport his audience to a totally different atmosphere on a vacant stage. Over dinner at my home in Paris he explained that this is the drama of the intangible. He practices in real surroundings for several hours, tangibly touching and feeling everything to totally internalize it all. The moment he comes to the empty stage, he transposes all the tangible aspects into his act, allowing the audience to feel and visualize them even as the stage is without sets. A critic once wrote of his ingenious "Youth, Maturity, Old Age and Death": "He accomplishes in less than two minutes what most novelists cannot do in volumes."

Marc Riboud

Marc Riboud of Magnum Photos, an international photographic cooperative, was famous for powerfully capturing fleeting moments in potent compositions. He happened to be connected to my design school, Academie Julian, when I topped a project. Afterwards, he invited me to Magnum where I saw his famous 1957 photo of Jawaharlal Nehru laughing together with Chou en Lai, obviously not anticipating the 1962 India–China scuffle.

Marc explained to me how the camera's view should arrest that exact memorable moment that can never become old. The visual direction should cover the 24 × 36 frame, with no cropping. The picture may be still, but it should look like it is moving. There is always the dilemma of whether to focus on the foreground, mid-ground, or background within a second. He trained me that the main subject can become a timeless intangible only by highly calibrating the focus dilemma. He said a photograph has to be so intangible that it becomes universal for all nationalities to understand at a glance.

Value beyond a price

Thousands of customers I interact with in my work deal with intangibles in different ways. As a poor child, I remember it was an incredible experience to sit in an Ambassador car and touch the steering wheel and pedals. A rich person is likely to have the same intangible feeling in a Rolls Royce. In the intangibles of love and affection you want to recall certain moments over and over again. The materialistic world of developed countries is highly driven by intangibles that you value beyond the price.

A brand's real value is its intangibles. But every brand cannot be for everyone, as something intangible for you may not be for others. In the same category, Lexus gives you more features but Mercedes commands a higher price as people value its intangibles. It is not cost that matters though. The US$30 Swatch watch has created aspiration as it is driven by higher intangibles of changing fashion than the expensive watches.

Intangibles form and grow from a product's rational credibility with functional advantage. It may remain totally tacit with the user, but its unspoken presence is too vital for business houses of any size to ignore. Starting at ground zero, your business can grow to become gigantic tomorrow if you have the capacity to uniquely deliver the customers' hidden desire for intangibles. For business results beyond the obvious, you must take regular baths in the ocean of the intangible.

3

Quality Customers Want

Quality Required to Poke with

In today's world any sustaining business requires an outstanding predictable quality that is recognized globally. That goes against the grain of jalebis as no one can predict its exact shape. If your brand does not figure positively via customers' word-of-mouth in their social life and regular repeat purchase does not happen, whether for FMCG or impulsive luxury goods, long-life cycle engineering products, or mass to business-to-business (B2B) services, your brand is drying up.

The huge quality lacuna in most Indian industrial products and services is possibly due to Hinduism's diverse culture with multiple gods and belief systems, no dogma. This democracy allows everyone to interpret everything his or her own way, including every customer touch point quality process. In single God cultures such as Catholicism, Islam, and Buddhism people have the discipline to follow one religious way. The oldest 2,000-year-old religious administration of the Vatican remains intact today. From this same belief system, Western industries have *been able to maintain highly defined quality standards since the industrial revolution. Due to one-belief-system discipline, they had no scope to tinker around it by themselves. None of this reflects my view or criticism; it is just the intrinsic nature of different cultures. So how can we deal with it?*

To erase the negative effects of the jalebi in business, I have devised many tools, processes, and frameworks in the course of my consulting practice since 1984. Emotional Surplus is that extra benefit the customers experience which makes them go for repeat purchase of a brand. The brand must have the PUB Reflex on the shelf, "provoke" the customer to "understand" the product and "buy" it. What makes people buy is perceptible selling distinction (PSD) comprising word-of-mouth, first visual appearance, and actual experience. Discover a few more strategic poke doses here to help you cut those crooked jalebi ideas. Delivery of the product or service to customers should be molded with quality customers want (QCW) that requires the ReFinE mechanism.

Is quality cultural?

"Religion is the opium of the masses," said communism ideologue Karl Marx. Had he experienced the political scenario after imperialism and feudalism, he may have said politics is more than opium, it is anesthesia to make the population sleep. However, nobody can deny that a country's cultural base is always religion.

Nonvisible quality

I have been introspecting about why, collectively, India is not quite quality-centric. In executive learning workshops I try to project that as a deliverable's hidden part is its real quality, companies should stretch to score here. But this nonvisible quality area gets scant attention from participants, both senior and middle management. They appear not to seriously consider it, although QCW continues to be an ongoing concern. Being at a loss to understand this, let me hazard an analysis with religious roots. Please take my analysis without prejudice; I respect every individual's faith and that starts from my mother who is religious.

France, my adopted country since I was 19, is Catholic dominated. Here God is one and good and bad values are well established. It is the only credibly anchored religion existing in exactly the same administrative way for 2,000 years in the Vatican. Christianity's doctrines and dogmas have underlying rational factors that bind 2.2 billion Christians in a strong belief system. Catholic rules were so strong that in 1559, refusing to go to church attracted a 12-pence fine. Religion does not allow killing, yet politics found a way to eliminate enemies. They had legitimized political death sentence by pulling in a Catholic priest to certify that society is sacrificing its evil side. The guilty is told that society will be cleansed when his death sentence is executed. However, before his death the priest pardons him for his misdeed by saying, "God will save you." This clearly proves that politics anesthetizes society beyond religion.

Freedom for the mind

Before the Church gave freedom of expression in art, litera-
ture, and science in the end of 15th century, people were not
allowed to think, create, or write anything beyond God. Using
this liberalization, Western society mesmerized the world with
invention after invention that defied nature to have control
over the universe. But their value system called *valeur rationelle* is always recognizable. All, believers and atheists alike,
consciously follow cultural cue and attachment to one God,
one principal rational belief system; for believers to avoid
God's wrath.

If you extrapolate Christianity's single God and belief factor, you will find it exists in Islam, Buddhism, and Judaism.
These believers in any country have the same understanding because their known indoctrinated practices glue them
culturally. To enter the faith you have to convert through a
religious ceremony. When a mix of Catholics, Muslims, and
Jewish live together there is constant friction, as we witness
in Europe today.

One God

In developed countries, not everyone regularly practices
religion or believes in God. But their single-minded collective focus in one nonvisible God is so strong that everyone
can easily strive for one goal. They can cooperatively sub-
sume subjectivity toward a common discipline. Sex is taboo
in Catholicism, allowed only for procreation. A section of
Christians revolted against this denial of sex and abortion. But
in spite of disruptions and perversions, a religious principle
binds believers to their nonvisible God and his representative
sits in the Vatican.

Religion of multiple Gods

Coming now to Hindu-dominated India, we find hundreds of Gods and Goddesses across South, East, North, and West. Hinduism is a way of life. There is no compulsion of religious dogma. Everyone is a Hindu, every individual's inclination toward God can differ by personal choice. Inside a region or family, two persons can worship two different Gods. This miscellany, along with all other religions that secular India accepts, makes us a vast multiplicity of people requiring no sanction from anyone. So by religion itself we are democratic, even before we claim being the world's biggest political democracy. Appreciation of this liberty is the birth of Hare Krishna movement and hippies in the 1960s when Western Christians sought sanctuary from religious domination and materialism. They looked eastward to find spirituality.

Only in this open-minded milieu of India can you nurture flexibility to drive a US$75 billion (in financial year 2013) global business. That is the strength of India's IT industry which year on year unleashes thousands of engineers to service MNCs in every corner of the globe. Free-thinking and tolerance have unparalleled value, collective discipline becomes a challenge in this egalitarian culture.

Quality customers want

Industrial business systems require quality delivery without deviation and QCW requires collective focus. The collective valeur rationale of societies having the culture of following one God as their single-point focus has made Western business practices very strong in the objective of providing or surpassing QCW.

In multi-God India, different people have different interpretations of any one job. This snowballs into a huge concern in the business arena. India has no QCW standard in any domain. Traditional handicrafts is India's forte, here your expectation is not quality, but folkish representation. Is Hinduism's diversity making it more of a challenge to achieve QCW than anywhere else? My research and sensitive inquiry reveals that Hinduism's go-as-you-like system is subliminally ingrained in the majority of India's population. So collectively, one standard quality has not been easy to gain.

It is normal for every company in India to have employees of different religions and beliefs. But as company culture, how do you align them to a single-minded, common quality drive? In the globalized world where the scale of product and service reproduction is the big business game, there is, now, a clash of understanding the valeur rationelle or nonvisible QCW. The only way to address QCW in India is for every industry to define its quality parameters by filtering the QCW in that industry in their competitive environment. An internal process has to then stringently drive these filtered points as a single company culture.

QCW leads to repeat purchase

After all, what is QCW but the straight route to customer repeat purchase? Living in the West has disciplined me to obsessively ferret out nonvisible factors that strengthen quality in any delivery. My urge is to always fortify the root working process of every product or service by incorporating QCW.

Businesses in India, both domestic and foreign, require huge QCW discipline. Cultural flexibility was thumbs up for the IT industry; but QCW is the surefire win for each and every company's growth. Indian companies will succeed in competitive global markets only when employees mandatorily drive each company's identified QCW parameters.

Intelligent industries push the quality button

It was not customers who took the initiative to want quality. Entrepreneurs with business ingenuity as well as visionary industries, seeking an edge in the customer's mind, surprised them with quality they were not expecting.

Customers in a commanding position

Today, customers have already lapped up the new that businesses offered them. They have reversed industry's dominance over them. It is the QCW and customers have learnt to command it, making industries bend backward to provide QCW.

Changing service rules

Let us go back a century to see how industry raised the quality sense of the customer. In 1907, a 19-year-old Jim Casey borrowed US$100 to find a six-bicycle messenger service that later went on to challenge United States Post Office (USPO) in existence since 1775. Calling the company United Parcel

Service (UPS) from 1919, UPS totally surprised people with faster and quality home-delivery couriers. Just imagine, up to 1906 nobody even bothered to think beyond the post office to receive parcels. This quality business model educated American masses that an alternative beyond USPO is possible. It kicked off customer expectation in another way.

Sensing opportunity, competition then jumped in with distinctive services. From there, courier service ballooned into a big industry, compelling the government's US$65.71 billion USPO to downsize every year by closing down post offices. Conversely, the top three courier companies continue to grow such as UPS with US$53.1 billion, FedEx with US$39.3 billion, and DHL with US$52.76 billion in 2011. UPS alone now delivers over 15 million packages every day to 6.1 million customers in more than 220 countries. To stay in business, industry has no choice but to provide better and better QCW.

World wars raised the quality bar

Two bloody world wars that claimed 80 million lives contributed tremendously to upgrade industrial quality. Quality obsession was tremendous to win the war. The Allies were not prepared for Hitler's war weaponry aimed to prove Germany's technological power. America had to beef up research to make weapons of higher quality. From 1942 to 1945, Allies versus Axis was purely a quality fight of weapons' superiority.

Hitler's ultimate dream was 1,000 years of worldwide Nazi rule. Even the simple barbed fence pillars of Auschwitz concentration camp were accurately well built, although they were rapidly constructed in 1940. The conclusion we can draw from historical evidence is that defense industry during the world wars also raised quality bar.

Japanese changed European auto industry rules

Even dropping the atom bomb in World War II could not crush Japan's collective ingenuity to come out from the destruction. They have taken a single-point value addition to the world which is quality. Europeans invented the automobile, the Japanese invested in QCW.

I remember on my various US business trips in the 1980s, I had become fascinated with Japanese cars booming in the US markets. Japanese cars, however, had a hard time entering Europe as protectionism discouraged a Japanese manufacturing hub there. My French auto dealer would say, "Careful, if you have an accident you have to wait 2–3 months for Japanese spares. Also, insurance cost is exorbitant." In those days, Europe was selling a bare-bones car; you had to pay extra for options of accessories such as air conditioning, music system, right-side mirror, sun visor, automatic window-glass opener, and other features. Industries regulations were galore. You had to drive the first 1,000 km at a certain speed, service it after 1,500 km, pay for the second service starting 5,000 km, and so on.

In one fell swoop of ingenious quality, the Japanese handed over the car keys to the buyer fully loaded with all features. The car offered free service after 10,000 km and you could drive at whatever speed you wanted from day one. The Japanese simply showed customers how to increase their "want," established QCW in Europe, and changed the rule of the market.

QCW for push-cart or BMW?

One day in Kolkata I found a flamboyant person driving a sophisticated BMW convertible. Alongside him was a push-cart with a front-puller, a back-pusher, and three people in the center holding the merchandise. Both the rich and poor were enjoying Kolkata's winter breeze under the open sky. Which customer's requirement should the QCW of this road be based on, the BMW convertible that needs a smooth tarred road or a dirt road that would be fine for the push-cart?

Living with extreme tolerance in India's diversity, we have not been able to appreciate quality at the mass level. These past 60 years, the common man has been dependent on different party politicians claiming to represent the poor. There is no single point of good and bad, as laid down in non-Hindu, one-God religions, so it is difficult to identify the quality that politics requires in this heterogeneous society. Similarly, it is difficult to imagine what collective QCW to apply. Without commonly set standardized norms, it is clear that business houses have a great opportunity to drive the QCW delivery model.

Indian masses require advanced small machine for livelihood generation

In developed countries, invention through industrial design for different types of machines has raised the livelihood and lifestyle of the masses even during the Great Depression. India's masses similarly require modern portable machines incorporated with mechanical and digital engineering for their ease of livelihood generation. Everybody is not an office *babu*. The backbone of the country's working-class strength is the small farmer and independent entrepreneurs in multiple domains. This young generation of self-employed workers has a huge urge to grow in life but in the absence of contemporary machines to ease their work they cannot earn more.

For developing such engineering products, we cannot always go to developed countries to get designs done. That is because they do not quite understand the diverse quality definition of India's common people. It is time for Indian industry to lead the way in raising the exceptional quality bar for the masses. Quality consciousness of Indian workers has risen under the influence of globalization, television, and user-friendly mobile phones. So industry needs to provide these evolved workers high-quality standard machines that "reduce effort, increase comfort."

"Reduce effort, increase comfort" is a framework for engineering products I had established and wrote about in my book *Jalebi Management: All Stakeholders Can Enjoy a Bite.*[1] Engineering products' manufacturers can apply this framework for designing products this workforce can use. This will make the workforce more skilled with the consciousness of a new kind of QCW that the Indian industry can provide them.

Doing so can change the face of the country's economy in the next decade by developing poor people's working skill set and capability. Is it not high time Indian industry raised the bar as UPS and the Japanese did?

Sparkling quality, the global next mark

Indian industry is married to basic, technical quality processes, but not to perceptible exceptional or exciting quality in the customer's hand that Japanese and Korean companies deliver.

---

[1] Shombit Sengupta. 2007. *Jalebi Management: All Stakeholders Can Enjoy a Bite.* New Delhi: SAGE Publications.

Industrial technical quality processes are mandatory for achieving the standard

Implementing technical quality-process engineering is a hygiene factor that delivers no competitive edge. Unless the society's state of mind is driven by the consciousness of user interface quality supremacy, no quality system will fall in place for Indian brands to meet the challenge of global competition. Quality in the customer's hand first creates trust and in long-term usage it becomes believable. It is totally a nonvisible, hidden factor. The customer experiences this quality at the discretion of the enterprise providing it.

In Executive MBA courses or customer-centricity training workshops for Indian companies, whenever I have tried to expose the hidden quality factor that creates customer trust and loyalty, I have confronted a wall called quality process. R&D engineers, marketing, customer service, and top management revere International Organization for Standardization (ISO), Total Quality Management (TQM), Deming, or Six Sigma quality that translate to working in a system that brings discipline and defect-free processes. But when every company follows the same system in a category, does it create the distinction the customer wants to receive?

Quality spark

As a product's repeat purchase is dependent on customer choice, surely the paramount quality parameter to run after is the customer's appreciation of the "quality spark" beyond any process. A few professionals who have undergone my training sessions in India are now working expatriates in Germany and Korea. They have called me to say that they are actually experiencing what they could not appreciate in India: that customers want this "quality spark."

After realizing the value of quality as the rational factor for a customer to confidently and repeatedly buy a brand, one professional wrote, "Developed society is highly differentiated, products are matched minutely to specific customer unstated needs. Their ecosystem is driven by quality that world-class products and technologies compete to provide." Another's comment was, "Pent up demand is huge in India, and low price is the driving factor. Industrial development has accordingly been based on need, not experience or expression. Products are considered okay when it satisfies the basic intended purpose."

Hidden rational quality

Neither manufacturer nor employees easily understand or focus on the hidden rational quality. They call Mercedes, BMW, Louis Vuitton, and Mont Blanc, among others, as costly lifestyle and status brands, but never ask how they have become so recognized globally. No education or training system has apprised them of the invention, innovation, and sustaining quality guaranteed on the life cycle of these products. I have never heard anyone here talk about the many trials, failures, tests, and customer clinics these brands have undergone. They admire the brands only in the form of visible glamorous advertisements with their global reputation only.

That tells me that India's cultural experience ignores the grid of quality excellence. In general, saris sell on weaving style and folkloric designs from different states. Sari shops give no guarantee on color as they say there is no single processed cleaning system. Customers happily street shop beautifully designed footwear at amazingly low prices. They do not bother with quality, they just consider design and color. In jewelry, weight of gold is the first check, next is design. Rarely do women focus on the clasp's robustness which is intrinsic to quality. Unhygienic selling conditions at kirana stores or small eateries are tolerated if the food tastes fine.

These few examples among others show that quality consciousness is vulnerable. Will Indian brands be sustainable in future when global brands fiercely compete in India with sparkling quality and affordable price?

My long experience in Europe has taught me the importance of hidden quality, which is their cultural phenomenon. Whenever I have probed out of curiosity, the answer I get is that meticulous keeping of historical records creates the grid of benchmarking with the best. That grid established Mozart as the master music composer of all time. George Stephenson is respected for his invention of the steam locomotive, although that has since been bettered with the Chinese CRH380A becoming the world's fastest train running at 302.8 miles per hour.

From making industrial production in unlimited quantities, the West became conscious that customers expect impeccable quality. Quality that cannot be questioned is sustainable over the long term, and so the product's reputation spreads. Product development with differentiating character requires time and money. The more solid and unparalleled the quality of reproduction compared to competitors, the more you can sell eventually. The longevity of the product improves its market, and this can be encashed for high returns on investment.

"It works well for me"

If a customer utters these words, it means the functional factor of a product or service delivery is satisfactory. Functionality is the prime criterion of a selling proposition. Development of human society happened always after achieving excellence in functionality in various products and services. From copies made through stone lithography to carbon copy, cyclostyling to photocopy to digital scan, wherever functionality improved with better technology, it made earlier versions obsolete.

"I believe in it"

When customers say these words, it means they are addressing the key rational factor. I have found it difficult to make people fully appreciate that. Rational means nonvisible quality support for emotive and functional attributes to sustain product longevity. In the hospitality industry, for example, if a hotel uses sophisticated German sanitary ware but the maintenance is poor, you have to hold your nose to get rid of the stink. This totally bypasses the rational factor in the service industry and mitigates the heavy spend on sanitary ware to look good.

"It looks good"

This is the fragile emotive attribute that instantly differentiates a product or service. But repeat purchase cannot happen if functionality fails, for example, if a perfume bottle looks beautiful but the spray jet, the functional part, hurts your body, you will never buy that perfume again. To make the functional part soothing requires the initiative to find superfine technology that customers cannot see but can experience. This nonvisible rational part is the manufacturer's good judgment initiative to make the spray system acceptable.

You can experience functionality upfront, see and appreciate the emotive factor. But for the product's intrinsic quality, you have to trust the company's brand at the moment of purchase. How do you build that?

I do not believe people regularly buy a product or service based on emotion through its ad or sophisticated product or service presentation only. Customer believability for repeat purchase lies on "sparkling quality" that is nonvisible. Quality is the assurance of the product's functionality during its life cycle. So you need to define QCW specific to your brand in the competitive environment.

Ignite QCW

The biggest hunger of global brands across industries is how to make low-priced products that have unique QCW, the key to repeat purchase.

Every category has its own QCW

Impacted by the high standard of global brands in India, customers are experiencing and getting habituated to elevated quality where the efficiency of rational factors is exposed.

Let us take three sectors where QCW is enjoyed at affordable rates: McDonald's offers an American burger lunch at ₹25 in air-conditioned and extremely hygienic setting. Several budget hotels of foreign brands provide perceptible quality of comfort and ambience at three-star hotel rates. Toyota's Quality Revolution is setting benchmarks for the automobile industry.

The QCW illustration in Figure 3.1 shows that in any given category customers have their own or influenced perception of the quality spark. Switching to QCW brands, customers are making several Indian brands that were ruling the roost in the license-raj era lose their market leadership. In automobiles or customer electronics, Hindustan Motors or BPL, among others, dominated the market till the 1997. Today, people willingly pay a higher price for competing foreign brands but they will haggle with Indian brands in every market segment when QCW is not perceived. Sony, Samsung, and LG conquered the customer-electronics market, bringing in new technology, customer focus, and perceivable sparkling quality from reliability (rational factor), functionality, and the aesthetic (emotive) edge.

The clash emerging now is that India is following the lifestyle of developed countries where rational factor efficiency is very high. Take a look at Point 3 in Figure 3.1 regarding industries that impose the trend. Examples of trendy brands are McDonald's in fast food; Louis Vuitton, Gucci, and Rolex in luxury products; and Apple, Google, Nikon, Facebook, IBM, Microsoft, and Samsung in technology. In personal care it is L'Oreal; in magazines Forbes and Vogue; in financial institutions HSBC and American Express; in apparel Zara, Esprit, and Hugo Boss; while coveted vehicles are Harley Davidson, BMW, and Audi; and sportswear Nike and Adidas.

Figure 3.1 How QCW Gets Formed

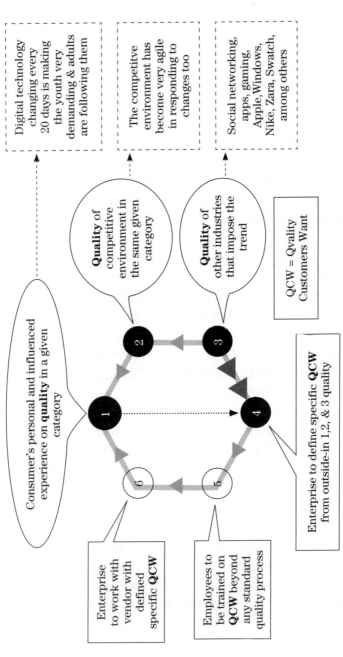

Digital technology changing every 20 days is making the youth very demanding & adults are following them

The competitve environment has become very agile in responding to changes too

Social networking, apps, gaming, Apple, Windows, Nike, Zara, Swatch, among others

Quality of competitive environment in the same given category

Quality of other industries that impose the trend

QCW = Qvality Customers Want

Consumer's personal and influenced experience on **quality** in a given category

Enterprise to define specific **QCW** from outside-in 1,2, & 3 quality

Enterprise to work with vendor with defined specific **QCW**

Employees to be trained on **QCW** beyond any standard quality process

Source: Author's own.

Want control over nature

Through inventions that go against nature, Western society created products and living style that reduce effort and increase comfort for people in every domain. Whatever social culture we may follow, we cannot ignore the comfort standards provided in the refrigerator, automobile, mobile phone, and the lift to Facebook, among others, in our daily life. The more our country develops, it is obvious that we will minutely follow the well-defined, materialistic lifestyle of developed countries. So the only choice Indian brands have to become sustainable in the market is to uplift the rational quality spark along with incredible user interface of the functionality.

Make no compromise on the rational quality factor

Every company has to take into account the customer's perception of quality, competitive environment, and trendy industries that influence the customer. Working for Indian companies, my priority is to sensitize their employees to make the nonvisible rational attribute of a product or service flawless. Employees have to be trained on QCW beyond any standard quality process. To actually achieve QCW, the company has to inspire, train, and control its vendors. The purchase order has to precisely define the QCW.

Most global brands outsource from China giving precise quality parameters and China delivers accordingly. But Indians often criticize Chinese products. That may not be China's fault as they admit they will compromise quality standards based on the cost the manufacturer bargains for.

Offering high salaries, MNCs in India are stringently imposing their proven processes and customer-centricity to bring global quality standard. I have heard that Indian professionals are leaving MNCs to return to Indian organizations that have revised their salary structure to keep up with MNCs to get greater freedom at work.

The catch here is if "freedom at work" means ignoring QCW, how can Indian companies improve? According to me, business cannot be sustained, whether it is corporate performance, brand, industrial product design, or organized retail, if the quality spark is missing. Indian brands need to ignite QCW to ensure repeat purchase and be globally competitive and recognized.

Quality beyond its process

You can have multiple ways to look at QCW. Appearance, functional experience, and trust are QCW parameters of any product or service.

The cart-vendor's QCW

When you see a cart-vendor shining his customer-facing apples to always look inviting and sort them to avoid any defective one on view, you know it is not just an ephemeral emotive factor. An apple looking good gives quality assurance. So you want to instantly bite it. Its appearance seduces you to buy it. When you devour the apple, experiencing its succulent taste as functional quality, you are simultaneously convinced psychologically about the high quality of this breed of apples. This was not visible at the time of purchase. But on biting, if you did not like the quality of experience, you will automatically stop eating it and lose confidence in it.

So only looking good is never enough to win the trust of quality. From looks to the bite function to the root that allowed quality growth, all have to be orchestrated for the customer to experience quality. There could be a catch on bite enjoyment, which can be disastrous if the produce is bad. Or another nuance could be customers preferring a different type of taste. Some like the juice to sputter when bitten, others like a grainy bite, and so on. What this proves is that one quality parameter cannot be suitable for all.

Customers have four types of requirements

The four different quality parameters are (1) expressed need and (2) expressed desire, and (3) unarticulated need and (4) unarticulated desire.

Products or services in a category always require different pricing segments. For example, a woman's handbag can cost ₹200 from street vendors and up to ₹200,000 from Louis Vuitton; both are available within a short distance in the same market. Today, we also have trendsetters such as Apple, Google, Facebook, Nike, and Samsung, among others, that influence every industry. They have changed the customer's habit, perspective, and expectations in everyday use products and services.

If you use the QCW framework, it will oblige you to very specifically diagnose the customer's psychographics in micro detail. Let us elaborately look at the four types of customer need.

Expressed need

Women are more conscious about falling hair than men who are generally resigned to the inevitable loss of hair. Can she ever accept going bald? So any therapy on hair care is an expressed need. Science continues to evolve on how to protect hair fall. The combination of science and naturalness is tangibly believable; the market scope of this factor will always be there. This market often faces a traffic jam with multiple lifestyle advertising showing beautiful women with plenty of hair. But is it so easy for brands in this category to make customers believe without showing tangible benefits? Customers will never pay attention if products in expressed need areas are not disruptive and scientifically proven.

Expressed desire

When people learn to walk in childhood, their first desire is to run. Health professionals set the trend in running; people have followed them in the hope of overcoming health issues. That is when intelligent industries put the treadmill in the market. Continuing running from open natural surroundings to a treadmill in the gymnasium's limited space is the real conversion of expressed desire.

This expressed desire, which is another angle of QCW, can be raised to become more desirable. The treadmill can be made to calculate performance, body and pulse movement, and further, for continuous addition in the expressed desire category, even a touch-screen TV system can be put. In future you will be running in a treadmill in front of a virtual life-size screen image taking you to different countries or situations virtually.

Unarticulated need

After Thomas Alva Edison invented sound duplication in the 19th century, the entertainment industry expanded with endless varieties of music, with a phenomenal array from rhythm to cultural contexts in different countries. When we have so many collections of old vinyl records, cassettes, or CDs, will we ever listen to them through different playing instruments? Will we ever have the time or inclination to go back to different periods of our music collection?

By simplifying all applications, Apple iPod responded to this unarticulated need of experiencing any part of one's own musical collection anytime, anywhere, with a fingertip. We can carry diverse and unlimited musical entertainment in the pocket. Apple did not invent any musical paradigm, merely catered to an unarticulated need.

If perfectly designed with simplification, any unarticulated-need product can make obsolete a lot of standard systems in the world. The iPod practically killed the cassette, Walkman, and CD player. By grabbing society's latent trend, you as an entrepreneur can always create a new habit by giving birth to a new unarticulated need in any domain. To do that, you have to submerge yourself in a continuous QCW bath.

Unarticulated desire

Do not ignore the human desire to see everything in magnified size. Pulling the chewing gum to experiment its stretch ability, or blowing bigger and bigger bubbles in the mouth is an unexpressed desire. That is why inventions like the magnifying glass, binoculars, telescope, and even the microscope have been so successful and used for such diverse purposes.

All these enlarging habits already exist. Taking habit and putting it in the telephone screen is unarticulated desire.

By inventing the picture or smooth text-enlargement system
in the smart mobile phone, Apple fulfilled this unarticulated
desire. With two fingers you touch an object on the screen;
move your fingers apart and the picture will enlarge. This
action feels truly hedonistic. This trend has become like a need,
so people have the tendency to see if this progressive enlarge-
ment is there in other products where there is a virtual screen.

The possibility of transferring some human habit in one
industry to another industry can change the whole category.
If QCW drives the quality process and discipline in your
enterprise, you can address perceptible value in any of the
four needs of the customer.

Industrial reproduction needs QCW oxygen

When I was a sweeper in a Paris lithography print shop from
1974 to 1976, I sometimes had to rub two very heavy stone
slabs for hours to create the texture for lithography. One day,
renowned French painter Lucien Fontanarosa, who had come
there for his lithography and knew me as a painter, was very
sympathetic seeing me, a skinny artist engaged in hard labor.
He raised my spirits saying the reproduction I was sweating
over was very noble work.

Route to industrial reproduction = QCW

Fontanarosa explained how reprduction first came from
German Johannes Gutenberg's invention of the printing

press around 1440. Gutenberg made it possible to precisely duplicate written words in large quantities for people to communicate far and wide. Then in 1796, a Bavarian author, Alois Senefelder, invented a method for reproducing paintings through lithography copy by using stones or metal plates. French inventor Joseph Nicéphore Niépce produced the first permanent photographic image in 1826.

Then an American, Thomas Alva Edison, invented sound reproduction in the phonograph, 1877. Reproduction for industrial assembly line production was innovated by American mechanical engineer Frederick Winslow Taylor. His famous Taylor System in the assembly line at Ford Motors changed industrial efficiency for all time.

From here to the vinyl disc to xerox and cassettes, Microsoft to the iPod, a huge industry has been created for large-scale reproduction. In the backdrop of such inventions, the biggest headache Western companies had faced was introducing an uncontestable, sustaining quality parameter. They had to ensure that QCW across geographies would always be met. Actually this mass industrial reproduction ended up as globalization.

Reproductive power was transferred from the West to Southeast Asia, first Japan, then Korea and Malaysia, and now China is the big manufacturing hub churning out high-quality duplication. The quality of the reproduction product is often not visible to customers during purchase, but without QCW, a brand will never gain global acceptance. So it is clear that the inventive Western reproduction model simultaneously addresses quality through product durability in its life cycle. Southeast Asia is excelling in quality reproduction. Will India remain a user only for lack of quality-reproduction ability?

QCW is different in the digital era

The digital world has totally changed the QCW concept for industrial reproduction. From providing durability and functionality in the mechanical era, the quality customers now want is better user interface through innovations, for example, what iPod has provided. Digital reproduction is easy and cheap now. In fact, it can make a bad sound copy into a good one by erasing noise, or it can clean up a picture's background. However, as industry is still largely oriented to physical manufacturing, industrial duplication will continue to need the QCW oxygen.

Mathematical quality system is stale, not QCW

Indian companies often make quality processes boringly routine, akin to pure mathematics which merely gives a count, and never delivers anything by itself. Human intelligence and inventions have changed the world by using mathematics driven with physics, chemistry, and economics. QCW is that vast chemistry–physics–economics combine of the customer's spending logic and pattern.

Traversing the multiple QCW avenues can change a company's perspective. Samsung's meteoric rise within 20 years to acquire top-of-mind recall in customer electronics across the world came from delivering the QCW value. Up to 1990, people only knew of Grundig, Philips, and Sony; now Sony has sold 50 percent of its stake in an LCD joint venture to Samsung.

Leaders unnecessarily force an inside-out approach

Often your company's quality system may compel you to follow an "inside-out" approach which you may not like to disturb as it puts you in a comfort zone. At the same time, you will be asked to create distinction in your product or service delivery for better market share, growth, and profit.

The root cause of why many inventor companies such as Polaroid or Kodak in the photography print domain have become obsolete is sedimentation in their QCW delivery. Digitech is bringing newness every fortnight. Only an "outside-in" approach can measure up to market reality commanded by QCW. Customers are experiencing products and services from diverse trendsetting industries such as mobile phones and cameras, so the QCW quotient grid is changing and evolving very rapidly.

Be sensitive to the unseen side

I have taken an expensive brassiere to different executive learning workshops for engineering to show that QCW also means addressing areas that are not visible or apparent. The bra demonstrates how women are ready to splurge money on the quality value to get tremendous inner comfort and beauty in a garment that is not exposed to the public. That women spend on nonvisible fashion proves that a product's hidden glamour can evoke extreme hedonistic desire.

The inner finish of products often lacks QCW. If you were to lift the smart seat of a stylish car, and it does not look as terrific on the inside, would you not be disappointed? These industrial reproduction areas require huge improvement in India. As do mass service areas such as toilets in our new malls and airports. Many even have imported sanitary ware, but they stink from poor maintenance. Service that has to be reproducible also has a front and reverse side, and both merit to have QCW.

My priority is to sensitize Indian companies to make the rational QCW attribute infallible for industrial-duplication products and services for the masses. It is the unseen, "I believe in it," part that creates customer trust, bringing in repeat purchase. Duplication is an inherent part of business. So driving QCW with latent trends will always be relevant to bringing the future near and creating the "surpass mark" in industry.

Aspiration at the fulcrum

The QCW is balanced by aspiration at the fulcrum.

What does an Audi R8 GT mean?

After finishing a daylong corporate meeting in Chennai one evening, I went to Marina beach to breathe the cool evening breeze. Suddenly, a huge Audi R8 GT stopped. The driver emerged, next a khaki-uniformed policeman-type man, and then a 60-year-old owner wearing a *lungi* (sarong) folded in half. His large family followed, tumbling out on to the beach.

In the West, the most expensive Audi R8 GT is bought for the intangible of personal pleasure to experience its power, technology finesse, and craftsmanship. In India, rich people buy the Audi, but a chauffeur drives it, proving that high-status symbol is enjoyed even as the car's intangibles escape the owner. Lifestyles are moving toward status.

Cost, quality, and aspiration

Aspiration and quality can be equated to human rights, while cost is like a religious sect that follows its own obligatory rules and regulations. If cost is the fulcrum of a deliverable, employees naturally focus on it, even at the cost of paralyzing entrepreneurial business skills. This may satisfy promoters, earn the employee a good appraisal, but it directly affects the brand, reducing it to a substandard quality.

Cost, quality, and aspiration cannot be compromised in any selling proposition at any price point in today's digi-tech market. In seeking aspiration, quality is taken for granted. No longer is she asking, "What is the price?" This was her query before 2000, when savings was her top concern. Post 1991 liberalization, international brands started entering the country. By 2002, new-generation teenagers and the previously deprived-of-choice customers became exposed to high-quality international products. India formally agreed to Trade Related Intellectual Property Rights of WTO and by 2005 markets became flooded with foreign goods. Faced with vast choice, the consuming Indian's standard became of international quality and aspiration. Intense competition brought down prices, making price a hygiene factor.

The West has always gone against nature's given conditions, preferring control over nature through science and technology. This made them invent, irrespective of whether they destroyed the planet's ecosystems in doing so. The human comfort this brought gave rise to the free economy with economic power on one hand and understanding intangibles on the other.

Living peacefully with nature

It is possible that Indian philosophy never sought to change the universe as god-men have always eulogized the benefits of living with nature through systems such as Ayurveda and yoga. So if Indian brands are getting accepted in developed countries, it is merely for cost advantage. This can be dangerous for sustainability. It indicates Indian industries do not understand how to create intangibles in a brand. Western brands justify high price by weaving in aspiration and quality that people accept and pay premium for. Even if they reduce price, aspiration and quality remain.

There is no question that profit is priority in business. But an organization's sustainability demands continuous customer bonding. If structuring cost only through operational efficiency satisfies you, the customer's key aspiration and quality needs remain unaddressed. Quality then becomes a mundane jargon manifested in quality policies hung on factory and office walls.

Volume brings down cost

Looking at the market through aspiration and quality, you will find volume decreases the cost factor. Developed European countries did not factor in volume when they concentrated on aspiration and quality. Consequently, products of aspiration and quality got aligned to high cost. They became sophisticated premium luxury products.

Americans introduced the concept of mass-scale consumption of products. Adopting that scale for mass-consumption products, Japan and Korea injected them with aspiration as priority, with quality inbuilt. Price was used to segment product categories into different customer targets.

Toyota's oobeya

I hugely admire Toyota's extreme sensitivity to cost that is never at the cost of aspiration and quality for customers. Toyota did not invent the automobile. Toyota redefined the automobile's connect to millions across the world. Let me share their *oobeya* with you, a new approach to planning and engineering that promotes more innovation, lower costs, higher quality, and fewer last-minute changes.

Corolla carries the Toyota DNA of quality, reliability, and affordability while evoking customer aspiration. In 1998, Toyota's Chief Engineer Takeshi Yoshida took on the task of redesigning Corolla for a price under US$15,000. Simultaneously, the renovated design was to add high-tech options to win young drivers. Yoshida adopted oobeya, which means a big and open office in Japanese and stands for the power of open minds. It allowed Toyota to cut costs and boost quality. Cross-functional teams from design, engineering, manufacturing, logistics, and sales came together, tore down silos in engineering and manufacturing and created more communication among people.

"We had never looked at a car that way," said Yoshida. "In the past, each of us had a budget, and we were fine if we stayed under that." Subsequently, they realized savings in all areas, big and small. Toyota was making Corollas in North America and bringing the sunroofs from Canada. When logistics told manufacturing that transporting sunroof-equipped vehicles south from Canada cost US$300 per car, executives revised the assembly process at a cost of US$600,000. This unexpected expenditure ended up saving millions for Toyota in the long run.

The under US$15,000 Corolla was ready in March 2002 with first-time-right-quality, unheard of in the automobile industry. The design quality was so perfect that not a single change had to be made in reaching the car to the market. Explains Yoshida: "There are no taboos in Oobeya. Everyone is an expert ... play a part in building the car ... equally important to the process, so we don't confine ourselves to just one way of thinking our way out of a problem."

Design the cost

To get the best advantage on cost, don't compromise on the product or service you deliver to the customer. Look at the multifold activities in your enterprise. You may then find an ingenious way to cut out waste from some function and improve the cost. It is essential to try every method and wisely manage vendors as an extension of your enterprise. Be careful not to make the vendor become the loser, make the vendor a winner. This will ensure you get long-term support from the vendor. In the 21st century, those who design their cost factoring in customer aspiration and quality will become sustaining winners in the future. When you design the cost, you are obliged to design the total deliverable where aspiration and quality become integral. But when an enterprise engages only in cost cutting, it becomes like a butcher of customer sensitivity.

Genesis of Emotional Surplus

Brands actually survive the long term when they ooze with aspiration and quality and cost is just right. Through the 1970s in Europe, I observed several new brands take birth, like rabbits breeding, but just as fast they would disappear into the market's oblivion.

Advertising in the mid-1970s

Ads then had poster girls and boys trying to mesmerize people for all customer products, be it food, personal care, automobile, detergent, home appliances, and fashion, among others. In 1977, I had just shifted from my sweeping job in Jacques Gordon's lithography print shop near Paris, and started work as an advertising paste-up artist. I spent a year in advertising, and concluded I was a misfit in the advertising world. So I changed professions to gain expertise in branding, industrial design, retail design, strategy planning, and hard-core consulting. But in any assignment, when sensitivity to the masses was not at the forefront, I would feel lost. After all, without customers where is business?

In those days, advertising only talked of emotion, conjuring up big sentiments in 30-second commercials. People were abuzz with big brands but not all heavily advertised brands made corresponding stir in product sales. My discomfort was that customers do not buy the ad, they buy a product or service which is the composition of quality, functionality, and the good-looks factor.

The quest for substance through the decades

The underlying mood through the decades laid the foundation for the quest for substance and sustainability in the European market. It went like this:

- 1940s saw devastating war ravages and Nazi atrocities.
- 1950s was repairing what was lost in World War II.
- 1960s experienced revolt against war and discriminations in society leading to the 1968 Students Movement in Paris. The hippies took forward the anguish against war by professing love and peace with drugs.
- 1970s had consumerism raise its head as a stress buster. Both husband and wife started working, earning more money, and the masses took on a new dimension centered on lifestyle. As consumerism flourished, so did brands.
- In 1980s the market began restructuring. European consumers were becoming more aware of the product's rational base where quality comes first. They wanted to return to the authentic root of customer products to realign with the origin they believed was being bypassed by marketers in an attempt to sell them superficial emotion.
- 1990s saw the start of the digital era.
- In 2000s, globalization is on the roll.

Quality time with customers

When people were revolting in the 1980s against the outward glamour of products, and brand advertising was making more media hype than selling products, I had started spending quality time with customers. I had quit the drawing table and meeting rooms to visit people's kitchens, living rooms, and dining rooms to understand their way of life. I had already worked with sociologists, psychologists, and historians previously, and got the essence of the value they bring to customers. Since I did not have formal degrees in marketing and management, I proactively took the initiative to observe, understand, and learn from people, with huge passion, by working day and night.

How do people experience products?

These learnings of how people experience products grew to become a passion in me. I was convinced the way to go was not through the current route being followed: think-tank strategy presented with an overhead projector (OHP) and downloaded to the masses through advertising. The offer to the customer must have some extra benefit that is perceptible in the product or service itself. From the moment of purchase people should experience that extra benefit the product promises.

Instead of selling intellectual creativity, I was sensitizing clients to the customer's way of life. The customer life cycle goes through stress, high or low morale, daily routine, economic crisis, health problem, work tension, family stress, social pressure, general depression, and monotonous life. In all this, what is their moment of decision or purchase? The European market found my perspective quite disruptive.

They started to reflect me as *casseur de code* meaning "the man who breaks the code" and my approach that of an "outsider." But my clients were hypnotized as my disrupting platform brought them results.

Genesis of Shining Consulting

Keeping the customer at center stage and making disruption as the core principal, I started Shining Consulting in 1984 in Paris. My competitor professionals expressed grave doubts about how long we can sustain our disruptive-thought reputation in the market while providing branding, industrial design, retail, and corporate-culture-change solutions.

Our disruptions in the European market included breaking the code of the white yoghurt with green branding and creating the probiotic Bio (later Activia). In 1986, that was a culture shock. Shock after shock followed for other brands too. Activia has since become the most profitable food brand in the world. It is perceived as a high-value-added product even while being in the generic category.

In the 1990s, professionals were finding our delivered work to be not just disruptive, but sustaining in the market. That is when several global management institutes and professional bodies in different countries invited me to seminars and conferences to explain my adventure with disruption. Intrigued with my uncommon experience with customers at home, in hair salons, entertainment functions, park benches, and shopping areas, different small intellectual circles would ask me to speak at their discussion sessions. They, in fact, encouraged me to develop my Emotional Surplus platform which delivers extra benefit to my clients and their customers.

Since 1992, I have formally created the architecture of Emotional Surplus. We continue to use Emotional Surplus to front-end our creative business strategy that leads to purchase and repurchase of products and services.

Tangible quality cannot be sacrificed

Brands will become vulnerable if they do not pay primary attention to their tangible quality differentiation. People should be able to differentiate the brand, even in a blind test. In India, I find corporations spend too much time in advertising, media planning, without addressing the perceptible differentiation a product or service will have in the customer's hand vis-à-vis the competitive scenario. In the FMCG category, the local and small player will always rustle up a war as customers rarely see the difference between their product and a national brand. Another upcoming phenomenon growing in the market that is already in the West from past 30 years is private label.

Aside from such threats, looming over them is the added danger the FMCG category faces of a large percentage of their brands being sold through wholesalers. This means that manufacturers have no control over the conditions under which the brand will sell at the kirana store, the biggest selling point in India. A huge number of these mom-and-pop stores have deplorable hygiene conditions with cockroaches and rats. What is the point of making a good looking or good quality product if its retail presence where customers buy from is horrible?

Applying Emotional Surplus

A repeatedly admired subject in society can be measured in the Emotional Surplus frame as I had explained earlier. That is the high combined surge of three attributes: quality (nonvisible, rational factor), functionality (experience that is relevant), and the emotive factor (looks good).

The root, trunk, and fruit/flower

Bringing a gift when invited to an evening party at home is among French social rituals I have experienced. Bouquets are common as elsewhere in the world but Francis, a florist near the beautiful forest park of Vincennes in east Paris, presented me a small Ficus plant in a pot and explained how to nurture it. Francis plays the flute, and being a fan of his music, I would often go to his pop concerts. When 30 years ago I had invited him home, he wanted to give me a plant that would solidify our long-term friendship. Ten years on, visiting me at home again, he was delighted to see the plant's growth. He hugged me saying, "Our friendship is solid now." Although I have not met Francis for some time now, the Ficus, just as our friendship, has taken strong root.

Landing in Hong Kong for a global conference in 1993, I lost my baggage with all the OHP slides of my presentation on Emotional Surplus. It was horrifying. How could I tell the organizers who invited me that I do not have my material? That is when the concept in Francis' Ficus tree gift came to my rescue. I bought a bouquet of roses and a rose plant in a flower pot.

I explained to the audience that if you gift a bouquet, it momentarily looks beautiful and evokes alluring emotion in your hosts, but the flowers will soon wither away. That is fragile emotion. Presenting a rose plant in a pot, the flower may wither in a couple of days, but new flowers will bloom again as the plant will grow. Even if the gifted plant has no flower, the host knows that flowers will come. I explained that as flowers in a bouquet have been cut from the root, their stems have become dysfunctional. But the potted plant has the nonvisible foundation of roots that nurture the plant. This rational factor helps the stem circulate sap internally to bring alive the plant's functionality. So the stem is the functional element.

The sustaining link of root and stem together empowers the cyclical blossoming of flowers. This repetitive flowering that is sustainable is Emotional Surplus. The audience was very curious. Every speaker had a presentation they used projection for, but here was I, presenting physically with flowers and a pot in hand in front of a large audience. People enquired whether I bought the flowers in Hong Kong and I said, "Yes, of course! Emotional Surplus exists everywhere. I don't have to bring it from Paris!" It is unlike the ephemeral emotive factor of the bouquet. Let me now narrate a few examples with this ideation of Emotional Surplus.

History as Emotional Surplus reference in the cricket world

A cricketer had a test-batting average of 99.94 in his career, statistically the greatest achievement in any major sport. He used to practice alone with a golf ball and cricket stump against the wall to sharpen his batting quality, which is the rational factor. Scoring with almost every ball is the functional factor where his performance responded to the immediacy of time. Being shy, he would never show off in glittering after-game parties but be discreet, which made him rare and sincere. This was his emotive factor. He consistently sustained these three elements, scoring and drawing record spectators in 20 years of playing.

After retirement he was an active writer, selector, and administrator for 30 years. Today, he is acknowledged as the greatest batsman. This was Don Bradman. With just 20 years of active sportsmanship, his sustainability is proven as he has been upheld as the reference of cricket for all time.

A manufacturer's self-surrender of quality defects sustains Emotional Surplus

A car manufacturer recalled millions of sold cars when sudden failure or defects were detected in them. This high sensitivity to address the rational engineering factor that is not visible to the buyer proves that the company is proactive and extremely conscious about quality. Competitors have predicted its downfall, but customers have not walked out. They are confident of always being delivered the high balance of rational, functional, and emotive attributes without anxiety. When you are sincere to your customers, your mistake is considered as learning. People have never forsaken Toyota.

If you consciously address the three attributes on higher ground, a sudden fall can also revive Emotional Surplus delivery

A thoughtful inventor went through turbulence, even quit from the company he created after a power struggle with his board of directors. He next founded NeXT, which his previous company bought in 1996. So he returned to become CEO again in the parent company.

A few years ago this company's balance sheet was in the red. Applying intensity in innovation, he injected very high-quality functionality, beyond expectation, and outstandingly sober looks into their new-generation products. Customers held their breath and this company became synonymous with how commoditized digital-technology products can acquire value leading to high aspiration for all classes of people in the world. It even entered the arena of entertainment that Sony had dominated for two decades. Sony has since declared that it can no longer keep up with the digital market. You guessed it! It was Steve Jobs and his sinful Apple.

Dazzling advertising cannot sell high-priced branded daily products that lack Emotional Surplus attributes

In my different interactions with customers, they have often expressed that they do not see any quality and efficacy difference between big brands and lower-priced products. After watching TV advertising they may buy the branded product once or twice, but they easily shift to local or pirated products as they find them cheaper and with similar quality. When a big brand pays no attention to higher performance through product engineering in blind tests, either for quality or functionality, it falls into the trap of growth and profit saturation. Glittery TV commercials with film stars cannot compensate product deficiency. That is why such brands cannot enjoy repeat purchase in a sustaining way. A number of brands in India are suffering this trauma.

You may spend huge amounts of money for market research to get some report. But if the managers do not go out to share the experience of customers from the bedroom to the toilet and kitchen to the living room, they will never be able to appreciate the real deficiency customers feel. In India where brand piracy is common and low-priced products proliferate in products of everyday use, it is extremely important to distinguish with a scientific and high blend of rational quality, perceivable functionality, and adequate emotive factors.

Bollywood-style marketing can be dangerous. You see a film once or twice but have to buy the product or a brand on a regular basis as repeat purchase. The mistake people make is considering marketing to be flamboyant or glamorous. It is actually a job that is very laborious, down-to-earth, and all about following trends and how people experience life. That is why Emotional Surplus has the very tedious and hardworking job of bringing together the combined surge of quality, functionality, and likeability.

Business sustainability = perceptible selling distinction

Roadside fruit sellers with carts have an inherent sense of exposing perceptible selling distinction (PSD). They consciously entice passersby with fruits shining fresh, temptingly ripe, and ready-to-consume. These entrepreneurs are their own controller of supply chain, sales, finance, administration, and public relations, negotiating space with police and city authorities. Cart sellers can teach corporates a lesson or two on differentiating from competition through punter pulling and selling skills that are explicitly visible.

Unique selling proposition

Earlier, the marketing world used unique selling proposition (USP) for differentiation. According to Wikipedia, "USP is a marketing concept … to explain a pattern among successful advertising campaigns of the early 1940s. It states that such campaigns made unique propositions to the customer and that this convinced them to switch brands. The term was invented by Rosser Reeves."

In the 21st century's digital era, USP concept has become obsolete. When USP was invented, most big innovations emerged every 20 years; global corporations did their own manufacturing and industries dominated over buyers. Today, buyers dictate their requirements to industry; innovations are happening fast and plenty, almost every 20 days. In the rush to introduce products, creating distinction is taking a beating. Marketers are hard-pressed to find USP which, as per Reeves' theory, makes buyers switch to the brand best differentiated.

USP in advertising does not answer how a buyer will switch from one brand to another today. Can you expect buyers to switch to your brand only because of USP advertising and vice versa? Is your brand content otherwise hollow? Mere advertising display of USP cannot win buyers. So in the contemporary world you require PSD.

Purchase factors

What is it that makes people buy? It is PSD with three critical factors: word-of-mouth, first visual appearance, and physical experience.

Word-of-mouth

Word-of-mouth goes beyond hearing and getting influenced by others, up to the social networking space. Backed by the authenticity of previous excellence, corporations launch new products. The two-day advance queue for iPhone's launch in Japan is a great example.

Sometimes, even when you know what you want, at the point of purchase another, more expensive product can change your mind, not because it is expensive but because it gives extra advantage. That is PSD which entices customers at the first visual appearance. You may not have come for this, but seeing it, you know you must have it. This is what's happening in the digi-tech world today. At the same time if real experience is not exciting, customers will not go for repeat purchase. So you always need to verify if PSD responds to repeat purchase. In this case, you need to rectify deficiency that has possibly crept into your offer in the gate of PSD. I have always experienced that it makes a great difference if we involve customers at every stage of product development. Also, continuous monitoring of performance vis-à-vis the competition keeps PSD alive.

Repeat purchase, the must of marketing and product development

Spectacular product launches are made, but after three to four months, repurchase generally dwindles. Why? With buyers increasingly demanding new and extraordinary experience, innovation by competitors is on the fast track. Several products of similar performance proliferate in the market.

The solution is to engage the buyer with the product's intrinsic properties that reflect PSD so that they are ready to repurchase. In the category where repeat purchase in a short span of time is the customer necessity, you should not wait month after month. You have to immediately verify where the PSD deficiency lies, and plug that in.

PSD to the rescue

To keep pace with buyers' mood, PSD is the potential solution for marketers who are challenged with their own non-distinctive products. What exactly does PSD stand for? It is an "outside-in-out" approach that leads to purchase and repurchase. When you involve buyers from the inception of product development, you create distinction that buyers perceive, value, and want. The buyer's requirement is your outside-in perspective. "Outside-in-out" is what the company subsequently delivers to the market that makes buyers buy and buy again.

Demanding buyers pay little heed to jargons, showy advertising, or flashy people in B2B. They seek quality first, but not the ISO 9000/14000 variety or your extrovert salesperson's talk. They may like a product's look, but to evoke repeat purchase they need to perceive distinctive extra value, better than competition offerings.

PSD is key to sustain growth

In the competitive scenario, "perceptible" is the intrinsic tangible quality, "selling" is the product's functionality relevant to the buyer. "Distinction" is the surge-up of nonvisible quality and functionality that makes the product look good in the competitive context.

A distinguished chef meets his customer's "stated need" by doing multiple trials involving people who taste his food and give their judgment. In continuously fine-tuning, it is all about how he adjusts ingredient dosage to balance his dish. Similarly, your every offering has to arrive at a certain balance. To start a new market for the customer's "unstated need," you have to simulate an experience. Create such a discomfort of newness that the buyer's mind totally shifts to the product development as shock of the new which has PSD. It's possible that not everyone will immediately connect to your product. The consuming market has driver customers and follower customers. Once the drivers have co-opted the unstated to become an obvious need, the followers will follow.

In the product development research lab where you involve buyers, do not force fit a proposition by applying reason and bulldozing these buyers. Until the buyer implicitly accepts the proposition, it is a risk to go to market. Well-polished visual differentiation is the external shell. Buyers should subliminally accept a perceptible substance embedded in a proposition. Only when the five human senses appreciate the proposition as implicit can repurchase happen.

When organizations lack PSD

The symptoms of PSD deficient enterprises are as follows:

(1) Topline is growing but bottom line is stagnant or degrowing
(2) Top and bottom lines are both under stress
(3) Bottom line is good but topline is stagnant

To overcome such situations your operations need to drive change through PSD. In some critical pocket, you have to make a pit stop for tightening up your enterprise's internal system. It does not mean total operations standstill. Only your ego-centric racing against competitors to gain market stature has to take a break. The analogy is you cannot repair a car while driving it. Let us look at the three symptoms separately:

(1) *Topline is growing but bottom line is stagnant or degrowing*: This means your product is facing huge competition in the market. Your brand is doing too many tactical-building activities in the sales field. The company is motivated only to push volume to get linear, stagnant profit. In this situation, the more you grow your liabilities become costly because your earnings are falling. This is a typical Titanic syndrome. Here the product PSD has a serious abscess.

Take the product's PSD in a disruptive platform, and go to market with high execution excellence.

(2) *Top and bottom lines are both under stress*: This is a serious problem PSD faces. Two epidemics can happen; either PSD deficiency or an alternative in the market is changing the consuming pattern. Apart from PSD, here you need to create companywide discomfort to change the gear.

(3) *Bottom line is good but topline is stagnant*: Here you may check that your product PSD may not be matching to the extended customer profile. Perhaps the younger generation does not like your product and that is why you are not growing. There is boredom in your product, so you need a PSD injection while bringing new customer profile to enlarge the market.

To make your brand a transnational brand, make PSD the center of gravity of your enterprise. Big brands become a rage not for their dazzling image but for PSD at any given time. For creating a new product or service or improving an existing one, you need to involve a certain number of buyers as a sounding board from the initial stage. When your buyers say, "I believe in it, it works well for me, it looks good," it means they have repurchase motivation.

You may prioritize your enterprise, vendor, supply chain, analyst, and channel, but in renovating or innovating a product give first priority to the buyer. Otherwise, today's evolved set of buyers will not see perceptible distinction in your offering. Without an assured buyer, where is your business's future? For mass-scale product marketing and selling, PSD is the only solution that will give you a strong topline, bottom line, and market-share growth that will sustain.

How the West has won

PSD was at the root of Western marketing and product development. Let us look at how it developed.

Evolution

Historically, Western management know-how has evolved from the Caucasian gene that has produced incredible inventions. All these inventions have gone against nature. Light was invented to brighten up nights, clothes to cover up human bodies, aircrafts to cross continents with, and pacemakers to fix an ailing heart. Western countries also exercised immense power over several countries in the world in the last few centuries. Their commanding position emerged from their capacity to thwart, lead, and rule diverse kinds of people through royalty to slavery and colonialism.

Business management took inspiration from this socio-politico-economic control they had assumed. Several models were innovated to scale up business. They experienced trials, tribulations, tests, and failures. Then their fallacies got proven, models got established, and their applications in business became successful. In business practice, the West is quite intolerant of mistakes.

Why are Western business models so good and sustainable?

You may argue that there has been a fall in the last few years. But it has not been as disruptive as the 1930s which led to World War II, post which they returned with invention after invention that have dramatically changed the world.

Since Medieval times, European monarchs and the Church have sought power for achieving living and governing comfort. A Roman emperor's first priority on conquering a new state was to establish a highly efficient water-supply system. Just imagine how many ideators, engineers, builders, and workers had to work at that time to construct 220 m high brick structures surrounding a city for water supply. Those systems are still strongly maintained as historical monuments. They prove ingenuity in technological advances over different eras. The Romans constructed numerous aqueducts to supply water to cities and industrial sites and to aid their agriculture. The city of Rome was supplied by 11 aqueducts with a combined length of 350 km.

When life was becoming boring and incestuous, Europeans went in for world discovery. With a handful of people sailing the high seas, they would land their ships in different continents and manage to somehow gain enough control to rule over native populations using skills and developed technology. Dominating different countries, they strategically plundered civilizations, became opulent, considered themselves superior, and started slavery. Such experience seasoned them on how to enslave, handle, or use manpower across the globe for enriching themselves. History says the Chinese explorers discovered North America 69 years before the Europeans did. But they did not invade the country, they merely observed like a tourist and left. That shows the difference between Asians and Europeans in their hunger to rule.

Church was the roadblock

European inventors, however, did not have an easy time at home. Art, science, and invention had to fight the Church that disallowed activities not sanctioned by Church authorities. Ideators defied nature and pressed science and engineering to make incredible inventions. Every century is marked by the kind of shift inventions brought about to provide greater comfort for living. The 19th century is represented as the mechanical era, the 20th century brought the electronic era, which shifted to digital technology in the 21st century. Tomorrow they will reverse science to bring alternative solutions to protect the very world they are destroying with wars and environmental pollution. Why and how do they do so?

Action oriented

Western philosophy being rooted in the here and now is very action-oriented. Every individual in Europe wants to accomplish everything in his/her short lifespan of average 83 years for men and 86 years for women. They question life and existence, but in every invention they ingrain a grid metaphor to enable its future continuity. The objective is always to go against nature and disrupt what has become acceptable to change the human living condition in search of a new height of mental or physical comfort. They created and abolished slavery, crafted auto-mechanization and now digitalization for a new way of life. Europeans in Europe were never allied, they were parochial. Even today all European countries live their own culture, but came together with the Euro currency to protect being swamped by American and Asian economic power.

When European immigrants went to America, it is possible they created the melting pot of invention, translated it into business in North America, and revolutionized science and technology. Multi-blended and experienced American society created the business frameworks we use today. They devised the business culture, from branding to handling large-scale businesses and globalization. History says that it was very difficult to align the two Allied army generals, Montgomery with Eisenhower, in World War II. Their command styles were totally different. But as per BBC's archives, coordination was possible only because General Eisenhower was an open-minded American.

Strengthening the core

The legacy of either fundamental or applied innovation or renovation is what most of the famous global brands of American and European descent have. The reality I have experienced in the West is that renovation means "I change myself" while innovation or invention means "I change the world." Following the Western business process, the Japanese and Koreans rigorously made a dent in the world with delivery-execution excellence. In the 1970s–1980s, Europeans used to caricature Japanese brands as copy masters. Japan or Korea never did present themselves as inventors or innovators; they proved they were best in the world at execution.

When you compare Indian-origin enterprises with such references, are there any gaps that need addressing? You often hear of enterprises restructuring or rebranding, but very often this is a feel-good exercise, not quite driven for global business requirement of distinction. When multi-conglomerate Indian corporations get ready for globalization, can it be possible they do so without first defining their core? They try expanding into new verticals without having that core competency to grab the emerging opportunity. It is not always possible for a business to run and sustain merely by investing money and hiring professionals who do not have the requisite capability.

Till today, leading corporations in the world that drive the trend are all unifocused on their core, whether it is Microsoft, Google, Walmart, Apple, Toyota, IBM, or Accenture, among others. Will unsynchronized Indian conglomerates be able to sustain the effect of being a conglomerate in the face of global specialists in each domain? Will their next generation of the family business have the capacity to run a conglomerate, or want to do so?

Build your core, globalize your business

Strengthening the core is the obsession of every business, yet do most business schools emphasize that?

My HR manager says recruitment at MBA schools exasperates him. That's because when he asks students in the interview if Bata can make jam, they smugly reply, "Of course! If a cigarette company can make food to cosmetics to *agarbatti* (incense sticks), why can't a shoemaker?" It is scary how Indian business schools are adulterating the marketing courses they have copied from the West. Our license-raj heritage of unsynchronized additions to the conglomerate seems embedded in India's business practice. Do business schools or such organizations understand what their perceived business core is?

Root, trunk, and fruit analogy

Let us look at this devise I have defined since 1994 on how an organization can sustainably grow with high top and bottom line. Every corporation, like every tree, has to have its root and trunk aligned to sustainably produce healthy fruits. This alignment meets the end-customer's needs and desires in today's phenomenally competitive environment. In analogy, the root is the perceived core with precedent and inherent value as practiced by the enterprise. Its end-customers experience and recall that core. The trunk is the direction its operating systems need to be driven toward; the fruit is excellence of its delivery execution to end-customers.

End-customers will perceive a single point of an existing company as its core. Their repeat purchase from this company, instead of from its competition, makes that core evident. A start-up's core comes from how it studied the market for at least a decade to find its unlimited potential and business viability there. You can consider the business you are trying to enter as your core only if you can match your personal expertise and competency with it, and have the stamina to encounter hills and dales there. Refine that every three years on how your end-customers perceive your core.

Need to concentrate on the core

From my personal experience of working in several countries, I have understood that seeding and nurturing the core makes business sustainable, and distinguishes it from trading business. Indian enterprises driving one corporate brand for multiple industry opportunities will face enormous problems in establishing their perceived core. In global business that is already in India today, not driving with perceived core focus can be a stumbling block.

Nobody prohibits an entrepreneur from entering multiple industries. When you have money, you can go wherever you want, but with a single brand it is tough. Do end-customers know that distinguished brands Cartier, Dunhill, Van Cleef & Arpels, Piaget, and Mont Blanc are all part of Richemont holding company? Each business keeps its perceived core separately. Similarly Louis Vuitton–Moët Hennessy (LVMH) has 60 autonomous luxury brands from Louis Vuitton to Dior, Moët & Hennessy, Sephora hyperstore; while Pinault-Printemps-Redoute (PPR) luxury group drives YSL, Gucci, Puma, and Fnac.

Traditional Indian conglomerates with huge countrywide awareness often drive the corporate brand for every category.

So when competing with specialists globally, their brands will never be competent. This shortcoming is the historical consequence of the protected economy. Industrialists with clout used to grab the limited business opportunities the government licensed out, so their diversified companies became big brands bought by non-evolved domestic customers. To compete in today's customer-driven global free economy, it is not enough to have large numbers of Indian Institutes of Technology (IITs) and Indian Institutes of Management (IIMs), youth power, skilled labor, and immense opportunity in India, unless companies have sharpened their perceived core.

The story of BSN to Danone

Here is how the US$12 billion French conglomerate Boussois-Souchon-Neuvesel (BSN) globalized by honing their perceived core. With acquisitions, BSN grew to have 14 verticals by 1993, but profitability was 2.5 percent only. Among their businesses, Danone dairy had high operating margin. And health is the promise these dairy products gave to the consumer. Launching *Activia* brand with *bifidus actif* bacteria in 1987 brought huge value to Danone. So they took a strong disruptive strategy to seed their core to become global. Using "Active Health" as the perceived core, they changed the name to Groupe Danone. This allowed focus on three "head" businesses related to health: dairy, water, and biscuit. They discontinued all "tail" categories and kept biscuit up to 2007 for critical mass.

To reinforce the perceived "active health" core, Danone expanded inorganically into baby nutrition and medical nutrition. Today Danone is the world's number one dairy company with a turnover in 2010 of US$22.62 billion and profit margin of 10 percent. This is called a core-loving corporation for globalization. Just imagine how strong their guts were for disruption! It proves that if you do not have a perceived core, you can define it for your business now.

The Indian market is growing, but the near future will see severe global competition. When Indian companies meticulously build their core and discontinue with tail businesses, they will become winners tomorrow. With strong sustainability they can encash high profitability both locally and globally. Here disruption and execution excellence are key factors.

Rejigger failure with curiosity to succeed

In discarding the "tail" business, focus has to be on growing the "head" business. But to my dismay, I have discovered a school of thought in this part of the hemisphere that supports understanding of failures, not to learn from them, but as standalone case-study subjects to avoid risk. People here do not enquire about how successful companies have achieved their triumph.

Look at success factors

Success can be gained from in-depth understanding of failures, though not necessarily their own, then rejiggering them with dollops of useful, differentiated value. Failure in a company could have one or several reasons ranging from misjudging market potential, strategy mismatch in company culture, marketing, and production or quality flaws, vendor management, procurement, and sales activation to just plain wrong communication. There is no reason to suggest that a strategy that has failed in one company will also fail under different conditions in another company. You will never know details of any failure's root cause as nobody will reveal it.

The failure of a high-quality product needs to be studied with curiosity and from all angles. If you bring positive energy into a failed subject you may refuel its success. Was the French Concorde a failure? Was it not extreme innovation that could fly over Mach 3, close the distance of an ocean in half the time of normal aircrafts? In business, the word failure does not work. Japan announced in 2005 that they are now working on a supersonic aircraft to reduce sound and increase seats while cutting 50 percent of current flying time. They have suffered a few setbacks and are now collaborating with research done in France and the US.

Study the competitor's nitty-gritty tactics

Customers of emerging-economy countries are enjoying a heightened lifestyle. Transnational companies are flocking to their recent open markets with novel product offers. However, in consulting with companies there, I find them to be slack in responding to competition. When a globally reputed company unveils a competing product, the emerging-economy company merely questions complacently, "Will it succeed? Will our customers pay so much? Is such sophisticated innovation required?" Instead, should they delve into that product's origin of success to rejigger their own product to meet customer aspirations? Such questions are baseless and judgmental. Customers with money are always open to alternative choice and better options.

Innovation in business has to be a passion of curiosity to change the world, not to question it. As an industrial house in an emerging economy, you may modernize your business to compete, but unless you inquire into why your global competitor is winning in your economy, your market growth will merely touch the surface, and not sustain.

During observation, no criticism, no preconceived baggage allowed

The Japanese, since the 1950s, have been exceptional in seeing things differently. They link microscopic observation to quality in product development. In the early 1970s, I remember seeing Japanese groups traveling around Europe, always with cameras. Collective discipline makes them process the microtones of their observation into high-quality deliverables. Microtone is a Western musical term where multiple instruments play different chords with different tones to converge into a harmonious melody. Any miniscule mistake in these chords or tones can corrupt the musical output. That is the power of a microtone.

During the period the Japanese observe a subject, no criticism is allowed. The subject is kept intact for holistic understanding, without distorting its shape or substance with preconceived thought baggage. When you observe with curiosity, you go in-depth into the subject to find the processes, struggles, and exhaustion it has gone through. The Japanese delve into the total package, not its surface. Having thoroughly understood its complexity, they top-up with added value. The object's first and fundamental innovative system is kept intact.

The Japanese reinvented the European motorbike and conquered the world with it. They renovated the piano. This sophisticated European acoustic musical instrument needs perfection at every stage. The German piano is acclaimed the world's best, but the piano most rock, pop, classical singers, or musicians use on stage anywhere in the world today is the Japanese Yamaha. You will see Yamaha blinking on the piano's side, the brand showing off its popularity where it counts.

When would India be capable of producing a world-class product that will replace the best that is available? South Koreans are following the Japanese route with fantastic visible results. They are competing globally, taking leadership in areas such as hybrid steel, customer durables, electronics, and automobiles.

Chinese discipline

In my experience in China I find Chairman Mao Zedong has sharpened focus on their national character of discipline even outside politics. With stringent discipline, positive mindset, and following in Japanese footsteps, China is overcoming its product-quality deficiency and stigma with radically improved quality.

In 2002, Jean Michel Jarre, the laser and electronic entertainment musician, did two spectacular concerts in China. Son of celebrated music director, Maurice Jarre, whose "Dr Zhivago" and "Love Story" have become the world's standard in easy listening, Jean Michel's concert was unique because he wove together the Beijing Symphony Orchestra, Chinese National Orchestra, Beijing Opera Chorus, and notable Chinese rock musicians in his open air Western music concerts. He amazed a billion Chinese stage and TV viewers and everyone else in the world by using Chinese musicians and traditional Chinese instruments in Western music style.

Enjoying the show on DVD, it proved to me the Chinese capability to enter a new realm with calculated ease. They have command over discipline, and their curiosity will make their nation the future business driver of the world.

We are proud to be an intellectual society in India. But can our collective intellectual power, not individual intelligence, help us attain world-class business processes and products? Billion-mindset economies such as India and China need a disciplined business mentality that can dissect success. To challenge the market, our professionals must collectively understand how and why innovation happened in developed countries. This will orient them toward the very foundation of the innovation mechanism.

The PUB Reflex

Make no mistake! The PUB Reflex is not about emptying jarfuls of draught beer down your gullet in a pub. Nor will it increase or diminish your reflexes when afterwards at the steering wheel, you have to stop at the cop's bidding and imme-diately roll down your glass as he sticks a breath analyzer into your face. My PUB Reflex can make you drunk in unlimited ways. You become an addict to creating the unarticulated and unseen to surprise society with, or to further business or sci-ence. It is about rejiggering the odds and failures to succeed.

New-connect system

Mass marketing the mobile phone has dramatically changed the human-connect system. Earlier you had to reach a landline, condition yourself into a certain telephoning posture, unhook the fixed instrument, dial, and then talk. You would recreate this landline-phone-conversation ritual every time and cost-consciously talk less. But today's little mobile device frees you. It is an extension of your life. Just face a mirror to discover how you change your bearing and gestures under different contexts as you chatter away on your mobile phone. You send/receive umpteen messages when you do not want to intrude, do not know how else to say those words of love or bereavement, or just to keep in touch with festival greetings or forwarding jokes. City-bred teenagers say they can send 500 SMSs daily, even continue texting up to 4 a.m. "How come?" Their reply is that provocative subjects beyond the ordinary invite instant reflexes. In contemporary social networking and mobile-phone usage, provocation spreads the message and creates interest.

The offtake pull

In business, PUB Reflex helps empower your proposition so people buy it. It avoids your having to sell it. Selling and buying are not the same. Hawkers or hookers sell you generic wares, but when customers buy a product, or employees buy into a process on their own initiative, it is the PUB offtake pull. Customers buy because of their own self-judgement without any hard push sales tactics being applied.

Corporate contamination

Everyday life in the corporate world is contaminated, peppered with boring words such as balanced scorecard, go-to-market, or acronyms Measure of Performance (MOP), ROI, and Management by Objectives (MBO), among others. B2B industries in particular use stereotype words in heavy-loaded business proposals. Repetitive jargons of incredible pollution are used globally by corporations to bulldoze employees and create a generic effect that is devoid of emotion and compassion for people. They contaminate people to become robotic rather than provoking their interest to understand and buy. Compromise (31–45 years) and Retro (45+) generation employees get addicted to such contamination and find it difficult to reverse the contaminated jacket. But the below 30 Zap generation is different. They do not connect to corporate contamination. So they have two roles. The moment they leave work they change their jackets and breathe freedom socially.

You have heard and sung "Happy birthday to you!" a thousand times, it is standardized yet emotional. It provokes a person's nostalgic celebration of birth. It also proves that when words acquire social meaning, there is neither fatigue, nor monotony under any circumstance. Is the lengthy fashion brand name French Connection United Kingdom provocative? It is for those who know that the French and British never see anything eye-to-eye. French say Brits do not know how to dress; Brits reply, French are froggy. But for everyone else, abbreviating it to FCUK provokes a new language in global fashion. Customers can easily pronounce it and understand its naughty meaning. Provoking with FCUK is the PUB Reflex example of how a small brand can overcome boredom and become very big in the world with word-of-mouth and extract the low-cost, high-mileage effect.

Adultery

When both husband and wife go to work, it dulls them into the daily grind of transport, children's education, kitchen, and bed. This kind of relationship is imminently vulnerable to contamination. Tomorrow, when women in larger numbers start earning economic liberty, consumption will grow to accommodate a comfortable life. But so will the egos of husband and wife erupt in search of independence.

It is what has happened in Europe. The 1950s cleaned up World War II's mess, the 1960s was clinical productivity. When women joined the workforce in the 1970s, they earned more, spent more, and consumed more. From the 1980s, it was adultery on both sides. The independent wife no longer sacrificed for the husband's sexual pleasure, she wanted her own hedonism. They understood each other mechanically, but provocation was missing. To exit boredom, adultery became obvious.

Reaching out

Without provocation, the innumerable messages people receive every day really do not register. Enterprises dole out big advertising bucks, try correlating ad spends to product sales, but they will be shocked to know the statistics: a miniscule percentage buys the product from seeing the ad, many do not understand the ad, or feel bored seeing it. They enjoy the ad, but that does not translate to purchase. This is the PUB Reflex gap in communication.

Very few companies, Apple, Google, Microsoft, Nike, FCUK, and Cisco, among others, have understood that provocation makes people comprehend product benefit and register the brand. They have created sustaining global trends because their continuous new language provokes the masses, makes them understand value, and buy the product. Their internal corporate processes are driven in the same non-boring way.

Walking around in Mountain View, California, I saw cyclists with Google colors whirring on their wheels. Sure enough, the Google office was less than a kilometer away. This provocation gave me the pleasure of visiting Google, which was not in my agenda.

Provocation for provocation's sake has no sustaining power

Provocation has to magnify the context. An evolved stimulus can transform a vanilla context into a gem that delivers differentiated, quality substance. Understanding the selling or seductive proposition has to be a by-product of the provocative subject. This then automatically translates to the buy-in.

From corporate house to family and social life, the stronger your provocation of substance, understanding becomes more intense, and the result is desire fulfillment. I call this the PUB Reflex.

Decisive, regular repeat purchase makes a brand

Here is how you experience the reverse of PUB Reflex. The so-called customer-care service of one of India's largest mobile phone operators calls me regularly, and then asks, "What's your name, sir?" Their intention to perhaps offer additional services may be good, but their insensitivity is appalling. Having been their subscriber for the last 10 years, obviously I am in no mood to reciprocate enthusiastically to reveal my identity.

Locking the bond

Clearly demonstrating tactlessness, such companies ignore per capita growth because market-penetration possibilities are high in populous India. Running after new customers in new geographies is the quick-fix business expansion route. Do companies glance back to seal the existing customers' emotional bond to the brand? Business houses relegate that job of acquiring emotional connect to television ads. Not on their priority agenda is the understanding of who the customer is. Failure to connect to existing customers may shut the door on what makes business sustainability thrive. That is clearly customer's decisive, regular repeat purchase.

Your brand's regular, repeat purchase can be extremely volatile as it is dependent on the customer's capricious decision. Unless the brand knows how to lock him/her in, he/she can move away at whim.

Purchase cycles

The character of different products and services demands relevant purchase cycles ranging from daily to short, mid, long, and extended terms. Milk, bread, and petrol may be purchased daily, FMCG products weekly and apparel every two months. Flamboyant, gizmo-lover or novelty-seeker customers may buy mobile-phone handsets every six months, others every 24–30 months. Television set or AC purchase is long term, every four to five years, while automobiles are changed in five to seven years, aircraft purchase falls into extended term of 20–25 years. In services, you could do fortnightly business of air tickets, courier, or bank transactions; leisure travel hotel bookings once or twice a year, or for business every other day.

Per capita consumption of your product or service gives stability to your business. If your brand does not figure in the customer's decisive, regular repeat purchase cycle, you have not read her subconscious mind. Korean refrigerators successfully occupied her mindshare to make a durable product into a consumable. From buying one every 20 years, people now change their refrigerators within six to seven years.

Irrespective of any buying cycle, your brand's biggest danger is the infrequent buyer, lapser, or those who swing at the last moment of purchase. This happens because industries pay scant attention to their customers' ecosystem. Businesses spend time in backend management, acquiring assets, but leave customer centricity to hypothetical assumption. Have they compulsively enquired, "Who is my customer? Why is she my customer? What is her social standing, family, health, education, earning, and living condition?" Do businesses have pictures of their customer profile pasted on company walls to invite employees to become sensitive to them? Instead I have often seen paintings, company policies, or HR initiatives on office walls. Poor infrastructure in India makes FMCG industries dependent on wholesalers who generate 40 to 60 percent sales. Keeping track or trace of this buyer is totally unknown.

Buying loyalty

Businesses are beginning to put in customer-loyalty programs, but at a very transactional level. Colorful fliers or frequent emails are sent to gently bulldoze members into buying. But none of these loyalty programs try to understand the customer's psychological makeup. Going back to the mobile operator, the biggest ambition is to bundle offerings for winning the price war. The telemarketer offers the best promotions to subscribers, there is never any talk on service quality.

B2B businesses such as India's IT services exports mistakenly consider that understanding the end-customer's ecosystem comprises the business-to-consumer (B2C) domain. They do not seem to realize that at the end, the end-customer is delivered a product. Not knowing the end-customer's purchase cycle prevents them from understanding their client's business. Their clients are under regular pressure to sweep up their end-customer's decisive, regular repeat purchase as per industry norm, and get per capita priority and up to penetration growth.

Lesson from kiranas

So I return to basics. Modern industry should take a cue from the Indian kirana retailer's immense customer knowledge, minus his poor hygienic sense. Prioritize your brand's activity and investment in understanding the customer's intangible areas first.

To get your target customer's endorsement of "I believe in it, it works well for me, it looks good," your brand has to excel over competitors in quality and functionality. Once these two factors are satisfied, it is easy to make the product look good to induce repurchase.

Everybody cannot be your customer

Define your core customer who contributes 70 percent to your business. Capture his/her psychological, social, family, health, and economic aspects and cater to his/her predictably. He/she should not become a lapser or your business will get peripheral and attract satellite buyers only; they are ad hoc, infrequent, swing, or take trials only.

Global fashion brand Zara from Spain has completely understood the customer's hedonistic mind frame for a fashionable differentiated wardrobe. Accelerating industry practices to satisfy her desire state, they change the entire stock in the store every 15 days. With complete control over creativity of their 200 designers, manufacturing, distribution, and retailing, they increase per capita purchase through strong word-of-mouth spread. Instead of buying different brands, their customers indulge in decisive, regular repeat purchase.

It is important for industries dependent on mid, long, and extra-long purchase cycles to penetrate to new customers for everyday business. If these industries have defined their core customers, and they are satisfied, they will become the brand's strong word-of-mouth ambassador. Internet social media can then be activated for real penetration. Such customers are more powerful in attracting new customers than advertising.

Ads only create awareness, satisfied customers create the pull factor. So give second priority to assets. Instead invest time, money, and effort to understand the customer's physical and intangible aspects to get your brand's decisive, regular repeat purchase.

Customer! Demand your due of craftsmanship

Outstanding delivery will happen through the COA factor: Deep "curiosity" leads to high-quality "observation" that results in differentiated "action." Japanese and Korean products display amazing customer perceptible quality through COA. But can it end with high caliber craftsmanship alone? What is the first experience when the customer takes that exceptional product home? How can you hold your customer for that repeat purchase after this?

Rigmaroles in the fix

In my different customer-service-experience research in home décor and purchase, I discovered a nightmarish example of installing a flat TV at home. It is not like old times when you place the TV set and fix an antenna. Now the dealer brings the set, but not everything else. You have to wait for the company representative to bring the fixture to fix the TV set on the wall. Next the direct to home (DTH) service provider with his set-top box has to come to connect you to different TV channels. Then you have to have your own electrician around also to set up wires for the surround-sound speakers, amplifier, and connect the DVD with the TV monitor.

Guess who has to coordinate among these four sets of service people? You are right! You have to take a couple of days off from work for this. You have just made an exorbitant full payment, yet there is nobody taking responsibility for installation. The DTH has to match the TV output, which has to match the DVD player and amplifier. And there you are stuck in the house waiting endlessly as nobody keeps to the promised time. If you try to be clever, plead with and juggle everyone's time in advance, fix appointments with them so they arrive together, you can be sure that you will be outwitted. Two of them may arrive two to three hours late, and another may not show up that day. Excuses will vary from traffic jam, motorcycle-tire puncture, rains flooding streets, public transport too crowded to take, too much work, the head office does not care for us, and so on.

The worst is yet to come, that is, shoddy craftsmanship. Each service provider will send two young people who are clever, but seem like trainees with raw behavioral skills. There is hell to pay from wiring to programming to getting connection. The early comer can barely set up his system, but he will not touch the other service man's area saying, "That's not my job." Then you wonder, "Should I have paid so much for a world-class brand associated with so many service providers with no coordination?" To get a good final output of clean installation, you, dear customer, have to struggle. If you are not demanding, they can leave you a patch-up job.

No after-sales service training

The customer electronics retailer should coordinate the way an automobile garage provides service after sales, managing different features from different vendors. TV brands promote hallucinating pictures in the showroom for the customer's instant buying decision. Yet scant attention is paid to synchronizing among servicemen to make your installation hassle-free.

Japanese and Korean companies need to give rigorous training to build up their Indian servicemen's knowledge.

Otherwise customers somehow feel cheated. Apart from better entertainment, as an integral part of design and invention, the flat TV has another purpose. It is sleek, not a boxy equipment taking up space in the room, so the idea is to mount it on the wall like a moving painting. With craftsmanship and price so much higher than the old TV, is it not the TV maker's responsibility to fit it in the customer's house without a mess? The customer's tolerance level is too high in India, so such hardware and software companies get away doing what they want. Every customer should revolt at this kind of unreliability. Only then will the industry change and craftsmanship grow. Global brands in India are eliciting consumerism, but they must refine and upgrade customer expectation in service too.

Responding to high customer expectation

Unlimited customer expectation in developed countries has obliged industry to sharpen craftsmanship, be inventive and highly competitive. So you get on-time delivery and sustaining value. If you do not raise your expectation bar, industry will not raise the craftsmanship of delivery people.

Let me narrate a personal experience in craftsmanship. When I was studying graphic design in Paris, Western calligraphy fascinated me. I learnt its grammar and alchemy, right from Gutenburg, under the tutorship of world famous Hungarian typographer Paul Gabor (1930–1992), who had invented several fonts. He trained me to study not the black fonts but the white space in typography. This white balance harmonizes typography, letter by letter, word by word, line by line, and paragraph by paragraph.

Gabor was a tough taskmaster. Only five of us from the original class of 30 survived to learn that the width of words A to Z is not the same, the capital and small letters zigzag in a word. You needed passion, desire, and learning hunger to persist with him. After two years, he advised me to work in a type-print shop where old-style steel letters were used before computers arrived. I worked for free for three hours, four days a week for six months and achieved control over craftsmanship in spacing, lining, and white balance in calligraphy and typesetting. Since then I could so inspire my team that all the brands we have created in the world have been hand-designed typography. This is a proactive call, clients will never ask for it. But it protects the copyright of their brands so that their authenticity cannot be challenged.

As a customer, everything is in your hands. Do you, for example, check the homogeneity in the floor tiles of the expensive apartment you have bought? Every joint section showcases craftsmanship of design. When customers increase their demand, service will improve and the selling proposition will assume tension-free quality and aesthetics. But you have to impose your requirement before making payment or you will achieve nothing. Do not get convinced by the showroom salesman's warm smile. Close the deal but pay after the work is done. Your exigency will alert the manufacturer.

Make quality inspirational and emotional

Did you know that the housekeeping staff of most five-star hotels in Mumbai lives in the slums? I did not believe it either, until I befriended a few of them in my different stays there and managed invitations to visit their homes.

Training the working class

No, it is not high officials at corporate boardrooms or head offices who alone nurture the vital space of a company or deliver its products or services. In any business domain, execution is always in the hands of the shop floor, inhabited by common people. Wide disparity in our socioeconomic living context ensures that common people have little mind space to understand quality excellence, and hence know little about it except what is taught at workplace training sessions. Working classes earning a maximum of ₹20,000 per month save for food, medical expenses, and children's education. From among them, an emerging new breed now spends ₹500 for an outing two/three times a month. Their homes are mere covered shelters, TV is their entertainment source.

All these workers deliver from Lux to Mercedes Benz, the way five-star hotel housekeeping staff in Mumbai lives in slums, but delivers luxury lifestyles. The stark difference in hygiene of where they work and how they live is incredible. I marvel at the superior training system of such hotels. They have made people who have not been entitled to minimum hygienic and civic comfort put in the effort to project society's wealth.

Making and delivering outstanding quality in every sense in business can create a huge social impact. It can change India's economy, industry, and global reputation, making it a value-led global hub of outsourcing in every domain. The common man's way of living can change too, as also those with no understanding of the right parameter for global quality. The government has taken no serious initiative to drive hygiene quality. No mass-scale education system enlightens anyone of quality benchmarking systems. So willy-nilly it is the organized industry that has the responsibility of inculcating quality sensitivity into ordinary people.

This reminds me of the Sony chairman's determination after World War II. His vision was that Sony will be the first among Japanese companies to reverse Japan's image of being the maker of low-quality products. With fantastic, game-changing quality initiatives Sony has proved today that Japan rules the world in quality. Even Toyota says "Quality Revolution."

Political victory through hygiene

Let me narrate how hygiene can lead to political victory in a developed country. Paris is the world's most beautiful city, but Parisians, in the name of walking their dogs in the promenade, have an obsession of making their pets do their bio-business in front of the neighbor's house. Jacques Chirac who twice served as the prime minister always harbored the ambition of becoming the president, but failed to get elected in 1981 and 1988. He finally won in 1996, before which he was mayor of Paris. During this time he tried to prove his administrative ability to French citizens.

Suddenly one day we started to see big specially designed motorbikes with white and green uniformed riders reaching every corner of the city to perform a service. They operated an automatic vacuum cleaner—like sucking system attached to a storage bin at the back. The bikes moved throughout the city and very elegantly "schwhoop! schwhoop! schwhoop!" sucked in every big or small pile of doggy poop on the road. He understood that asking Parisians to change their habit may make him lose his electorate, so it was better to find a proactive approach that innovatively kept Paris clean of dog shit. We used to call these bikes *moto merde* (shit bike). However, Mr Chirac became the president after Mr Mitterand's death in 1995 up to 2007.

Raise the living-condition bar

Every month I travel alone or with my team to underprivileged areas in India to understand the psychographics, living
style, economic, and social factors of this human ocean. The
hygienic situation is pitiably different from my Parisian or
European experience. When I present my research findings to
gauge the market potential of my clients here in their sophisticated corporate meeting rooms, I wonder if the management
understands the practical living conditions and aspirations
of these low-income people. Is a corporate house only for
board meetings, production, advertising, and selling? In what
condition does it sell?

Every company puts up quality messages as picture boards
on the premises. Yes, quality training is imparted to scale up
industrial production, but unless quality training is extended
to their personal living style, will employees ever internalize
quality sensitivity? Can industry raise the bar of our society's
living condition? I am not talking of luxury living, but just
habituating people to better hygienic and civic conditions. It
is not easy, but as an industrialist you need to look at the living condition of your workers to change their attitude. They
should demand quality conditions at home. Only when quality
becomes important to them can you improve the perceptible
quality of your deliverable.

Perhaps the basis of the annual bonus can be to oblige workers to raise the level of their living condition. Such an initiative
can change the Indian paradigm of quality excellence. Your
consumer will be benefited. They will not need to pay more
to get five-star quality in every purchase.

Can a beautiful Indian advertisement made abroad with
a famous film star, a hullabaloo communication spend in all
TV channels and cinema halls justify ROI or define the quality parameter? Your product at the retail may still be in some

horrible and unkempt condition. What is the meaning of dogmatic ISO 9000-type cultures, unless the customer's purchase experiences has real perceptible value that upgrades his/her quality of life at the point of purchase?

Making the working class highly sensitive to hygiene, civic, and aesthetic sense will automatically boost quality of your deliverable. These three fundamental attributes combine to impact positively on people's work in delivery sensitivity. This should have happened before economic liberalization. Raising the consciousness of the masses can ignite them to demand better implementation of our hygienic system. Otherwise dirt will spread unabated like it is doing today, huge housing developments have drains with floating feces, yet nobody cares.

End-customer desire enterprise

Better work and living conditions may uplift product quality for sale to the person we eulogize as "customer is king!" But are you sure this jargon is right?

Customer king is as free as a bird

That is because a king has aura, by law everybody pays him obeisance and he has administrative responsibilities, but the customer is a free bird. This free bird wants no cage that binds him/her to duties. At the same time he/she wants to be caressed by a brand to experience its human sensitivity. Very few companies in the world can drive with end-customer desire. An enterprise, big or small, often loses this criterion by giving too much importance to backend engineering when installing the value system. By itself an enterprise is an asset, its goodwill is the end-customer's desire and inclination toward its product or service.

What is the meaning of a brand's human sensitivity?

In an Indian airport you suddenly see a famous German automobile company, publicly exhibiting its new vehicle. Written prominently beside it is, "Do not touch the car." What can this mean? You are exposing the product in a public place to eventually encourage sales; simultaneously you are giving a monarchical order to the public. In a museum you are conditioned not to touch any painting. But this is a mass area, yet sales are targeted to high-income customers. To resolve this dichotomy you pretend that your demo-advertising is in a museum.

The other day, flying with Air India to Kolkata from Delhi International Airport, I saw the same German company demonstrate a very futuristic vehicle. This time a sales representative was by the car. From a distance I watched several very simple people going toward the vehicle and very quickly returning from it. The representative gave them no importance. Not a single affluent-looking person went near the car in the span of half an hour.

Being an automobile engineering fan I was curious to see the car. I asked the salesman about the car's speed and cost. His first question was what my budget was. That totally turned me off and I immediately left the demo site. I am not giving the brand's name as my intention is not to criticize it. This is an example of customer insensitivity. Clearly the manufacturer's approach is of an arrogant lord, claiming the product is its asset, goodwill, and museum piece.

What is the meaning of exposing the car in public if it is not friendly with people? Everybody should be allowed to experience the car, irrespective of being a customer or visitor. You may say this kind of exhibition is to inspire people, but that is questionable. Rather the brand establishes a distance by its insensitivity. Alternatively, the car should be exhibited in five-star hotels according to its target customer focus. This is context of service.

I checked the Internet for the vehicle's cost, which is ₹2.25 crores. It can run 370 km per hour. On the highway it gives 8 km per liter, city driving is just 5 km. Is this a farce or Formula 1 racing? Making cars guzzle so much petrol in this day and age is quite criminal. What happened to being environment-friendly? Was it mere lip service to collect brownie points from environmentalists? In India, where would you drive such a car? We are not in Germany where the roads are paradise with no speed limits. I am sure some Indian will buy it for status and show it off as a museum exhibit.

Human sensitivity is a big factor in any industry today

After all, everything is handled by human beings. If you are a heavy industrial machine maker with lots of sophistication and automation but without human aspect, you will find that today's Zap generation would not like to work here. A medical instrument cannot inspire a patient unless it looks totally different from a medical instrument. Nor can a vehicle feel secure to sit in or drive unless you feel and experience the safety features. Just knowing its safety features will make you admire the vehicle.

Twenty-five years ago industry was the god that surprised people with new products. But the scale of end-customer surprise intensity has gone down drastically. End-customers always want a positive surprise such as inventions to miniaturization that happened in the last century. Now is the time for humanizing a product or service. I have entered all layers of end-customer society in diverse industries across the world, both B2B and B2C. What I find is that in selling IT services, soaps, or cars, among others, believe me all levels of customers say that they want to be treated with consideration, that is, without ignoring their human touch.

Trust is most important for repeat purchase

The end-customer's "I believe in it" factor is super important to create instant trust for a product or service. But this is not enough. The decisive purchase factor comes from "It works well for me," meaning the service or product has been totally customized for an end-customer's need and desire. End-customers understand extreme functionality of any service or product that brings progress to society. This is where human sensitivity has a serious role. The third customer need of "It looks good" is the easiest of the three needs to deliver. But customers will not return if the product's functionality doesn't match expectation, and if the unseen quality factor is missing.

You may research a thousand end-customers, but that is considered a hygiene factor. An analogy: A technically perfect singer does not necessarily attract the public. Even without a perfectly trained voice, you need other values like charisma to pull in masses. In the same way, irrespective of the industry, to perfectly connect to every end-customer, his/her work, transportation, marriage, family, home, social cauldron, education, and health all count. No product or service can exist without some human benefit. Singer Elvis Presley did not have technical training in music, but he reached millions of people. His ecstatic human connect went beyond everything.

Your enterprise may have every technical system in place to process and reproduce your market offer. But are your employees sensitive to how human beings accept or react to your offerings in the market? The passion to understand people is the core that drives an enterprise into a futuristic path. Once you have instilled human sensitivity, consider it your real goodwill value that will contribute to your company's growth and net worth.

Why should the customer sacrifice?

Enterprises supposedly pander to the customer's desire, so how come customers in India are suffering unhygienic experiences, erratic price, and irregular availability in daily food and FMCG products? Small farmers are suffering as the middleman is depriving them a fair price. Politicians opposing FDI in multi-brand retailing are shouting that kirana stores need protection and customers will be cheated with high prices. Is that really so?

The question of 100 percent FDI

India has allowed 100 percent FDI in lifestyle sectors such as automobiles and customer electronics, among others. That has raised customer choice and desire levels sky-high. Fast foreign motorcycles and cars are dangerously dashing down appalling road infrastructure in urban and rural areas. Customers are flouting minimal safety and traffic-control norms, hiking up fatal accident rates. Before allowing this FDI, did the government first secure the roads, safety, and traffic-control measures? Did political parties make a noise then? Yet when customers and farmers would gain price advantage rather than remaining in the sacrificing dock, some political parties are barricading FDI in multi-brand retailing. Of course the powerful trader middlemen will be eased out when this happens, is that the stumbling block?

Experience of other countries

Countries such as China, Vietnam, and Chile that initially hesitated but have since opened 100 percent FDI to multi-brand retailing are today enjoying the investments, job creation, introduction of technology, processes, and infrastructure. Customers are benefiting from better pricing, better quality, and better shopping convenience.

As per Chinese analysts, entry of Walmart and Carrefour has changed the way Chinese companies manage business, from farm procurement to logistics. Local Chinese retailers such as Shanghai Bailian Group, Suning, Gome, and Dashang still dominate the retail market as they have quickly learnt how to set up new supply-chain systems. In fact, small retail outlets have risen in China from 1.9 million to 2.5+ million since 2004.

US market researcher RNCOS has projected that Vietnam's retail market sales will increase from US$39 billion in 2008 to US$123.8 billion by end 2013. In 2009 alone, FDI in Chile was $6.21 billion. Similarly, Argentina, Brazil, Indonesia, Malaysia, Russia, Singapore, and Thailand have allowed 100 percent FDI in multi-brand retail since 1990s. According to a Columbia University study, 10 years after Indonesia opened FDI, small traders continue to retain 90 percent of the business.

The lot of small farmers

The large majority of farmers in our agrarian economy own a mere 2 acres of land per family of about seven members. They barely generate ₹50,000 per year, input costs can reach ₹30,000. Poverty deprives them of transportation means, so they are dependent on intermediaries to sell their produce. In a bumper harvest, wholesale market prices dip drastically, leaving the farmer unable to recover his cost. For a kilo of tomatoes, farmers in Barpeta, Assam, have earned a mere 50 paise, whereas Guwahati customers buy that tomato at ₹25 per kg. Farmers may even jettison unsold produce, as carrying that home would entail transportation cost. Both farmers and customers lose here, the chain of middlemen dealers from farmer to customer clearly wins.

Unemployment leads to trading

No government has resolved unemployment, so common people set up kirana stores as a route to survival. The government grants them license, but without establishing any inspection system on the conditions in which they must sell products. Take the case of edible oil where about 68 percent is unbranded and sold loose. Mom-and-pop stores are a kind of godown for simultaneous stock and sell. Unhygienic conditions prevail in a large number of mom-and-pop stores because commodities sold loose from sacks and tins attract rats, lizards, cockroaches, ants, and other insects. It has been reported that when a rat falls into the open loose oil tin, retailers merely strain out the oil.

The poor customer becomes the victim when there are no mandatory checks on quality standards. Unlike organized retails where you can interface what you buy, mom-and-pop stores actually exercise an anti-democratic consumption pattern. Manufacturers spend excessively for brand promotion, but customers are always dependent on the counter salesman's recommendation at mom-and-pop stores to get the product, especially if they do not know a category.

Customers pay less

Organized multi-brand retails, particularly hypermarkets invented by the French, have the extraordinary mission of benefiting customers through lower cost and higher quality. Economies of scale make this possible. Large retailers go directly to the source, especially with food products. Here the farmer, retailer, and customer all benefit with competitive pricing. In the West, such retails became gigantic only because customers get the benefit.

In the 1980s, when retailers found that manufacturers were continuing to raise prices for their own interest, they challenged them with the private-label concept. Retailers created private-label brands in different categories and offered them to customers at 30 percent lower cost than national brands. Customers found no quality deficiency here and lapped them up. The result is that FMCG category private labels comprise nearly 60 percent market share in developed countries.

Like several developing countries did, India will gain from 100 percent FDI for multi-brand retailing as it is the biggest sector for the economy's growth. A new hygienic discipline will be put in place for everyday consumption products. Customers will enjoy outstanding choice in a self-help purchase pattern, competitive pricing of national and international brands, highly discounted private-label pricing, and a regular loyalty program. Small farmers will get a fair deal in directly selling to retailers. Retailers will have massive control over short duration perishable products.

Current mom-and-pop store employees with their acquired knowledge of retails will get better jobs in organized retails. Intelligent mom-and-pop store-owners will learn how to convert to elegant convenience stores by selecting the in-case requirement of customer merchandise or become franchisees of foreign convenience stores. Their standard will improve, they will not be wiped out.

Customer demand is so high in developed countries that industry, government, and politicians cannot ignore it; they have to respond in accordance. Actually it is not only manufacturer magnanimity that offers customer benefit, huge pressure from customers has ensured that customer benefit becomes the bottom line in retailing. The time has come for Indian customers to stop sacrificing and start demanding. Let us enjoy the future with 100 percent FDI in multi-brand retailing, freedom of choice, and spend less money at the multi-brand retail.

4 Human Ingenuity for Business

Poke to Bring Organizational Change

The jalebi will taste fabulous if the jalebi maker has the right craftsmanship to deploy the process, takes fresh ingredients in correct proportions, and uses appropriate tools for its preparation. Any failure here will highlight the jalebi's twists and turns that people in India often use as a negative figure of speech. In Western society the equivalent negative image is the banana skin.

The term human resources is outdated and basic. In an enterprise, the business catalyst is the function of human-ingenuity builders. They have to build leaders of two kinds while retaining the outside-in dynamics at every moment:

(1) Back-end leader to maintain a rigorous process that is always latent, never obsolete

(2) Front-end leaders in the open environment who know how to have all selling propositions of the enterprise on a disruptive platform and deliver with execution excellence

The job of human-ingenuity builders is to train people with the V-metaphor which is never blocked. That is the character of the letter V, it is open-ended and so has innumerable business possibilities. The confrontation of the competitive environment is so high and frequent that if ideation of leaders is not V-minded, they will fall into the cul-de-sac of grey business results.

The disciplinary culture in business is different from military discipline. Here the discipline is the outside-in approach that keeps an enterprise in tune with the times. When all employees mentally imbibe and tangibly practice the operating values of an enterprise that are outside-in driven, complacency gets reduced, and delivery and financial results get sharpened. Another big job of human-capital builders is to eliminate the complacency of leaders within an enterprise, which can be a bonus. If all selling propositions are 100 percent right, never give the scope of complacency to sediment. That is really not good for continuous improvement. So promote prohibition of complacency.

Our education system confirms to the social order. Taking on the connotation of being as crooked as a jalebi, rote learning is a permanent blight here. We require students to conform and deliver standardized answers to questions, rather than independently ideate solutions to problems. They learn merely to reproduce the taught, and carry that technique to the workplace. On the one hand is the totally ad hoc, massive unorganized sector; on the other are foreign brands changing people's habits. Without a disruptive platform, what can you do between these two juxtaposed sectors? What human-capital builders need is to invite people to operate on a disruptive platform with execution excellence. This will help to discontinue with the comfort zone. Human-capital builders, in particular, may like to consider the different poke doses here.

Drive infinite V, achieve vision

Arithmetical number crunching in business always has its limitations. Perhaps that is why the first alphabet letter A looks blocked, sans a horizon. But the letter V opens wide into infinity, it drives unrestrained vision for achievement that is sustainable.

Infinite V-drive of innovation

When an enterprise has the guts to put its product or service in the infinite V-drive, intelligently weaving in end-customer driven innovative R&D, success becomes obvious. There could be lots of turbulence on that journey, but a win is certain. This is what happened to Apple since its incorporation in 1977. The company remained coherent in the infinite V-drive of innovation. Apple is among the world's largest technology firms selling customer electronics, computer software, and commercial servers, with annual revenues of over US$60 billion in 2010. The iPod continues to make addicts from different generations.

A sustainable vision is the winning character of a business. Business can have unlimited projections when the prospect is open in the V-act. Of course, execution can be done arithmetically in stages, with products getting improved in different generations. If corporate or product strategy is put into the infinite V-drive, you bring continuity into different generations of deliverables in a boundaryless timeframe.

The two-finger V-sign gesture was used to represent victory during World War II. In the 1960s counterculture protests against US involvement in the Vietnam War, "V" was adopted as a sign of peace, which John Lennon popularized on a poster and in a song. But my adventures into different human dimensions culminate in an aspirational direction: What makes you strive for vision achievement. In the clash of negatives and positives that stimulate the neurons in your brain, you can win smoothly with a vision if you avoid mere number crunching.

A is closed

The open-at-the-top letter V is powerful and visionary whereas A is for arithmetic, the oldest, most used, and most elementary branch of mathematics. It can encompass advanced science and business calculations too. We cannot advance to the next level without "A," yet it is symbolically constrained when you look up.

Using statistical information alone can give you a narrow "A" vision, either in professional or personal life. Take the concept of globalization which Pankaj Ghemawat of Spain's IESE Business School says has surprisingly low global integration indicators. There are only 2 percent university students outside their home countries, just 3 percent people live outside their birth country, rice traded across borders is only 7 percent, while foreigners as directors of S&P 500 companies is a mere 7 percent too. Of global GDP, only 20 percent is equivalent to exports. Vital for globalization are air travel and ocean shipping, but bilateral treaties and cartels restrict their free-flow operations.

Infinite V strategy will take you far

In contrast, the infinite V of globalization has unparalleled innovation, as happened in the West in the last century, from aircraft to the Internet. Society went through exceptional turbulence as well. Was discomfort intentionally generated to create a hunger for innovation where the innovator gains as well as imposes his power? Innovations prove the strength of human intelligence to enhance living comfort. Toyota's Corolla grew robust in infinite V scale since 1966, connecting to customer trends by upgrading value. Placing corporate transformation or product design in the infinite V-strategy from inception can make you unique and take you to an unlimited path. Even in personal life if you continuously nurture stimuli in the infinite V-strategy, your intellectual capacity will build up to take you into leadership mode without limit.

Living in France for over 35 years, I have absorbed the unbeatable mechanism of the infinite V and have learnt that without putting the infinite V into action V-achievement gets left behind. Considered among the most cultured of societies, France uniquely incorporates innovation and philosophy, nurturing intellectuals and inventors such as Pierre and Marie Curie, and 20th century innovations, such as Concorde and Train à Grande Vitesse (TGV) that have vastly contributed to the world's progress.

Yet, over centuries, very little of French innovations were converted to business. Closeted parochially in their geographical hexagon, France does not engage in global public relations to publicize the country's innovative power. Other countries have converted France's innovative recipes into application and business and money.

Infinite V to achieve vision

French inventors Joseph Nicephore Niepce and Louis Jacques Mande Adgurre ushered in modern photography in the 1820s. It was American John Wesley Hyatt who commercially used celluloid photography in 1868, and George Eastman invented dry photographic film for commercial use in the Kodak camera in 1888. In contrast, American inventor Thomas Alva Edison commercialized most of his innovations such as the motion-picture camera and the light bulb, and created one of the most successful corporations, General Electric.

Human innovative power resides in the ever-widening V-sphere, which needs action to make contributions to society. In any field, the maverick's vision, knowledge, and skill will always be ahead of its time. Society should always encourage deviant ideators without conditions, so they can contribute by becoming more and more groundbreaking and victorious in their own specialized fields to support infinite V.

Top 10 21st century innovations

It is about time that out-of-the-box innovations in the V-drive bypass the destructive ways of human beings and nature, and cater to a higher level of human need and desire. The top 10 21st-century-innovation topics according to scientist Eugene S. Meieran at Intel, US, are reminiscent of how to take society forward through energy conservation, resource protection, food and water production and distribution, waste management, education and learning, medicine and prolonging life, security and counter-terrorism, new technology, genetics and cloning, and global communication. A new type of struggle must emerge in this century so we drive-V, achieve vision.

There is appalling imbalance on the innovative platform among people from different parts of the world. Caucasian Western society has been able to usurp superiority status up to now through inventions. If all emerging-economy nations in Asia, Africa, and Latin America dive into innovation, global power equations will change and a balanced power equation will result between the West and the rest of the world. How can this be done?

Keep the A-platform for arithmetical number crunching, but make it subservient to the guiding infinite V. Infinite V is for vision achievement that is endless.

Middle management drives Japan

Everyone participates in the V-drive in Japan. Individuals take ownership. Here is an experience etched in my mind.

The extreme politeness and service orientation of the Japanese completely bowled me over. After some casual conversation about the fascinating Japanese breakfast at my hotel in Tokyo, as I was getting off the lift, one of the reception managers rushed to touch my feet. Totally unnerved, "What, wha… ?" I stuttered, stepping back immediately. I discovered that my shoe laces had opened, and he was trying to help tie them.

Discipline and long hours

Never have I seen such courtesy, except perhaps on Japanese trains. Unlike the underground or metros in different parts of the world, in Japan people are quiet and gracious. I have never seen anyone speak on a mobile phone when traveling. They readily accommodate one another so everyone can travel together in comfort. Even in the wee morning hours or midnight, black-suited young, middle aged, and old men stand out in plenty. As do formally dressed women going to or from work.

"In America my father would come home for supper every day, and we'd spend two weekend days together," said Kuniko, an office clerk at a store in Tokyo. She recalls her childhood spent in New Jersey. "Our family bonding was joyful like Americans. But when we moved to Tokyo, my sisters and I barely meet him for weeks together." Being the head of a gas station, her father goes to work on Sundays too, "He'd never ever come to our school events, and I hardly know my father now," she says.

Actually her father is not very different from the thousands of office goers in Japan who board an underground train at 7 a.m. and return home at midnight. The Japanese passion for hard work is legendary; being a workaholic has emerged as a corporate culture that is appreciated. The longer employees stay at work every day, the better rewarded they are with bonus and overtime perquisites. You are in your boss's good books if you leave office after him, which generally means 11 p.m.

Women quit work to raise a family

Not being able to cope with the demanding 14–15 work hours plus family responsibilities, most women prefer to quit work on getting married or to raise a family. Kuniko speaks excellent English and had risen to become a section manager of the departmental store she worked in. After childbirth, she first returned to part-time work, so was given a lower, clerical position. "When I started leaving office at 6 in the evening to pick up my baby from the crèche, people would look at me like I was an alien," she recounts. "For me, my family is my first priority. Even if I get more salary, if I have to stay long, I will not take up that job. I need to balance and manage my family and work."

No promotions have come her way since, although she is back to normal hours, while her male counterparts have leapt ahead by burning the midnight oil. Although such gender discriminations exist, Japan's traditional society is averse to litigation, and social attitudes respect women's household role.

Immediately after World War II, Japanese women started to participate in the labor force. Today, about 50 percent of all women have paid work in service, wholesale and retail trades, eating and drinking places, and secondary industries such as manufacturing. This percentage is higher than most countries. But reaching positions of authority in managerial roles largely remains the preserve of black-suited salaried men.

According to the International Labor Organization, women held just 6.6 percent management jobs in Japanese companies and government in 1985, which rose a mere 10.1 percent in 2005, whereas in the US at the same time, women held 42.5 percent of all managerial jobs.

Middle management takes ownership

Japan's demanding, morning-to-midnight corporate culture is the expectation of its dominating middle management where productivity is very high. According to a 1988 study in the *Journal of Applied Psychology*, management-development systems in Japan's leading corporations have produced executives and managers who are commonly acknowledged to be among the best in the world, although how these systems operate is not well understood. Although the Japanese always listen to their superiors, when it comes to decision-making, they discuss a matter threadbare and have several consensus rounds. Everybody in the room has to agree to a point, and unless that happens they do not move on. In contrast, the Chinese are very shrewd and quick; and in America, the senior most has the authority to take decisions.

The top management can be quite different in Japan, they move about on business trips, socialize at business lunches and dinners to develop relationships with their customers. The middle-level stays stodgily at work, shapes policy, sends more than 100–200 emails a day, with lots of conferences and meetings and drives the Japanese working style. They take the responsibility to maintain harmony so employees can work together in an *uchi soto* or "us and them" situation. That means working in groups and teams. This term can also translate as "we Japanese" dealing with an international "them" in the global situation.

Cities differ in business cultures

The business and social cultures in Tokyo, Osaka, and Hiroshima are a bit different from one another. In Osaka, they talk a lot, joke, laugh, and express their feelings directly. But people are more reserved in Tokyo, which is more commercial. As a society, the Japanese are humble, they are polite, understated, and do not shout. In fact, in their wonderful fast trains, nobody talks, but you will observe a large number of commuters extremely engrossed in reading novels. The Japanese characters are in large print in these 4" × 6" books, and I found a lot of them are illustrated comic books.

Sitting next to an old gentleman as he pored over the comic book, I got curious and peeked into what absorbed him so. Lo and behold, it was a pornographic comic book! A thought flashed by: If Japan with 99 percent literacy, as per UNDP's 2009 report, needs illustrations for easy comprehension of this subject, how long will it take India's piracy pushers to deliver the same to the 44 percent of our people who are unlettered?

Soft skills, IT bottom-line booster

Japan's hardworking middle management has perfected productivity process; but when it comes to delivering services as in India's IT business, a very different requirement comes to the fore, that of polishing soft skills.

Behavior has to co-opt cultural nuances

Driving US$75 billion (2013) of the arguably US$800+ billion global IT business, India with 2 million IT professionals has certainly flourished in the demand-led market. The prime benefit offered is low cost with good management, and the ability to handle large-scale operations. High technical skill set is the frame that carries the business, but without soft skills the delivery remains a skeleton with no flesh. Tomorrow's route to acquire better brand value and restore better bottom line is about anchoring soft skills at the core.

Techno-savvy engineers travel the world delivering IT services, but far too often they are oblivious of how to behave in different cultures. This lack of understanding can mar many a business transaction. In a neck-to-neck competition, if the

Indian manager shakes a woman client's hand with his gloves on, the discordant feeling can be a major reason to lose the contract. The apprehension could be, "How will we handle cultural differences in future?"

It is certainly not fair for organizations to leave employees to pick up, interpret, and perform in culturally divergent environments. Just as technical training is not negotiable, so must an engineer be made culturally fit with relevant soft skills; mere learning how to correctly hold a fork and knife at the dining table is just a hygiene factor. Gender equality is a big topic in the West, yet it is culturally right to hold a door open for a woman to pass through. Undoubtedly Indians are very polite, but soft skills and politeness are totally different subjects. Our tendency to push through in India does not even allow people to properly exit a public toilet, train, or bus; we rush in before others can vacate that space.

Service is at a discount

In the service industry, soft skills and subtlety create 60 percent selling value, the balance 40 percent is technicality used to deliver the service. In a country where service does not have high admiration culturally, soft skills can be picked up only with hardcore, effective absorbing training. To buy an on-the-spot ticket in most airports, you have to stand outside. When counter attendants dillydally, I have sometimes asked them what they think of how their slow service is affecting customers sweating outside when they are in air-conditioned comfort. Of course they have not designed the counters, but are they sensitive to customer service? Unfortunately, their nonplussed expression conveys that such a thought has never crossed their minds.

The employee is the brand

India's IT industry can yield a tremendous global reputation and image boost if highly processed soft-skills coaching becomes a corporate priority. Wearing a monkey cap over a formal suit in winter in a Western developed country is not a representation of soft skills; nor is having some religious sign on the forehead at the workplace. The client may wear casual clothing as per his country's culture, but the servicing partner should not follow suit. A corporate dress code will better define the on-site engineer and his company's seriousness. It is not good manners to bring traditional smelling food to eat at the worktable. That can disturb your client's corporate and social culture although they may not express it upfront.

When located on-site at the client's premises, you become the face and brand of your company. Do not become a temporary immigrant who huddles in his own community, but mix freely in their cultural and business environment. Americans nowadays talk of the US becoming an exporting rather than an importing country, and unemployment is rife in Europe. So people should not perceive your being there as depriving local people of jobs. Display your individual identity here, your value distinction at work, so that you are not just a coder the client has contracted for from a foreign IT-services provider.

Twenty soft skills to hone

Your on-site posting is a huge opportunity to enjoy a foreign-country stay with a strong mentality of integration. This learning will add more value to your CV than your work experience. Here are 20 soft-skills areas to process and productively use in the IT industry:

(1) You have to be adept at integrating with foreign colleagues on-site.

(2) Be confident in the spoken language even if you are not perfect at it.

(3) Have a congenial attitude and behavior.

(4) Your manners must address the clients in their societal context, and not what you are used to in your culture.

(5) Wear the right workplace attire to always appear elegant. Even if casual wear is appropriate on some days, be sure you appear neat.

(6) In terms of work execution you have to learn how to understand a client's deeper business activities to avoid jarring him with lack of knowledge.

(7) Make a client speak elaborately to encash valuable insights, and make him feel satisfied that he has contributed to your personal learning.

(8) Gauge a senior client's personal sensitivities to better bond with him.

(9) Address clients in their own business language, as per the business culture of the company and the country.

(10) You will achieve deal-making only when the client is sure he can take you as his/her confidant and can deal with you in future.

(11) You need soft skills to deliver the nitty-gritty of daily work such as facilitating the client's team to adhere to the mutually agreed action to get your work done smoothly.

(12) Take the lead in interacting with multiple nationalities so that the work team can bond well.

(13) Understand and interpret technicalities with a palatable story which is illustrative for everyone to grasp.

(14) Work toward magnifying a business delivery so
       that the client perceives it as higher than its basic
       substance.
(15) Be alert and quick in managing crisis with equanim-
       ity, not anxiety.
(16) Soft skills pop up in gender matters, how to interact
       with colleagues of the opposite sex is important.
       There has to be trust in professional relationships.
(17) Generally men have a stereotyped image of women
       being subservient and are unable to come to equal
       terms with them in the world of business. If you are
       a woman boss, see how you can get men to work
       without their resentment.
(18) For your own pleasure, comfort, and recognition, soft
       skills are important in how to be integrated, and not
       have an immigrant's feeling of being an outsider.
(19) Be perceived as a leader in your profession. Soft skills
       play a part in you ensuring that everybody finds out
       that you are knowledgeable and so can naturally lead
       them.
(20) Be involved in diverse activities and acquire admira-
       tion for your prowess in them.

Celebrate with your host-country friends

When you are posted in a foreign country, you can always
invite your host-country clients and friends to celebrate India's
festivals, dress traditionally, and use your religious rituals.
Your guests will be thrilled to learn about your culture. But
the workplace cannot accept this.

In India's high-economic disparity, and diversity in culture,
religion, language, and geography, soft-skills grooming is not

part of our social fiber. Not many people would thank an auto-rickshaw driver, nor would they expect him to say thanks. The West is so exuberant about soft skills because they have consciously abolished slavery and learned to respect the service sector. When you are working for them, you have no choice but to follow their etiquette.

Indian IT companies have some soft-skills training, but does that make you persuasive enough to convert business during a high value strategic business pitch? Relevant soft-skills coaching will improve marketing and sales relationships and reverse perceptions so that Indian companies can work toward becoming proactive strategic partners to global clients.

Do soft skills exist in Indian organized retail?

Want proof that soft skills bring business? Just watch this salesman, within five minutes, 30 saris were swiftly unfolded and draped extravagantly over his outstretched arms. This spontaneous selling demo at a typical traditional store mes-merized my British friend, Paul. He quadrupled his purchase intent of a sari for Christmas for his wife in Liverpool, to taking sari gifts for her sisters as well.

Paul wanted clothing for himself, so we entered a modern Indian fashion apparel store. As he walked alongside the merchandise shelves, he found a salesman shadowing his every step. This was embarrassing, he asked the salesman to stop following him. The man stepped back, but kept a hawk's eye on his customer, purportedly to help him. When Paul did turn around to ask a question, the salesman ran to his boss to verify the veracity of his answer.

No sales tactics or glib dialogue

So what was the point in following Paul if his merchandise knowledge was so sketchy? Obviously his training was not just inadequate in facts and figures, but pitiful in soft skills. He had never been trained to read a shopper's face, or dialogue to help shoppers buy. Unlike the proverbial garrulous British barber who engages you in a constant stream of chatter as he shears off your hair, salespersons in modern Indian retails have no sales tactics or behavioral skills. So they just tail the shopper, not just irritating, but intimidating him, resulting in no expected business conversion. Shoppers who get tailed just take a round as though on an inspection tour and quickly hit the exit door. Those who actually buy come with a need-based agenda with prior knowledge of the store's merchandise.

Clearly modern retails require pragmatic soft-skills coaching and systematic review mechanism. India's social culture accepts the casual aspect and people interpret the same subject very differently. So following a Western model is difficult, as it requires conditioning, discipline, and review. Sales people have to be made accountable to respect every discipline from morning to evening, during the tenure of their presence in the store. A service manual for streamlining of training has to cover every moment of activity of every salesperson at the retail end.

Associative learning for retail staff

Ivan Pavlov's 1927 theory of classical conditioning can perhaps be applied here. In normal course, a dog salivates on seeing food. Pavlov's conditioning theory demonstrated that by simultaneously ringing a bell and giving food, the dog would salivate on hearing the bell even without food because it associates food with the bell. Training people by strengthening the stimulus-outcome association has proved to be very effective in the West. When teaching an individual a response, you need to find the most potent reinforcer for that person. It may be a larger reinforcer at a later time or a smaller reinforcer immediately.

Reading the shopper's body language

Retails design a planogram to evoke the shopper's subliminal desire for merchandise offtake as he/she walks through the retail. A simplistic example is placing accessories such as cuff links and neckties next to formal shirts or suits. Shoppers of various types walk in, such as a man sporting a ponytail in traditional clothes or Western suit, a woman with plenty of tattoos or in sophisticated outfit. How should the salesman approach these different personalities with appropriate soft skills for business conversion?

Individualization of service makes the retail great

On a recent US visit, my wife and I entered a large, crowded Walmart store. She sported a walking stick, having recently been operated for a broken knee. Suddenly a store keeping merchandiser woman came, hugged my wife with a smile enquiring after her injury, and gave her an electric shopping cart with a seat. She explained how simple it was to drive the cart inside the store and shop without walking. What heartened us is that she brought the electric cart on her own initiative and made us feel welcome in an overcrowded store. This warm gesture is soaked in soft skills.

Another day at Walmart, I was looking for a video-camera charger that I forgot to pack into my suitcase. The storekeeper searched the store and electronic inventory in vain, and asked for my mobile number. After two hours he called to apologize that they did not deal in this category, but that he had enquired and found that his rival, Best Buy, has it. He asked me to visit a specific Best Buy, gave me the address and saleswoman's name who was holding a charger for me.

I was totally overwhelmed; I did not know how to thank him. He humbly said he thought it was his duty to help his shopper as he could not provide the needed item. I went to Best Buy and got my charger, but my emotional bonding with Walmart increased substantially. I have now clearly understood how Walmart has grown to US$466 billion revenue within 30 years.

Salesmen can radiate a dynamic ambience in the store

What is the right mix for a retail to get quick ROI? The answer is low-cost real estate, high spend in soft-skills training for sales people, highly aspirational retail design, and appropriate merchandise that cater to entry, mid, and premium price tags and retails highly connected to their localities. For the store manager, the most important criterion is the retail's fresh look. The ambience is the pull. How promptly can the merchandise be rearranged after the previous shopper leaves? When a shopper appears to hesitate, can the salesperson help by taking on the confidante's role?

With FDI, when retails such as Walmart set up shop, the shopping culture will change. Instead of driving every subliminal aspect of shoppers, retailers are merely providing air-conditioned lung space for them in summer to prevent them from going and buying unbranded products from street hawkers or kirana stores. Is it not time organized retailers understand and diligently address the shopper's soft corners?

EMOD factor that India requires to appreciate the value of time

The umbilical cord of license-raj work culture has to be snapped off if Indian industry has to align to global trends. Every industry needs to blend its own corporate culture, chalk the operating discipline in every function and every layer so everyone follows it meticulously. The main job of HR function is to ensure this while keeping end-customer delivery as the key objective of EMOD. The objective of your enterprise vis-à-vis customers is twofold:

(1) How to get customers to return for repeat purchase of your product or service
(2) Expanding your customer base to new areas

A factor urgently required in India's business domain, EMOD is an actionable operational efficacy matrix to seamlessly interconnect the back end and front end of an enterprise to its market dynamics. This behavioral matrix comprises four human characteristics: attitude, behavior, action, and delivery. When applied in different enterprises the matrix will not change, but employees' articulation of attitude, behavior, action, and delivery will be different. The difference depends on the gaps they need to plug to coherently run the enterprise in their competitive environment.

Diversity leads to haphazard ways

Indian industry has inherited the license-raj work culture where time management was never an issue. Customers were used to waiting up to five years for their car or scooter to be delivered. This sluggish legacy has translated to crisis management under global competitive pressure. So strategic decision-making often happens at the last moment, forward planning is amiss, and being reactive in business has become a malaise. This business style started changing after WTO-TRIPS in 2004 with simultaneous arrival of global brands. With state governments empowered to grant FDI for multi-brand retails, globally successful retailers will further radically change the Indian consuming system.

The major reason why Indian brands are weak is that EMOD was not managed systematically, from top management to shop floor. When the business agenda becomes flexible, the value of time does not get recognized.

The multicultural people from different states have different behavioral habits, and everybody tends to try out operating discipline in their own way. That is why it becomes almost impossible to achieve alignment of an enterprise-wide discipline. Indian managements are lenient to individuals instead of making an enterprise-operating discipline a highly processed guardrail.

In my experience of transforming several corporations in different countries, the meat is obtained only when an internal rejuvenation discipline program is put in place with a stringent timetable. It is never enough to create beautiful internal communication without a core message of the corporate entity that is relevant to employees internally in an outside-in perspective. This has to be well illustrated, meaningful, and instantly understood by everyone in the enterprise. If it merely stays as a buzz with some ephemeral images, it's a management textbook that will not spark the real change required. Even when the message is changed, if employee behavior remains the same, the purpose of corporate change gets defeated. Only when it is driven by EMOD can corporate transformation be successfully managed. As an entrepreneur if you have decided on transformation, there was a fundamental logic and purpose behind it. But if EMOD is not put in at its beginning, you will not see results. EMOD is the point of departure of building a corporation's high worth.

When an enterprise launches a new identity, this corporate branding has to incorporate the back-end and front-end alignment of the enterprise toward its vendors and end-customers. To achieve internal rejuvenation employees must understand how they and their professional activities are linked to the new identity. The corporate identity drives business and becomes visibly manifest when it radiates the purpose of different activities. Corporate transformation that drives business has satellites as drivers that impact proactive customer sensitivity. These include the enterprise value system, business objective, corporate promise and vision, corporate and business strategy, and back-end and front-end alignment and operational execution excellence to achieve a message-rich, single-focus, and transformed corporation.

To establish and perfectly manage internal change, a central theme as a coherence nerve is essential to understand customers in the competitive environment. This sets the direction on how to win the customer's heart with a *fil conducteur*, which is a sensitive nerve that runs through and activates different functions in the enterprise. A coherent central sustaining nerve system can be drilled into employees of different functions as their EMOD.

ABoArD promise culture as a process

As in an aircraft where speed and rationality parameters are regulated, coming aboard a value framework for a continuous journey is the employee's EMOD in an enterprise.

A brilliant academic student may not necessarily get a higher rank in professional life. In practical business, it is not enough to score high marks; you need action and delivery. The quality of enterprise delivery and success depends on the enterprise attitude for boundaryless learning. That leads to appropriate behavior and puts into action a deliverable to enrich end-customers and increase business worth.

Indian enterprises give too much space for individuals to follow their own method of working. They need to follow a corrective working process. At the same time, they allow little opportunity to take decisions. You can achieve the competitive edge if with single focus you manage the attitude, behavior, action, and delivery promise of employees through EMOD.

EMOD drills to internalize mechanical procedure into employees to enrich customer experience as high quality, and increase the business of the enterprise. Let us watch it in operation when you board an aircraft. The flight crew commands you, with smiles and soft voices, on how you should behave during the flight. You have to maintain some order for safety and security purposes at different altitudes and for times such as takeoff, landing, and turbulence during the flying time.

So with your **a**ttitude, **b**ehavior, **a**ction, and **d**elivery for a safe journey as explained, you **ABoArD** the aircraft consciously to change your normal routine of life. Like this aircraft, where parameters are regulated for fragility, speed, rationality, and safety, employees must change their inherent normal life routine to ABoArD this value framework of an enterprise for a continuous healthy journey to overcome turbulence.

Attitude

Employee attitude to work can be articulated to match enterprise purpose and objective. It is important to be able to observe society and its distinct, fast-moving trends to extract and bring in the enterprise as continuous learning culture.

Behavior

A structured attitude will guide employee behavior that also needs to be articulated. There has to be coherence and pre-dictability in the behavior of the employee and enterprise that customers perceive.

Action

When the attitude and behavior of employees is streamlined in collective force, the enterprise can anticipate trends and take requisite action to overcome competitor activities to give a sustainable end-customer experience to its products or services. Action also needs to be articulated precisely.

Delivery promise

Customers generally select a brand based on its promise of delivered excellence. Such a promise is measurable. The interplay of the employee's attitude, behavior, action, and delivery results in the coherence of a fil conducteur. I am using this French term, which means an active nerve. These four progressive employee steps can be linked as an EMOD program, and be specific to every enterprise.

Elevated ABoArD

Business, however, is always at ground level, although its complexity and risk factors fly in high altitudes. Such high altitude risk can be equated to any type of competitor aggression. Take the example of how digital technology has shifted several social trends and marginalized a category like celluloid film for cameras. With top-notch know-how in one industry, an enterprise can enter another domain to crush a big category.

That is exactly what Apple did. From inside the computing industry, Apple bombarded the entertainment industry and demolished several strong players in this space. Attitude, behavior, action, and delivery form the foundation of a dynamic business culture. That is why the highly professional ABoArD way of piloting your enterprise with high precision and technology solutions will give you a better edge. So, EMOD is an enterprise's efficient time management of the individual and collective. ABoArD is the driver of cohesive culture of the enterprise to drive business forward.

Distinction in service

Attitude and behavior are intangibles that create distinction in the service business. Fashionable and excessively priced Parisian restaurants portray their superiority with impeccable service, following rituals ceremoniously for serving different wines as per the food and seasons. Waiters are trained to proactively keep an eye open to anticipate every small requirement at each table. This attention to service has to be cultivated meticulously because only when the value is perceived and appreciated can it command a premium price.

In India's diverse and plural culture, flexibility is a common characteristic across every way of life. Being flexible or accommodating is very positive for maintaining relationships, but extremely dangerous in business. It translates to the quick-fix application of *putti* (patchwork) approach, which is not sustainable. As attitude is driven from external effect, only an attitude that questions is conscious about discipline, sensitive to creativity and distinction, and can align a business process to deliver the quality customers want.

Regional language factor

There lies in India another exceptional aspect which may be unique in the world. All the states have their own mother tongue: Tamil is spoken in Tamil Nadu, Assam speaks Assamese, Gujarat converses in Gujarati, while Punjabi is Punjab's oral tradition. But the Hindi belt comprising Uttar Pradesh, Uttaranchal, Bihar, Jharkhand, Madhya Pradesh, Chhattisgarh, Himachal Pradesh, Rajasthan, Jammu, Haryana, and Delhi ostensibly have one language. This so-called common language takes away from the identity of each state's character and makes them homogeneous, which in reality is not the case. This kind of mixed culture encourages a totally erratic attitude.

As Hindi has been declared India's national language, although not everyone embraces this pronouncement, the mixed culture of flexibility has seeped into the functioning of people in all states. In a business enterprise, when employee attitude is so diverse, their behavior gets impacted with that erratic culture too. As attitude and behavior drive the core essence of a human being, the *chalta hai* or ok-mentality drives every action, so the delivery is bound to sink into mediocrity.

A hangover of our colonial past

A hangover of our colonial past is high admiration of Caucasian society. In response to that, many American management consulting firms have come to India to teach Indian companies the American discipline. They fail to take into account, conform to, or seamlessly mesh with the societal aspects of people here. Over time Americans have managed to integrate the different types of people from all over the world who call themselves Americans today by inventing an operating discipline that is stringent, has one culture, one language, and demands efficiency. In India, people do not have the same temperament. Yet we have to do global business and so need to practice discipline, creativity, or alternative ideas and process.

Ritual of the daily notebook

Ritual is the precisely coordinated attitude of forward planning. It maintains coherence at all times and empowers relevant teams to execute work on time. EMOD avoids crisis management, which is never good as there is a possibility of losing key elements in the hurry.

Writing every problem and solution in a daily notebook, either physical or digital, with the date brings in the very rigorous EMOD factor. When you drive EMOD by injecting the psychological and intellectual perspective, your attitude, behavior, and action follow a marked functional benefit that aims for distinction. In his/her first job, an employee is entrenched in family, societal, and college culture, which has to change to absorb and create interest in long, addictive work hours in an enterprise. This work culture influences and seasons both professional and personal life. If you don't enjoy your working life, you may not enjoy your personal life. That's because a large, important chunk of your time is spent at work. Also, success at work is directly correlated to your better lifestyle.

Today managers spend at least 10 hours a day at the workplace; his/her work starts to mirror the work environment. So it is important to infuse human sensitivity into this culture as it drives employee enthusiasm for action and their hawk eye for demanding and delivering quality.

In your competitive environment, define the unique attitude and behavior your enterprise is based on. This will enable you to dovetail the action of employees for delivering sustainable, profitable business. In sum, the EMOD time factor is driven by ABoArD that is about your human capital absorbing change for better, intelligent, and qualitative delivery.

Closed, incestuous environment versus happening, open environment?

In business we drive our attitude, behavior, action, and delivery with EMOD. In society, at large, we experience a contradiction between the open versus closed environment, both at the individual level as well as in the industry.

Employees have to be sensitive to co-opt what is happening outside their business area as all their customers reside there. At the individual level, art enlarges our imagination and digitization of technology has uplifted the value of human life. But digitization has also created linearity across society, commoditizing all products and services in the happening open environment. It is industry's big responsibility to inculcate the outside-in factor inside the enterprise to create a higher curve of employee learning.

Inside you is your closed environment

Take a look at how you, individually, have been groomed in your personal life. The education system expects you to write and talk English better than Britishers and Americans with no grammatical mistake. Your family would want you to come first in class, take up a "decent" job, and "settle down" to a respected family life. All this comprises the opium of your closed, incest-like environment. It makes you practice prudence in professional life, satisfying the boss becomes a critical activity, and making decisions is no longer your problem. The trend is to tote up the money you make, the job offers that come your way, or wallow in your job's stock options.

In earlier times, security came when you clinched a government job for your whole life. Since the 1991 economic reforms, the young generation is flirting with jobs. In each new position they are again cocooned in the same kind of culture, as though they are in the closed, protected, and family environment. People are averse to the discomforting risk of becoming an entrepreneur or having an entrepreneurial mentality. MNCs applaud this as they can hire people communicating in English here, which is very difficult in China.

Reforms bring change

So statistically, after China's 1978 economic reforms and policy change in 1987, that opened up private enterprise, the number of individual new businesses grew 11.04 million from 1989 to 2004. In contrast, as per India's Ministry of Corporate Affairs, from 1992 to 2006, the average number of companies formed per year was 33,835, thus taking the 15-year total figure to just half a million new companies.

How does one become an entrepreneur? We know Charlie Chaplin as a great comic, but he was among the first to take on an incredible entrepreneurial challenge in cinematography. He became the producer, director, screenplay writer, composer, mime choreographer, and principal actor in his films. He started early. His mother Hannah used to entertain rioters and soldiers in Aldershot theater near London in 1894, when she suddenly one day developed a larynx condition. They booed her off the stage; her career ended abruptly.

Watching her weeping and the audience angry, five-year-old Charlie took matters into his own hands. He strode up on to the stage alone. He sang "Jack Jones," a well-known tune of that time. The audience was spellbound. With thunderous applause they threw coins on stage for him.

Confidence is what education has to instil

Do our schools infuse this confidence in our children, making them independent minded? I recently met over 1,000 students, parents, and teachers across India while working for a company into for-profit education. Parents expect high performance results having spent excessively on fees. Most secondary-school students bemoaned that nobody understands their sentiments or counsels them. They are forced to study boring subjects they do not like and discipline that's relevant to their parents' time is killing them. Teachers decry a loaded curriculum and lack of respect from students.

I passionately listened to these daily-life crises and thought how fortunate I was to be born in an underprivileged family. I could go to Art College without any pressure even though art was considered a domain sans a career at that time!

From humble beginnings Charlie Chaplin's entrepreneurial talent took him places. When his half-brother, Sydney, tried to promote him to an American businessman traveling through England by boat, they suddenly found a young boy somersaulting toward them. So passionately engrossed was Charlie in his performance that he somersaulted into the water. Sydney had to dive in to save Charlie who did not know how to swim.

Chaplin went on to become an astute businessman determined to have full control over his creative career. He marketed his film persona as "The Tramp," and in 1919 founded United Artists with several prominent stars of that time.

The closed and open environment at work

To have control over productivity for efficient operations, enterprises carefully define their own introverted culture and principles in their closed, incestuous environment. Internal discipline was relevant 20–30 years ago when industry used to command the market. Digital technology has gifted them the Excel sheet for this modern habit that is making work culture quite insensitive.

Today, the public at large command industry. Stakeholders of an enterprise comprising end-customers, talent pool, suppliers, shareholders, distribution channel, and financial institutes all reside in the open uncontrollable environment. Technology democratizes this happening space, expanding its power into endless infinity.

New trends of new media and rapidly changing lifestyles influence this open environment. Enterprises may find it difficult to control this happening environment, but employees engaging in entrepreneurial challenge can certainly intercept society to ingeniously navigate business through this bubbling cauldron. Unfortunately, most employees exhibit a subservient character at work, just the way Indian children are tutored into dependence by parents and teachers.

Lacking this spirit of entrepreneurship, Indian business houses have not made a dent in world markets. Only the monopolistic, family-driven businesses make it, enter new areas even without domain competency. I salute the handful of exceptional people with no traditional business background who became successful in big business after Independence. Here I am not referring to the trading community with entrepreneurial mindset.

Micro, small, and medium enterprises (MSMEs) need strengthening

MSMEs form the backbone of most economies. A US study shows that 35 years after World War II, more than one of four young men and one of five young women became self-employed in the 1980s. But in India, I have heard many MSME owners say they do not see the future of their business as their children are not interested; they are happy working in someone else's major enterprise. So MSMEs remain contained instead of becoming big professional entities. According to

Business Today reportage, just 13 percent of small family businesses survive till the third generation, and only 4 percent go beyond that.

The closed-environment culture, whether at the individual or enterprise level, is the dope that kills the entrepreneurial urge. Being able to adapt to, integrate with, and flawlessly navigate the uncontrollable open environment will bring Indian education and business the platform on which to survive the future with entrepreneurial challenge.

Chalta hai is a no-no in business

Tolerance is a virtue for retaining good human relationships or upholding human rights, but definitely not for business. What business needs to forge ahead and to make money is the open-business environment, not the inward-looking closed one that will tolerate anything instead of trying to perfect the delivery for the customer.

Do not bandage the flaws

The mentality to accept the imperfect chalta hai (let it be) is a most deceptive and unwanted malaise in business. It destroys customer's value delivery and sustenance of business in the competitive environment. Refurbishing the bad by putting a bandage on it to make it look good is like giving propofol to Michael Jackson, American King of Pop. The pick-me-up power of this hypnotic agent is exhilarating, but when its short-acting effect wears off, it can be fatal with continuous use; the way it suddenly killed Michael Jackson in 2009.

Chalta hai is a slothful business

Currently, most industries in India are very seriously enjoying short-term revenue generation through volume business with low-cost wages. This trend is not good for the country's future as the demand-led working culture in both exports and home consumption does not allow entrepreneurs to be creative enough to craft to transform in the value-led market. A simple example of this malaise in our society is that we do not even produce a hard disk that tiny Taiwan can churn out in a jiffy.

The chalta-hai attitude exists in businesses where market demand is flat, such as traditional unbranded categories like fabrics, khadi, and utensils, among others. Having lasted decade after decade in dull categories, they have had no inclination for renovation. Whether the market is growing or not, profit is always under pressure.

Negligence of on-time market watch can bring dangerous consequences such as obsolescence because an emerging category enters and knocks them out of the market. If there is no technology obsolescence, the business can be transformed through intelligent innovation by adding distinction and customer benefit that is felt in the product or service. A disruptive platform is required to turn the business and organizational culture upside down. A successful disruption example is loom-maker Toyoda transforming itself into Toyota to join the ranks of today's global leaders of automobiles.

Opportunity, unless seized, is useless

As India is an emerging society everybody looks for growth with market expansion. This idea that we have a large enough population so penetration will resolve all growth woes is a lack luster solution. You can see how retail brands are opening store after store with no profitability in sight. In most domains, per capita consumption is far lower than in developed countries.

No business institution trains students on how to increase per capita consumption, which is the real indicator of brand fidelity that results in numbers. Per capita growth requires huge understanding of customer usage and purchase patterns. By following their day-to-day life requirements, we can intercept the gap and fill it, then increase the per capita growth.

Demand-led syndrome

In a demand-led market, all you need to do is supply as long as there is demand. In concentrating on fulfilling orders, you dangerously neglect to plan future strategy. Of course when good money is coming in, you should undertake this generic business, but have you realized that the customer has multiple choices when price is the only differentiaton?

Take India's IT-services industry, among our biggest foreign money-spinners today; it is a part of the extreme demand-led market. After economic reforms in 1991, the huge requirement from foreign companies for India's coding services became evident. So everybody wanted to enjoy the fruits, irrespective of how much competency and domain knowledge they possessed. In its honeymoon period in 2001, the business was giving operating profit margins of 35–42 percent. It was an easy entry ticket, luring company after company to jump in. They invested in whatever would grow revenues right away, that is, good administration, great infrastructure, and English-speaking manpower.

Then the foreign customers got smart. Not seeing any distinction in the generic deliverables from this competitive environment, they started haggling. It is human instinct after all to negotiate for better price advantage when the market is aplenty. Indian IT companies had to fall in line and give discount after discount to hold on to customers to focus only on volume. Quality of deliverables slipped, recruitment levels fell from engineers to just science graduates. Then the real demand-led market malaise hit them. Profit steadily dwindled to between 25–35 percent in 2006, and by 2012 margins had plummeted to 18–28 percent among Tier-1 companies. Obviously, the figures would be lower for the lower tiers.

Choose to deliver value

Indian IT companies do have a choice though. They can go against the wave to create value without leaving this business for another. Instead of being the "order takers" they are today, they can become strategic partners to their customers by adding premium value to the work they deliver. Such value can be supplemented with massive execution excellence and in-depth industry knowledge that will eventually help their customers to shape their business strategy. Once customers experience that value, they will be ready to part with a better margin.

Need for creative, disruptive platforms

Our business education system needs to impart training on creating disruptive platforms that can change the world. Delivery of out-of-the-box execution excellence by Indian companies to create the value-led market needs to be built up. That is not extra terrestrial or humanly impossible. The first step of leading the market through value is extensive research to understand the gaps in between. Certain investment in wide scale primary research and study is required to interpret those gaps and plug them with 360-degree improvement of products and services. This business model demands micro detailed qualitative insight and has to be handled very sensitively. To avoid commoditization that can easily destroy an established business, high-technology knowledge with skill set is imperative here. And innovation has to become a continuous process to see the future as up front as possible. Without passion in the agenda, an enterprise will not reach its objective.

To exit the demand-led market is very simple

Just ask any customer why he/she always pays a higher price for a reputed foreign brand in a given category. Is it for their inventive power, product quality, or advertising? He/she will definitely choose the first two options. So the biggest thrust the country needs immediately is how to create a generation of value-led market creators.

Rote learning versus inventive capability

"Made in India" is still to acquire an inspirational platform globally. Post economic reforms 22 years ago, foreign companies came in with global expertise and know-how. They suddenly roused the economy with inflow of investment. They outsourced Information Technology Enabled Services (ITES) supplied by low-cost human trade, calling it body shopping, and India gained the reputation of having a human supply industry. Yet the country does not have a value-driven brand that is recognized globally. We continue to have a demand-led market.

Other Asian brands are acquiring global value

On the other hand China, earlier known for cheap quality, today puts its "Made in China" manufacturing signature on the world's most coveted, inspirational brand like Apple. This means "Made in China" has become global standard for even sophisticated products today. Korea too, insignificantly tucked away in northeast Asia, has done a phenomenal job of mesmerizing the world with its brands, making Samsung, LG, and Hyundai, among others, into household names in every country. None of all these advancements have happened with any innovation or invention. They are all examples of outstanding application execution excellence work. They have been executed with hard work, elegance, high quality, and innovative customer interface.

Rote learning dulls the brain

India's basic education and professional learning system is driven by memorization or learning by rote. This hampers the quest for inventive application or taking a problem as a platform and focusing on how to bring a real, thorough solution. Mechanical mugging is done through "mug books" or a series of question-and-answer publications that show the way to score high in written exams. Students are required to conform and deliver standardized answers to questions, rather than have the courage to ideate for great solutions to problems. So they learn to place greater value on remembering and reproducing the taught.

The learning by rote culture has not declined in India. As per a McKinsey study, a very high percentage of educated professionals are not qualified for high-end jobs. They comprise 75 percent of engineering graduates, 85 percent of finance and accounting professionals, and 90 percent of professionals with other degrees. This means that only a few educational institutes equip students for professional competence. The balance 25 percent engineering graduates, 15 percent finance, and 10 percent other degree professionals are competent for high-end jobs corresponding to the degrees they hold because they got through by rote learning. A telling example is that only 3 percent Indian academics publish research papers in science as opposed to 60 percent US academics.

Evolution of learning

Before liberalization, the Indian market was "demand-less" or repressed, that is, the mentality was focused on saving. Post 1991, sudden economic power created the shift to a demand-led market. Tremendous choice was offered by foreign players and diversity in exports. So clearly an opportunity was there for value addition but Indian industry did not take it up. Again the root of this can be traced to rote learning as that pollutes the foundation of learning and does not allow people to be inventive in any situation.

A value-led market can only be created by continuous enterprise learning system that calls for deep dive analysis and encourages following a process for problem solving by individual and collective disruptive ideation. Most Indian enterprises are more focused and feel comfortable spending money in tangible assets rather than taking risks in greenfield areas to give a new shape to business. But the inviting market here has brought in global companies seeking opportunities in droves. They have set benchmarks, even changed our purchase and usage pattern. For example, Indians were proud to say their refrigerator lasts 40 years. But the Koreans arrived to usher in a change in Indian habits. With contemporary design and technology resulting in better functionality, refrigerators are changed every five years now to be aligned to the trend.

Inventive when outside the rote learning system

In practical life, people in India very clearly become highly adjustable where rote learning does not work. Driving on crowded Indian streets and off-roads with one foot continuously on the brake and a hand on the horn against all international conventions is an example of necessary adaptation. When I ask people why they drive in the middle of the road, the answer is that both sides have to be kept as walking paths.

There is the famous inventive use of the washing machine in busy roadside *dhabas* (roadside eateries) of Punjab. Instead of putting clothes in it, they efficiently whirr buttermilk or yogurt in bulk for making delicious, frothy lassi in a jiffy. In adverse situations when some waterlogged roads become streams during the rains, rickshaw pullers in Kolkata have managed to put rubber tubes that make their rickshaws float in flooded streets, again then run normally on non-flooded streets. So, clearly there is no dearth of intelligence; the education system where rote learning reigns supreme makes it very difficult for qualified executives to drive business through innovative application.

When a country is principally driven by rote learning, breaking the education mold is the only avenue for promoting inventive application. Already the education market is growing at 14 percent and here too foreign institutions are tying up with Indian colleges to offer different education programs. Focus on "employability education" is being attempted in a few schools, colleges, and universities across India, but this translates into a seamless integration with the existing system, not a disruptive entry that provokes innovation. Industry needs to disrupt executive education so that they can lead and create the value-led market in the tremendous business opportunities available in unpredictable India.

Disruptive platform with execution excellence

In praise of China

Learning by heart has been a malaise in China where six million students take exams every year. Yet they have been able to emerge from it to create value distinction in the market. Discipline, process, and creativity have played their roles proving that China has gone beyond the learning by rote pattern into significant delivery excellence.

Professor Ananthakrishnan of Pune University, former (retired) senior professor of Tata Institute of Fundamental

Research (TIFR), Mumbai, a fellow of all the National Science Academies, had just returned from eight weeks in China as a senior international visiting scientist to the Chinese Academy of Science, when he wrote:

> It gave me an opportunity to closely look at their educational system and I must say I was very impressed. They too complain of rote learning, but many of the students I met knew their math very well and could understand advanced mathematical concepts far better than corresponding level students in my MSc class in India. Their engineering industry works closely with academics and produces very high-quality engineering products although there's an impression, even inside China, that it is not high quality! In comparison to India, they seem to have surged far ahead. It would be total folly to compare India with China. Their focus and ability to achieve whatever aim they have set is certainly worth emulating, but I do not think that our political bosses have the capacity or the required technical background to do it!

American systems prevail

With over 50 percent population below the age of 25, and more than 65 percent below 35 years, India's opportunity to drive the world's future is tremendous, if only we exit the path of memorizing for recall. Most students enter India's mushrooming MBA schools directly after rote learning in graduation. They pay a hefty fee, but how can they become management professionals without any previous experience of how a company runs? Students of India's best B-schools mostly read American case studies like rote learning as part of their MBA course. If an Indian case study is utilized, American cultural norms are used to come to conclusions. That is why these case studies often have no business connect or relevance in India's industry and customer experience.

A shocking business case on European TV

On a business visit to Europe, I was shocked to watch a TV documentary on poor working conditions in textile dyeing outfits in India and Bangladesh. They cater to the Western fad of washed-out looking denim jeans. Fashionable brands sell discolored jeans, torn at the thighs exposing skin, or with worn-out back pockets so a teeny bit of panty can peep out. This distressed, used effect in denim cloth is creatively crafted in developing countries.

Using a spy camera, some journalists visited such workplaces and filmed people working in a highly toxic atmosphere using strong chemicals for tinting and fading fabrics. Most workers had lung diseases from poisonous fumes and many suffered from cancer. The objective of foreign media channels is always twofold: to bash big business as irresponsible for importing and getting their dirty work done in poor countries from people with no health insurance and, second, to supposedly protect their viewers by making them aware. The sensitive skin of the fashion conscious who wear these old-looking shorts and jeans could be affected by the toxic bath the fabric goes through. Slinky, sexy models were shown displaying the titillating trend for black lingerie. To prevent black cloth from bleeding color, even more powerful and more toxic chemicals are used. That is certainly not good for the health of wearers of these itty-bitty inner garments.

Understanding India-specific issues

MBA students should gather India-specific and practical knowledge and experience instead of learning from foreign case studies. If young professionals fail to understand quality or deficiency in Indian manufacturing processes, how can they be disruptive in deploying their learning to change nasty work conditions in future? In the construction industry, for example, do they know the procurement procedure, how a brickfield operates, or whether there is life-threatening risk in iron ore and coal mines from where steel comes and people work hard without asking questions about their life, health, and safety conditions?

Look at the supply chain of unorganized sectors such as staple food, fabric, or footwear that is really among the biggest drivers of our economy. As an Indian, you are happy with rice and roti, but as an MBA student, do you question the practices deployed to procure items from their source, produce them for consumption, and transport and distribute them, so that your mother can easily buy the products in her neighborhood kirana (mom-and-pop) store?

Contracting professionals

An eminent CEO in France was admiring India's contract labor or temporary workers system. He said it overtly seemed to exploit the unemployed, but if managed well, professionals can have the advantage of working in areas and companies of their choice. Companies can be rid of keeping people on the bench by hiring trained professionals for peripheral jobs as and when required. This way the company can focus on innovation, marketing, and sales and outsource everything else, even manufacturing in its own factory.

He bemoaned that many Europeans have become bonded to their companies because they refuse to relocate. People mobility in India is a great advantage for any business enterprise. He said many companies would be willing to even share their

competency values with contract professionals to upgrade
their quality of life and proficiency.

Disruptive platform required

It is clear that India requires disruption in business strategy
to bring execution excellence at the workplace. Why disruption? On the one hand, there is the massive unorganized sector
with a totally ad hoc way of working. On the other, are foreign
brands changing people's perception in different livelihood
and lifestyle domains. Without a disruptive platform, what
can you do between these two juxtaposed sectors? Young
graduates in arts, engineering, commerce, or science having
minimum four to six years work experience need a professional teaching model that breaks the mold of the current rote
learning process. They have to learn to disrupt and simultaneously bring excellence in execution in any industry domain.

   A practical, seriously India-centric experiential professional
education system is required to equip young professionals to
become disruptive in action while reflecting perfection in the
art of execution to present high value in India to the world.
Take a look at disruptive selling proposition in Figure 4.1.

Figure 4.1 Analogy of Disruptive Platform with Execution Excellence

This dessert using 2 simple bananas is an example of disruptive platform with execution excellence

A grand chef sells this for 25 Euros

2 Bananas cost 50 cents

Tangible

Intangible

These touch & visible points become intangible, providing ecstasy to customers

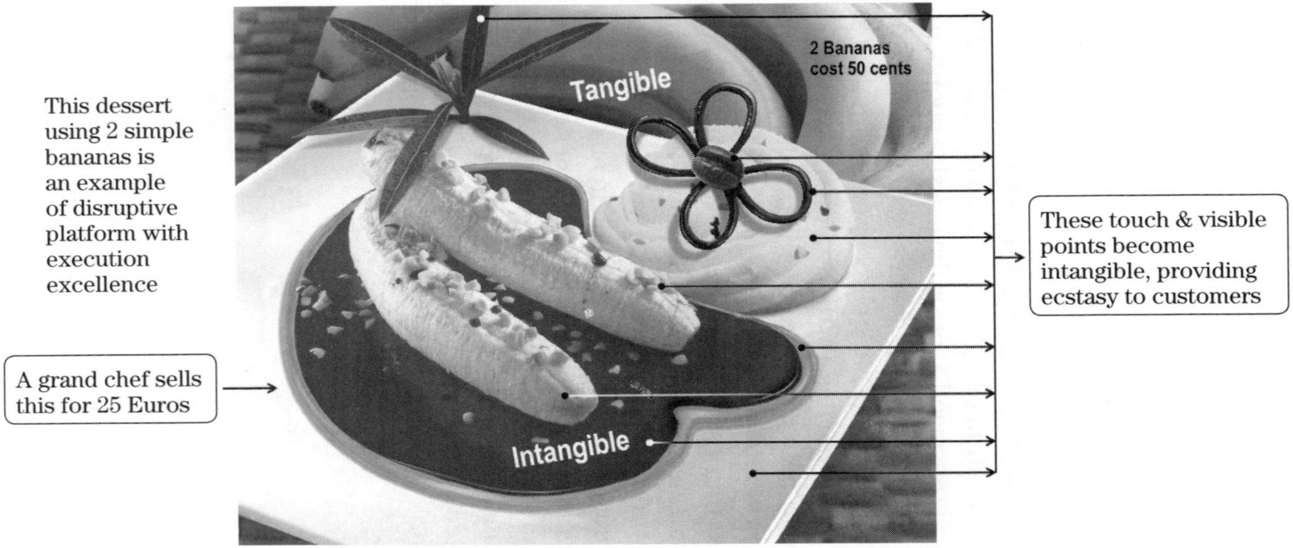

Source: Author's own.

5

Disruptive Platform in Business

Shock-of-the-poke for the New

How do people live their lives, what makes them spend money—decide which brand to buy among competitive offers—or shift paradigms in their requirement? Addressing this psychological sensitivity of the customer is the big, disruptive game the enterprise has to play.

Europeans are suspicious of the American dream that translates for them as a miraculous marketing myth and manipulation. They consider it like a jalebi that has multiple undulated patches; people in India say that is not straightforward. But from Americans selling Santa Claus to British royalty peddling their own legacy souvenirs, marketing is here to stay.

What about in India? Zappy marketing was born together with the generation born after 1986 into the free economy. They brought in a new lifestyle, from open sex to influencing every purchase decision in every home. They have given a new look to society, instead of being submissive they air their opinions, which is

*drastically new to India. Manufacturers, retailers, and the
service industry have not caught on to the implications of
this radical shift in attitude of this generation. So they do
not connect to this mobile-phoning Zap generation and their
changing trends and usage patterns.*

*Post-1991 liberalization, the IT-services industry has
played a huge role in changing India from the economic perspective, and the lifestyle of a few Indians. But three rotten
or uncooked jalebi dimensions are happening in this area.
I do not know what measures have been taken by India's IT
tycoons to step forward under the following circumstances:*

*(1) Developed countries will try to bring the service
industry back home to develop their own economies.*

*(2) It is obvious that Western inventive power will find
a solution on how to reduce the number of people
required for IT servicing. They will create computing auto-mechanization that will provide the service
or become the boss. In the last three centuries, their
inventive perspective has been to use less manpower
by creating auto-mechanization to avoid slavery, and
later to avoid dependence.*

*(3) There is enormous data storage through cloud com-
puting in every domain, which can impact the scope
for outsourcing.*

*When you ideate disruptively, taking on the swagger of
an uneven jalebi, many provocative ideas for potential new
businesses can emerge. A few could be as follows:*

- *Auto-mechanization of small machines that can kill
poverty for poor people so they can work with dignity
to gain their livelihood with less physical effort.*
- *Motorized mobile vehicles can revolu-
tionize the cart seller, whether he/she
is selling fruits, baubles, plastic goods,
or hot tea.*

- *Cultivating a fragrance culture in India, much beyond the traditional ittar.*
- *Remodeling of auto accessories so people can get their car's styling done without waiting for the next five years to buy a new car.*

Industry level

Is marketing a kind of manipulation?

Making one country's ruler globally loved is a humungous marketing job. And marketing, they say in France, is only manipulation.

Does marketing exist?

In the 60 years following World War II, consumerism started with marketing, the organized selling of mass-scale products. Americans formulated the marketing concept which their business schools have been promoting from the 20th century. But in reality, marketing was invented for and by religion: for gods, goddesses, spiritualists, and preachers thousands of years ago. Religious icons have left their extraordinary symbolic expressions for recognition by the social system century after century. And billions of humans follow and sustain it with reverence. This is the real form of marketing, which is beyond the obvious.

Marketing is all about creating a continuous need

Oranges, for example, originated in Southeast Asia centuries ago, but the culture of eating oranges on Christmas Eve was started and popularized in Europe from 1950s onward. Today, the top three orange-producing and orange-exporting countries are Brazil, the US, and Mexico. They benefit from good Christmas marketing, as well as the health and fitness trend that has made oranges a necessity across the Western world.

Ever since shipping turned global and scurvy became rampant among seamen living off salted meat and stale wheat, eating oranges or lemons has become a health factor. Take a different example of how an American multinational computer-technology corporation went into Greek mythology to pick up the name Oracle and marketed itself into toting up the third-largest software revenue, after Microsoft and IBM.

Santa Claus is a marketing tool today. Billions of dollars worth of Santa products and services are sold worldwide irrespective of whether the buyers follow the Christian religion. The fervent celebration of "Burra Din" is a British legacy that unites India. Even villagers and small-towners eat some version of cake, follow the gifting tradition, or go on picnics, while new-fangled shopping malls in metros sport Santa saying "Ho Ho Ho!" I do not think any other cultural or religious festival in India cuts across society so visibly.

Let's take a look at marketing and disruption in four industries: luxury goods, automobile, IT service and retail.

Luxury goods industry

Luxury market

The global luxury market, which was 212 billion euros (US$273 billion) in 2012, would reach 250 billion by mid-decade. Even the luxury retailing market, quite unknown earlier, has luxury products growing by 30 percent today. India is pegged to grow at 25 percent on a year-on-year basis between 2013 and 2015. And it may be worth ₹82,500 crores (US$15 billion) from the current level of ₹44,000 crores (US$8 billion), reveals the ASSOCHAM–Yes Bank study. Smaller cities are also becoming a big hub for luxury brands that are adapting to new Indian status conditions. For gifting on festive occasions, luxury brands are combining local and cultural elements into their own creations.

French luxury brand Hermes, best known for their ₹19,182 plain white T-shirts and ₹548,550 handbags, entered India with a line of fancy saris. Hermes expects to launch a perfume specific to India too. The government has allowed 100 percent FDI in single-brand retail so other luxury brands such as Italian apparel Emilo Pucci will start operations soon. Louis Vuitton is bringing in three premium brands; beauty retail chain Sephora, Singapore fashion company Sincere, and Hong Kong-listed Emperor Watch and Jewelry are ready to storm the market.

Even luxury goods keep up

The establishment and its doctrines do not work anymore today. Take the world of high fashion. Chanel, the French haute couture design house that Coco Chanel founded in 1909, had maintained an elegant, prim, and classical tradition up to the 1990s. Chanel's classic, rectangular-shaped perfume container was so coveted that it was impossible to think it could be disturbed. But even Chanel had to bow to the Zap generation. Their recent perfume called Chance broke Chanel's classicism by having a round bottle with a half-naked, funky young girl gracefully showing her beautiful legs.

To make the brand contemporary, Chanel radically changed its dresses too. Chanel now stitches jeans for Zap girls to look rowdy and sexy. Levis Strauss had popularized the cowboy logo for the jeans back pocket; now Chanel's "CC" logo also adorns back pocket of jeans. From archetypical French haute couture to jeans is indeed a daring step. By doing that Chanel has not reduced its brand value, rather it has been extended to the youth.

Another fashion example is reputed French designer Christian Dior, who started in 1946. His legacy was carried forward by YSL, and then Italian designer Gianfranco Ferré in Paris. After Bernard Arnault, chairman of the luxury conglomerate LVMH acquired Dior, he found Ferré to be too straitlaced. So in 1996, he appointed John Galliano, the most eccentric English fashion designer, for Christian Dior. Galliano had demonstrated the ability to redefine existing subcultures to create fashion garments for the younger, funkier set. "My role is to seduce," he confessed, saying that theater and femininity inspired him in his creations. He recreated some of Dior's period clothing for Madonna to wear in the film *Evita*.

Galliano's fashion radically shifted Dior's old classicism

The perfume, Miss Dior, has been a French classic. From such a gentle perfume, Dior went on to create the provocative Poison, a new departure in perfume. Christian Dior used to be dressed in very classy suits when on the fashion ramp with models; Galliano came to his first Dior fashion show showing a great deal of skin and you could openly see his body and legs in a provocative carnival dress. By doing this, the Dior brand has not lost its value in the world, but has instead connected to the Zap generation and contemporized its image for the continuity of the brand.

Critics did question whether Galliano's maverick reputation would appeal to Dior's established clientele. The designer shook up the haute couture world, infused energy into an industry that was showing signs of losing sales and customers. In his 1997 spring/summer collection, Galliano spun classic Dior themes around exotic African Masai tribal forms to fashion silk evening dresses. He used colorful choker-bead necklaces that injected a young image. But the Dior name remained glamorous and refined. Galliano's collections, complete with historic personalities and forces, have always enchanted or shocked audiences and have been huge commercial successes. These two examples, among many, show how connecting to Zappers is taken seriously.

Human odor generates business

The world of perfumery that attracts all three generations will continue to create intangibles because human odor will never go away.

Perfumes and toothbrushes

Fortunately the human body emits numerous smells considered unacceptable in civilized society. Like the thumb print of 6.5 billion people, there are as many different human odors in the world. Ask the dogs, they can precisely differentiate people through scent. The mega quantity of odor that human bodies produce per day is immeasurable, but whatever small portion has been captured generates a huge amount of business.

The US$30.5 billion global body-fragrances market in 2006 will be US$45.6 billion in 2018. Premium fragrances comprise 60 percent of the market and women's fragrances account for 66 percent of total sales. It is statistically known that consumption of toothbrush and toothpaste was lower in France, Italy,

Spain, and Portugal than in northern Europe. I have even heard that 50 years ago French homes used to have only one toothbrush for the whole family. Gauging the potential, American marketers flooded the market with "smiley" toothbrush and toothpaste communication, which proved powerful enough to change the "cheesy" French-kiss habit from one to multiple toothbrushes in the family.

If you are not a cheese connoisseur you may find little difference between merde and cheese Epoisses from Burgundy or Munster from Alsace. The dish called tripe, which is made from animal stomach offal, smells like ammonia in urine. What does this show? That odor may not always be gentle and a horrible stink is also a selling point. So good or bad smell is not only subjective, it is a measure of cultural preference too.

Underarms have taken the most strategic advantage in people's mind. There is roll-on deodorant costing a dollar to Clive Christian's Imperial Majesty Perfume for Men priced at US$435,000 a bottle. The 16.9 ounce limited edition signature scent is the world's most expensive, presented in handcrafted Bacarrat crystal with a five-carat brilliant-cut diamond. Globally, deodorants will grow from US$11.5 to US$13.5 billion in 2013. Economic prosperity is commensurate with higher social recognition and usage of costly perfumes in living areas up to the bedroom, kitchen, and toilet.

Scented toilet paper

The quality of toilet paper has a strong relationship with affluent living. I remember in my first Parisian job as a lithography print-shop sweeper, the stiff-style, one-side glossy toilet paper used to give me irritation. Going from the Indian water habit, this cultural and physical change was dreadful, but I had no choice.

One day in those days I was invited to an affluent family who wanted to buy one of my paintings. When I went to their toilet, its grandeur overwhelmed me. The toilet paper was called Lotus, and it was softer than lotus petals. And it was wonderfully fragrant. My big discovery was that sweet-scented toilet paper can cover up hygiene, bad smell, and replace water usage.

Catering to the mouth

Take a look at how many industries have popped up to address the body's bad-odor sources including underarms, anus, private body parts, hair, toes, and mouth with multiple scent solutions. Just the mouth has flavored toothpaste, chewing gum, peppermint, after-mint, mouthwash, mouth freshener, and even electric toothbrushes to reduce effort and increase comfort. Is it not useful that a small, out of home briefcase-pack mouthwash can be carried around for use before meeting a client or mistress after a smelly lunch? Even the dynamic smell that the human body can throw from the back, inside, or outside the toilet, can be concealed with dreamy air fragrance.

Cooked food fragrance

In Europe, specialized companies are working for edible food fragrance. Restaurants which are renowned for their gastronomy spray "roast duck" or "truffled mushrooms" scents just before serving such dishes to their customers. Investigative journalists have recently caught out a few famous French restaurants that claim to serve gourmet food made by their specialty chefs who select fresh ingredients by going to market at 4 a.m. every day. In actual fact, these restaurants were secretly buying readymade, beautifully decorated, highly specialized industrial food from one of Europe's reputed global food brands. This company has a supply chain division for café, hotel, and restaurant readymade food. This division's products are not publicized outside the small set of target customers.

The industrial food maintains its aroma consistently by using food perfume that is created by master chefs and reproduced on an industrial scale. Rummaging the backdoor dustbins of these sophisticated restaurants, the journalists found the empty containers of packaged industrially produced food and broke the scandal to prove how the public was being duped.

Ambient perfume

Closed areas such as fashion retails and hotels use fragrance as psychological addiction to get their customers to return. There is a trend to create sustaining perfume inside automobiles too. Experts in Europe are working scientifically to create harmless-for-humans industrial aromatics as their living conditions are always closed due to culture and cold weather. Ambient perfume remains for a longer time there, unlike in India where culturally everybody loves an open situation and the weather permits people to leave their doors and windows open. For India, ambient perfume has to be treated differently for it to remain a longer time matching with the weather, way of living, and culture.

Body hedonism

Royalty in every country patronizes perfumery as a luxury element. Western nations have taken it to the masses. With names such as Obsession, Nude, Delicious Feelings, and Intimate, perfumes today have a heady association with romance, sex, love, and affection. Not to mention aroma candles, overpowering incense sticks imported from Asia, and fragrant condoms. It would be interesting to know if kissing intensity has increased post mouthwash innovation. The big plus is that the fragrance industry faces no recession as stress leads to sweat, which increases human odor and has to be camouflaged.

Indian *ittar* or botanical perfumes, derived from Sanskrit *sugandha*, meaning aromatic, can be traced to the 5,000-year-old Indus Valley Civilization. But high quality, mass-level fragrance development as per social trends is still at a nascent stage here. This is not the technocrat marketing person's work; it is the domain of creating intangibles. Fragrance culture requires specialization that has to be cultivated. Manufacturing companies outsourcing from perfume makers will always be handicapped and dependent, as the alchemy of fragrance will escape them. Unfortunately, the business of fragrance is unrecognized and neglected in India, a mere outsourced process. It is time we learnt this specialized domain from European experts to drive the huge future opportunities here in food aroma, personal-care products, and ambient perfume for places such as retails, hotels, homes, automobiles, spa, hair-dressing salons, gym clubs, and offices.

Automobile industry

Change your car every so often?

Your car's fragrance has to match your personality; it is the final touch to your grooming for a date. The automobile is an adult's ultimate aspirational toy. People use it to stamp their distinction.

Expression you can ride

Look at how musician John Lennon expressed his antiwar philosophy in 1965. He paid £2,000 to a Dutch team of gypsy artists to paint his thoughts on his Rolls Royce. The car turned out so psychedelic it made it to the Ripley's Believe It or Not! Museum. Automobiles have inspired several artist painters.

Such expressions are normally visible in apparel fashion, but in the summit of painting their imagination, people extend fashion to the automobiles they possess.

On the 100th birthday of the automobile in 1986, pop icon and artist, Andy Warhol, was commissioned by DaimlerChrysler Corporation, Mercedes Benz, and BMW to paint a series about cars. BMW also had artists Frank Stella, Roy Lichtenstein, and Ernst Fuchs do art cars. But an automobile is a big-ticket item. How often can customers get designer cars painted by famous artists or afford to change their cars? Yet everyone wants to be different. Newer kinds of spendthrifts have emerged such as the sub-30 Digital Zappers. This generation flits from product to product, their needs are many and always changing, and they influence every purchase made in the home. Reshuffling change is their frenetic new habit, which is driving industries out of breath. They require something that they can change easily to transcend their zapping habit. Can industry consider this enormous opportunity awaiting a tap?

Epitomizing social changes

The major perpetrator to disrupt market rules with recurrent newness is the mobile phone. It took the landline several decades to change functionality, design, and aesthetics. Today's techno-savvy mobile phone has not just miniaturized itself, it has collapsed many industries into a single device in the palm of the customer's hand. You have all time access to the camera, TV, banking, Internet, calculator, music system, dictionary, pen, paper, phone, and many more functions. At home, the music system or refrigerator spent a good 15 years with you earlier, while the idea of discarding a TV set was unheard of. Then Japanese and Koreans arrived to turn topsy-turvy our belief that electric and electronic appliances vacate the trend-wagon every three to five years. If home appliances can be changed so radically, why not the automobile?

Connecting to trends

In this backdrop, auto designers would do well to rethink about how to connect to customers' changing needs. Long working hours in developing countries are making working couples spend less time with each other. Affairs outside of marriage are on the rise, as are social stress and divorce. Grappling to find pressure busters, people are more self-indulgent, and their high-spend patterns are taking them into diverse new areas. In the auto industry, in spite of digitalization, customers cannot change vehicles like they do mobile phones. Nor can the vehicle's development time be squeezed to below two to three years.

Style your own car

Regular-change auto remodeling accessories could be the auto industry's quick solution to participate in the customers' frequent changing habit. Certain physical elements can be altered to change the car's overall appearance, without disturbing its internal master engineering. These could be the bumper or steering wheel, bonnet, wheel cap, side mirror, gear holding, and upholstery, among others. Remodeling accessories should never be considered as replacement of damaged features. Instead, the auto industry should promote "style your own car" as the contemporary new dimension that takes car owners into the quick-changing paradigm. Customers generally keep a car for minimum three years, which obliges them to stick to its original style. For today's change mentality, that is an eternity; total frustration creeps in. Remodeling their cars will definitely perk them up. Multiple visible looks can be generated for people to use different remodeling accessories on different occasions. They need not go for superficial accessories such as crazy horn sounds, music on reverse gear, or stylish hubcaps, among others.

Easy-fix remodeling accessories can represent an India-centric trend

India represents only 3.5 percent of the global automobile market. Considering its 1.2 billion population, every auto manufacturer is focusing on capturing this throbbing potential. The scope for invention using India's unique diversity of culture, social, language, food, and geography is tremendous. With the economy-on-the-boom trend, people are looking for personal identification, status, or cultural difference. By testing and proving remodeling accessories in India, this new concept can open a new business horizon in the global market, and promote India's unique multicultural aspect.

Easy-fix remodeling accessories can redefine the service station. Creating a new dimension of activities, it can become a new revenue stream and brand-image enhancer for both manufacturer and dealer. Customers glorify the brand that allows them to transplant their own personality into the vehicle during their period of ownership.

Remodeling accessories must be relevant to socio-behavioral clusters

Over the past decade, we have tracked Indian customers and have identified eight socio-behavioral customer clusters in every income group. Society's drivers are the clusters of critical, novelty seeker, flamboyant, techy, and gizmo lovers. Remodeling accessories for this exhibitionist group can be complex, whereas for society followers, the low key, value seeker, and sober; they can be simple yet functional. A wide variety in each type will invite customers of every socio-behavioral cluster to change to get out of boredom.

Auto manufacturers can consider offering easy-fix remodeling accessories for at least 10 features in the car. Each feature should have four choices each for the driver and follower groups; for example, eight pieces of the rear-view mirror. These should all flaunt widely different characters to connect to these different socio-behavioral clusters of customers. Different packages can range from US$200 to a maximum of US$2,000 for an automobile that costs about US$12,000.

Rapid-fire change running across industries

Product planning for tomorrow's vehicle can have in-built design that allows easy fixing of remodeling accessories. This could start a new industry where quality, cost, and aspiration at any price point are not compromised. Avoid marketing them as gadgets. Take a cue from Swatch, an often-changing product, which was never marketed as a temporary doodad. Swatch is reputed as serious, low priced, highly aspirational, accompanying everyday lifestyle, and the mood-change driver of different people in the world. Remodeling accessories could be modeled after Swatch to change the automobile industry's perception where all vehicles look more or less the same.

American automobiles have a Barbie-doll image, Italians show off delicate women, the French ooze fashion, and English cars are a royal experience. German cars reflect hardcore sophisticated engineering, the Swedes stress on safety, and Japan stresses on quality and cost efficiency, which Koreans also diligently follow. This new idea showcasing diversity through remodeling accessories could acquire for India a futuristic image and be our contribution to the auto world.

Unlock their desire for an automobile

"Why the traffic jam?" I enquired. The hired car driver rolled down the window to expose the crowd of what appeared to be expectant reality-show watchers, who replied in unison, "*Modna* has come to Kolkata!" The driver nodded and knowledgeably repeated, "*Modna aaya.*" In colloquial Bengali *modna* means stupid, but that, as it turned, out was not the case. Rather, obtuse pronunciation was at play here.

Inching through roads thronged with excited multitudes, I reached the airport to find that Argentina's all-time great football legend Maradona had come to town, and not Modna. This is our culture, instant emotional people-jam by poor and rich alike. Similarly, the auto-industry has that aura that draws crowds. When thousands of visitors walk through New Delhi's Auto Expo, do not make the mistake of thinking the auto-market will flourish in India tomorrow. Take retailing as an analogy. People enjoy air-conditioned comfort on hot summer days at the big malls, but most leave with no shopping bag in hand. In nine years, retailers have made no money. Becoming numerous within a second should not be taken as business conversion.

Western auto-manufacturers have not understood India's diverse multicultural mentality and habit of physically surrounding any activity, be it a fight, jugglery show, or an accident spot. They have developed sophisticated or mass cars for the pleasurable experience of a long drive. But in India's pathetic road infrastructure, this emotion does not exist.

Sophisticated auto-companies think affluent Indians will flaunt money. That is possible in the luxury section where the big buy becomes a museum piece for that show-off factor. At the 2012 Frankfurt Auto Expo, I observed the future of the vehicle to be very clearly green, an area India is yet to appreciate.

Be relevant to different buyers

Trying to implement an automobile's previous success in the unidirectional West as a readymade solution for India will not work. Let me explain. To sell to the masses after World War II, vehicles were made relevant to different societies. Americans liked big-sized Hollywood-style cars. Italians had small cars to ride the small cobbled streets of their ancient cities, as well as the macho luxury vehicles corresponding to Mediterranean chauvinism.

Robust German cars were akin to their hardy culture where their autobahns have no speed limits but maintain the stringent discipline of keeping 50 m distance between cars. Sweden's population scarcity made sure safety is a must. Colonial British culture made the vehicle a royal divan. Even if that industry is sold out, that stature has to be maintained. Japan has always thought they will conquer the world, so long-lasting quality was important.

I'd mentioned in Chapter 3, European showrooms in the 1980s sold cars without features such as AC, sound system, both-sides mirror, headrest, or wheel cap. These were available as extra options. The Japanese stormed the market with "Take the key, and drive your car away." They gave away cars with all the inbuilt optional features. Inbuilt feature excellence with outstanding quality made Japan the world's number one automaker. They broke into the American market with the small vehicle, which Europeans failed to do.

To sell in different countries, the Japanese spend enormous time to study the physiology, psychology, and sociology of customers there. Korea has since followed them. There is an opportunity to produce and sell huge volumes of passenger cars in India which accounted for just 3.6 percent (2.3 million) of the 56 million passenger cars sold worldwide in 2009. The biggest mistake of Western automakers is not designing the vehicle according to Indian needs and desires.

What is the Indian trend to follow?

How do you translate "Indianism" into automobile design for the billion plus, multicultural market? For example, Henry Ford in 1930 incorporated the new US lifestyle of large windows at home by having big car windows, thus aligning the vehicle to societal context and social aspirations.

Mahindra's Bolero-type of vehicle appears to be right for India's mass population. It serves both the purposes of hardworking-income generation and lifestyle, suits India's rough roads, gives great mileage, is a value-for-money buy, and has good resale value too. The Japanese and Koreans have understood India better; that mobility is our biggest priority. Indians value qualities such as low-running cost, less service, easy maintenance, high aspiration, and earning potential. Suzuki, Hyundai, and Honda are doing a marvelous job in bringing India the small car at an affordable price.

Why should the vehicle for mass-scale sales be useful for livelihood plus lifestyle? At least 190 million households earn less than ₹200,000 per annum; their desire to buy a vehicle is totally locked. For them to even dream of a vehicle, auto-manufacturers have to become innovative. The vehicle must be suitable for different earning purposes, and marketed very differently from conventional sales methods.

Show customers the opportunity

But first, they have to educate target customers on how they can earn ₹15,000 more per month by utilizing the vehicle. For example, apart from the husband's regular work, the wife can commercially use the vehicle for jobs such as ferrying school children, doing home-delivery services for flowers, cooked food, tailored or dry-cleaned clothes, or running a mobile books/CD/DVD library. This way the bank Equated Monthly Installment (EMI) becomes affordable, vehicle-running cost gets taken care of, and family joyrides are a possibility. To incentivize them, manufacturers can offer a free driving license with training for a second person in the family within the vehicle's price.

Innovate to unlock desire

Three fundamentals are required to design this low-cost vehicle:

(1) A system of highly flexible features for multiple functionality usage. The inside space should be automatically or mechanically managed to make it relevant for earning purposes.

(2) Very elegant vehicle to match India's young generation.

(3) Low-running cost in any road condition. But low cost cannot mean ugly or bad fit and finish. All income levels want to enjoy the glamour of a vehicle whose aspiration value should sustain at least five to seven years.

Selling auto as a service, not product

Tomorrow's automobile industry can become a service industry. With regular EMI to the manufacturer, people can change their vehicle at any time. Engineering and technology have no choice but to rapidly change to find the best alternative energy system. That is why, only an auto-service industry will ensure the customer does not have to look for frequent version changes as in the software industry.

IT service industry

Disrupt IT for client biz-tech solutions

Identifying trends and creating the new, such as selling a car as a service not a product, can take business forward. What is the new waiting to be created in IT services?

Why outsourcing became a dirty word

After about 11 million Americans lost their jobs in the 2008 recession, "offshore outsourcing" has become a dirty concept. To win customer confidence and be politically correct, US companies are now showcasing their contribution toward American job seekers. American apparel brands are appeasing the public by advertising their product uniqueness to be "Made in Downtown LA, Sweatshop Free." They earn the customer's wallet share by emphasizing US manufacturing facilities, not outsourced from foreign sweatshops. Similarly, Starbucks communicates, "Every Latte, Every Cappuccino 100% Fair-trade Coffee" in every coffee cup, meaning they practice fair-trade in procurement.

Commodity business is not a profitable proposition

Natural spring water is a gift of nature; anybody can bring a container and, without struggle, collect water. The demand-led global IT market has been the spring under which Indian IT-services companies have placed their buckets. Consequently, they grew phenomenally in the last two decades. With cost advantage, good management of large-scale basic engineering, and hardworking English-speaking manpower, they established the IT-backend structures for developed country companies. But the needs of the Western market for such commoditized IT services is shifting toward value-led delivery. To make spring water into a brand, Indian companies will go through pain, struggle, idea, failure, and then success of global recognition if you can persist and sustain.

Offshore outsourcing is the uneasy gossip in the political climate of developed countries. The 11 million Americans who lost jobs during the recession are mostly still unemployed and economic growth is miniscule. In this backdrop, only a case for business performance or value as measured by revenue, profit, customer satisfaction, and market share justifies the significant, indispensable, and recurring IT expenditure.

Global IT and technology-services buyers are contemplating how to de-risk IT investment. IT has become commoditized like paying for water supply or power. From operational cost cutting, IT is now assuming a business-performance requirement, the only way for it to stay relevant.

Role change for chief information officers (CIOs)

IT services are still pretty much a buyer's market. The recession has increased the client's price sensitivity. At the turn of the century, a business-driven CIO in global companies was a rarity. Business now has no tolerance for CIOs who are only technologists. Although they still need IT understanding, new generation CIOs are compelled to sophisticatedly align technology for their company's business value and performance. The pace of change dictates that they must be part of the executive team, lacking which they may be relegated in the organization. How will Indian IT professionals, who are largely from technical backgrounds and horizontal services, fit here?

Global IT brands establish client relationships at a business level with the chief financial officer (CFO) or chief operating officer (COO), not necessarily targeting the CIO. So they are at a less competitive space; they get both high and low-end businesses. Indian-origin IT firms are very strong at working reliably and technically only with CIOs or their reportees. They fight it out as commodity players in that competitive price zone. How can they reorient and shift focus toward helping increase the client's business?

Need for proactiveness

There is some hype that IT companies are appointing senior professionals from different industries to present to IT-buying clients. But clients find such force fitting to be a gimmick, more like a façade to hide shortcomings of their lack of know-how. This move probably helps Indian companies to deliver better, rather than improve the customers' business performance.

When technology is continuously advancing, clients no longer say, "Write this code." What they ask is, "Help me optimize my supply chain efficiencies." In a rapidly shifting economy, if Indian IT companies proactively delve deep into the client's industry, they can find technology-enabled solutions that the client never thought of, and so increase the client's business prospects. By crafting new services or tweaking current service offerings to be more efficient, Indian IT can display innovation and thought leadership.

Surprise the CEO client

How can you as an Indian-origin IT company, make the difference? To be the client's technology mentor or strategic partner vertically, you have to understand his/her industry and core processes from the board room down to the factory floor. From a service delivery point of view, how does the client interact with his/her clients or end-customers? Find out where that chain is broken or not aligned, and fill in some of those holes.

To impress the CEO you have to know the few things that a CEO can make an impact with in his/her time in the organization. These could involve the market, resources, capital, and service offerings. When you vertically, not horizontally, integrate inside the client's business, you can find and fix those alignment problems to become his/her preferred strategic partner. Coming in with a proposal that you can do everything even if it is true, just does not work. Most clients do not want that, they seek focus. It is much better for organizations to reinvent themselves to specialize, have depth of service, and be narrow not wide.

Riding on the brand

The global IT companies use their branding on two axes, that is, relevant solutions and delivery excellence. Accenture's "High performance, delivered" is proactive and solution-oriented, indicating that the firm is at the intersection of business (performance) and IT (delivered). IBM's "Smarter

planet" is again a business orientation. Global brands take that
extra excellence in delivery and marry it on the front end with
excellence in solutions. To survive not being commoditized,
Indian-origin IT-services companies need to proactively provide the client with an opportunity, a point of view of where
the world and their business in it are headed. For example,
one global IT major has documented how cloud computing
is going to impact different industries, how will it play out,
and how companies in that vertical should think about it.
In essence, the domain point of view has been married with
technology understanding. Now this global IT biggie is ham-
mering home that it is different, cost competitive, and it
dominates with verticals.

India has to develop credibility

The business people still want technology execution probably
more than CIOs do, but that is at a business level. When they
want to connect the front end with the back end, Indian IT can
provide the technology execution of business. But are Indian
IT brands considered credible for entrusting high-end jobs?
By acquiring and exposing industry expertise for the client's
business advantage, Indian IT can run delivery discipline
through their go-to-market plan to give technology usage a
business-like perspective.

Aside from focus on vertical or industry centricity, the
areas crucial for Indian IT brands to address are relevant
soft skills at every customer touch point, outstanding delivery execution with high-technology skill set, and seamless
localization in their different countries of operation. With a
central passion to increase the client's business prospects,
challenging them with new market-driven ideas, Indian IT
brands can make that paradigm shift to gain a positive image.

Will cloud computing make Indian-origin IT companies into subcontractors?

Cloud computing was discovered in response to Chaplin's mimicry on automation. The last 100 years have proved that the West has always attempted to reduce excessive human interface in the routine work of business. The reason for this was to ensure perfect quality with no human interpretation and to never again practice human slavery. With fewer people, it was assumed that trade union problems will be avoided.

Global IT brand kings may sandwich others with cloud

India may be touting cloud computing as the next "in" thing without really considering where they stand in the pecking order of the industry. So it may sound absurd that new computing paradigms such as cloud can radically diminish the profitability of India's US$75 billion IT industry. Sunset may be knocking on the door of the golden age when Indian-origin IT companies provided demand-led IT services to developed countries (see Figure 5.1).

At the macro level, globalization and digitalization are affecting all industries; at the micro level, cloud computing and social networking will impact all companies. Since the industrial revolution, Western nations have ruled the world's markets using talent pool from their colonies.

Colonizing the IT world

I reckon that global brand IT biggies will colonize the IT world leveraging their brand worth. They localize in every country by ingeniously commanding business solutions using emerging

Figure 5.1   Tier 1 Indian-IT Companies Are Squeezed from Both Top and Bottom

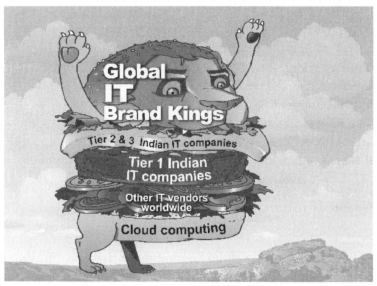

Source: Author's own.

Caption note: The Tier 1 Indian IT companies, the meat patty of the hamburger here, face a tight squeeze. The Tier 2 and 3 Indian IT companies (the cheese on top) as well as other IT vendors worldwide (onion and tomato slices) are in high competition. Riding high are the global IT brand kings (the lion's head) such as IBM and Accenture. The biggest threat is that cloud computing (lion's legs at the base) is gaining ground and threatening the entire foundation of the business for the Tier 1 Indian IT companies.

technologies such as cloud computing. Aside from several emerging technologies, they will command the powerful "cloud reservoir" to become the central hub monopolizing the IT ecosystem of global companies. Majors such as Accenture and IBM, among a few others, have tremendous clout as they already drive their clients' IT strategy on investment, innovation, solutions, and applications at the strategic CEO/ CFO and board level. They even manage their clients' other IT application subcontractors, including Indian vendors, so clients can sleep easy.

Companies such as Google and Microsoft, who are not big "service providers" in the Accenture and IBM sense, have access to almost every PC/Internet user in the world. They too will try and leverage their position to gain traction in the cloud world. I am sure emerging players, such as Facebook with 1.15 billion members (March 2013), are already working on devising strategies to have their play in the new world of cloud. Thus, Indian IT majors are squeezed (or perhaps sandwiched) between the global IT biggies with their brand and customer trust on one hand, and players with deep pockets and reach such as Google, Facebook, and Microsoft on the other. A sandwich typically ends up being a lunch.

De-risk IT investment

Recession has made global companies extremely price sensitive. The CIO is compelled to focus on business beyond technical requirements, converting the IT function from a cost to profit center. When technology is commoditizing yet advancing so rapidly, cloud computing is fast becoming the CIO's cost-effective solution to de-risk IT investment. When shared resources here are available on demand, the way we draw our electricity or water supply from a common grid, they effectively democratize and free the users from rigid and insular silo-like structures.

I foresee global brand IT majors inventively solving barriers to cloud such as security risk and 24×7 service availability. Capitalizing on their brand worth and reducing their own cost to be competitive, they will gain volume by delivering business value with strategic interface. They will use several IT companies, including Indian-origin IT, to run that marathon of providing commoditized services with huge employee numbers. Clients will naturally trust the reputed global brand as intermediary to cut their cost, reduce the complexity of synchronizing several vendors, and advance their business growth.

Indian-origin IT getting "clouded"?

So will Indian-origin IT companies eventually lose their direct customer base? Will they become third-party subcontractors of global brand IT biggies? Historically, Indian-origin Tier 1 to Tier 3 IT service has not paid attention to help shape their client's business strategy through technology solutions. Plugging horizontal basic knowledge areas, Indian IT companies have successfully grown by fulfilling the vast IT demand–supply gap when manpower was scarce and expensive for clients. Providing low cost, basic technical services, they considered this advantage would always be theirs, and expected to continue growing volume and 30 percent bottom line annually. This is total non-understanding of the Western world.

It is true that global companies cannot survive without IT support tomorrow, but the moot point is whether India's current IT-service model will remain indispensable. Global clients have always associated Indian IT as diligent service providers, having scale and cost advantages. They consider them "order takers" rather than consultative approach vendors who enhance the client's business.

Indian IT's current focus on global delivery model chases volume growth, scale, and utilizing capacity resources to maximize market share from current leaders. In going after quantity, they fail to strategize and invest qualitatively in imbibing best practices for long-term sustainable brand worth for better strategic growth and net worth. In working directly with clients when technology has become competitive and commoditized, a huge cost reduction is expected. Work volume could become very high, but bottom line will plummet to 5 percent.

Emphasize human intelligence in basic coding interface

The days of 25 to 30 percent bottom line in this cloudy world may be a thing of the past. A dramatic mindset shift is required toward becoming client-business centric. The only choice is vertical or industry centricity, diving in-depth into the client's industry to shape his/her business strategy with high-quality IT execution. Eighty percent of India's delivery-execution people comprise the Zap generation, below 30 years. They do not like to be software coders. After three to five coding years these IT professionals want to become managers who control teams. The IIMs have geared up MBA courses for them, but have never included teaching multi-industry centricity to help shape their customer's business in a global marketplace. So these engineering–management graduates do not imbibe high-quality technical skill or global marketing skills, eventually falling into the "order taker" trap.

Engage at the strategic level

Indian-origin IT enterprises also need to emphasize on making their brand globally accepted as a value differentiator. They fail to engage at a strategic level because of soft skills' deficiency among employees. All companies have soft-skill training which unfortunately is an ISO-type certification that their clients fail to perceive.

A further gap is non-usage of best practices and the vast knowledge experience that already resides in the company to build a globally reputed skill set. The collection and easy retrieval of the company's historical data is not managed for usage when required. Indian managements recognize time spent at work, rather than employees' productive quality.

These are best practices rationalized, where advantages of cloud computing, among other methods are used.

Be sensitive to menu than thali

To localize solutions, Indian-origin IT companies may borrow a leaf from how big star restaurants in the West serve customers. Using same ingredients, different chefs create their brands by embellishing dishes differently to sell at different prices. Western cuisine does not mix food like we do in the Indian thali system. From pre-starter to starter, the main course, dessert, and digestive, all are served separately by changing plates every time to restore each taste.

My point is to understand cultural differences, not criticize either of the eating systems. Indian-origin IT companies serve like the thali, where everything can be mixed. This generic global IT service caters alike to different industries. It does not sharpen focus for the customer's specific business requirements. It is volume business with standardized basic technology that is processed to benefit customers with reduced cost and people arbitrage. Such service is a commoditized one, like our water or electricity requirements.

All customer touch points that engage the customer professionally and psychologically, in marketing, sales, PR, or delivery execution are in a thali currently. Clients do not care for sales and marketing people, or large service-line numbers. They just need to enslave technology execution excellence in their own industry to grow their businesses better than their competitors.

Driving execution excellence will make Indian IT companies be recognized as global brands

Indian-origin IT enterprises will gain respect as global brands of IT intelligence, if they drive this menu:

(1) Exceptional localization in each country they operate in, from culture, business, and resource perspectives.

(2) Seamless blend of different human races of the world at work.

(3) Employees should be trained to become gold mines themselves, unlike the current transactional training for gold hunting. This global human capital practice ensures people stability.

(4) Deep focus on the client's business vertical with superior quality execution, the way Japanese and Koreans promoted their brands into new lands very successfully (see Figure 5.2). They have globalized several brands with high-execution quality, rather than claiming to innovate. This should be the grand route for Indian-origin IT; innovation and invention are buzz words that the world is not yet ready to accept from them.

Every effort of global clients is to build the worth of their own brands for gaining proximity of their products and

Figure 5.2   Indian IT Needs to Dive Deep, Not Swim on the Surface

Source: Author's own.

services to their end-customers. Global IT biggies are totally in sync with that and cloud computing may be an accessory. Indian IT has to drive execution excellence with human intelligence and interface that's superbly relevant to their clients' business growth. Without this move, will you still find Indian IT millionaires and billionaires tomorrow, or will they all become "clouded?"

Retail industry

Retail addiction

Global brands are always ever ready to know more about their customers and shoppers whose choice means everything to the brand's growth. The shopper's mind and eye are always in a yes/no mental wrestle. Have I made the right choice? Is the price right? Have I seen enough variety? Was my pricing satisfactory? Is there something here that legitimately substitutes my cost-saving temperament? Did I make a clever purchase?

Getting the shopper's eye

For organized retail business to be viable, you need to acquire and enlarge the shopper's eyeball space. Three types of competitors are trying to distract him/her: unorganized hawkers on the road or cart sellers visiting homes, unorganized local traditional retails with no price consistency, and small modern independent stores.

Organized modern retail business still has just 5 percent share of India's ₹2,250,000 crores retail size. Speculating with statistics, global consulting companies have created hype about the greenfield potential of India's retail industry.

Tapping this opportunity, Indian conglomerate business houses have focused on the real-estate route. They have set up large, plush, and brick-and-mortar retail spaces. But have they gone through the shoppers' sensitive core?

Like a rose, retail business is sensitive, fresh, fragile, and inactive in a place

It is different from manufacturing companies that can multiply its distribution to sell products in different geographical areas at any given time. Retail business cannot be mobile like that. If you miss out on the expected average bill per square foot and number of bills on an everyday basis, it means the retail is losing money. That is why the shopper's permanent addiction to the organized retail is the only solution for success.

The retail store management team needs to anticipate shopper's psychographics in product involvement and purchase behavior. She can be serious, bored, snobby, or show-off. She can be window shopping, romancing, perhaps love smitten, arrogant, speculative, impulsive, or just a value-seeker. By recognizing and addressing these moods you can expect an increase in the share of her wallet. Her shopper-centric retail experience means she gets what she wants and gets surprised to refresh her desires. A hypnotic retail façade and internal visual merchandise that cues shoppers to enter will attract footfall from both planned and impulse shoppers.

In-shop experience

In-shop experience can change the metaphor of a brand. The shopper's purchase act is linked to the type of outlet and its merchandise. It is not the same in different types of outlets. Store plan and merchandising create this impact, the outlet type defines the merchandise, and the purchase act responds through the psychological parameter. The more a store hallucinates from merchandise offers and display factors, the shopper returns to spend more. To retain the shopper and make profits, the retailer must provide an unparalleled shopping experience where some very useful merchandise is not available anywhere nearby. This will increase footfall, conversion, retention, repurchase, and increased wallet share. Merchandise that is unparalleled, coupled with the right price, can give you the power to sustain an ethical retail practice.

Maximize shopper's eyeball space

Within the next 10–15 years India will undoubtedly be the hub of the world's organized retail business. With FDI opening in India, fashion and fashion accessories' organized retails will face pressure on their brand worth. Global brands with strong brand image, quality, and product-sourcing competence will mesmerize India. These Indian brands will then be constrained to reduce price as they have not built aspiration beyond cut and fit.

Grassroots retail strategy is nothing more than a focus on how to occupy and maximize the shopper's eyeball space. What addiction will you offer the shoppers so they converge and occupy your organized modern retail space? To sustain business with reasonable profit, retailers will require plenty of patience and passion to understand the shopper's sensitive areas.

Can COA break business mediocrity?

To get the shopper's addiction, Japan, South Korea, and now China have reinvented shopper perceptible parameters in a new language. How did they do it?

Curiosity, observation, action

There is no rocket science involved, nor have they reinvented the wheel. They were just curious about the readily available invented wheel. This raised their observation quality to bring a paradigm change in their action. Only when an individual stresses on "curiosity," or an organization creates a collective process for curiosity, can you drive high "observation" quality, which leads to meaningful "action." This is COA.

India's young generation loves international brands in every domain. They find in them status, elevated quality, the latest aspect, and distinction with global flair. Till yesterday the "Made in China" label was synonymous with low-priced, mass-manufactured, and low-quality goods. But techno-savvy people across the world, including young Indians, are not questioning that the Apple iPod, the world's most in-demand product in their pockets, is "Assembled in China." Chinese products have no aspirational deficiency as most technology-efficient hardware comes from China today, not India.

Irrespective of what India's "business gods" with success-ful careers might try to establish that they have changed the paradigm, in reality they have delivered very basic work compared to global companies in developed countries. Individually they have made good money, their companies have achieved excellent valuation, but they have not added value to technology upgradation, invention, or innovation in the world. Yes, a bunch of people got jobs in IT, but does this credit go to our IT gurus or the global requirement for low-cost basic work?

The passion to ferret out the new

Why are Indian companies not paying heed to designing a service or manufactured product with unbeatable quality, functionality, and aesthetics? Perhaps we are missing COA centricity. Beyond the routine, curiosity will help unearth a new perspective. The passion to ferret out the new in every domain is the beginning of the search for brand distinction. It impacts a brand's action for breakthrough innovation, making it competitive in the "glocal" market.

Since ancient times, Indians have been sensitive in appreciating consistency in aesthetics with strong craftsmanship. Take the 13th century Konark Sun Temple in Odisha. Ganga Dynasty King Narasimha Deva-I (AD 1236–1264) built this exquisite temple as a royal proclamation of political supremacy. Just check people's work consistency then. Initially about 1,200 artisans and architects invested creative talent, energy, and artistic commitment for 12+ years in executing the design. Imagine, if Indians today meshed this legacy and caliber for perfection in meticulous design with great ideation and execution with contemporary digital technology, where a brand can go. Perhaps our people of multiple races interpret design in too many unscientific ways. Or are manufacturers not capable of eliciting passionate curiosity and high-quality observation among employees to compete globally?

The advent of change

In the last 22 years, customer approach toward different products has changed dramatically. An Ambassador car driver had to sit at a 45-degree angle to accommodate three to four others alongside him. Psychologically feeling the physical distance, people would yell "Hello" into the telephone when it rang like a fire-brigade alarm. In roadside public call office (PCO) booths, you had to wildly gesticulate to the caller inside to indicate the queue.

Today, you no longer own a 40-year-old refrigerator, the professional dhobi (laundry) has almost disappeared in the city, and most city airports are not old Indian railway station look-alikes any more. All such changes came to India from developed countries, when they brought their innovation/ invention on quality, functionality, and aesthetics. Have Indian brands contributed through distinctive value propositions when customer desire level has shot up? Explaining her expectation for her next vehicle, a 32-year-old woman said that an instrument-panel sensor should indicate with sound the minimum fuel in her petrol tank. When probed further, she questions the lack of a tire-puncture indicator. Just 15 years ago her father's Ambassador was all she knew. Her mindset change on engineering excellence has come from experiencing foreign brands. Such revelations prove that the protected economy merely empowered a few monopolistic industrialists who lived in comfort zone delivering substandard quality to customers.

But wait! There is convoluted drama here. People's buying behavior has changed but not their working and delivery style. There is lack of craftsmanship, finesse, enduring quality, connoisseur treatment, sense of aesthetics, and excellence of functionality in every domain. If the aim of companies trying to match up to global benchmarks is to chase short-term gains without discipline or holistic approach, they may not reach that level. Employee mindset has to change for incredible delivery to happen, but the responsibility lies with the willingness and drive of the enterprise.

Missing innovation

Since the 1991 economic reforms, the buying power of around 25 percent middle class has increased. Correspondingly, what has Indian industry addressed?

(1)   Responded to the demand-led IT market opportunity of fulfilling basic needs of developed countries. That

our British colonizers gifted us the English language certainly helped us here.

(2) Several companies are growing with the single-minded ambition of raising valuation to sell out to a global giant.

(3) Indian manufacturers are offering better price advantage in global competition. Basic employment has been generated, but when will India respond with innovation to mesmerize the existing invented wheel the way Japan, Korea, and China did?

When COA culture is absent, people want everything in an easy manner, not through struggle and tenacity. To avoid being inferior to global brands, Indian brands can imbibe COA, develop curiosity with extreme passion; while their observation dissection has to be powerful for a new blueprint of differentiation with substance. The brand can then act to astonish "glocal" customers.

At a COA workshop, I examined the threaded end of a ₹15,000 Mont Blanc pen. This was a solution to secure the cap at the far end while you write. The participants in my class figured Mont Blanc is expensive, so they could do anything. This is pure complacency. They did not appreciate the simple breakthrough idea that provided customers with distinction and extra benefit of not losing the cap.

It is a pity that Indian companies are not taking excellence of global standard delivered model seriously. Being this shallow can make India like a Middle East country where only international brands dominate the economy.

The retail industry requires this most important adjunct of communication to function optimally. Let's take a look at the impact of communication that touches every aspect of life and living.

X Vram Vrook

Curiosity and observation lead you to action with which you have to connect to people to be in business. Communication conjures up a pictorial image to catch the mind's eye, information equips you with knowledge, while a technical description tells you what something is. These three bases of societal connect are often cluttered in our extravagant digi-language society.

Let us experience them through global brands. Apple brand is communication; its name provokes you with imagery that can be infinitely interpreted. Coca-Cola being a combination of ingredients from kola nuts and coca plant is informative centric. IBM is a technical description earlier called International Business Machines. It spells out its global power of innovation.

Technical description

Trade-marking trends in American and British businesses before World War II were driven by technical description, identifying themselves with technical processes. Britain started the 1750 Industrial Revolution, but industrialization with highly efficient processes first started and scaled-up in America from the beginning of the 20th century. That is reflected in trade-marks such as GE and UPS among others. They later changed to acronyms GE and UPS to storm global markets. British companies added royal nomenclature, such as Imperial Tobacco Company and Imperial Chemical Industry, among others. After relinquishing colonial power they democratized to becoming ITC and ICI, respectively. The business logic of these two nations was different, but both created technically descriptive corporate entities initially.

Today, technical descriptive brands are a basic requirement in society, corporations, politics, education, and entertainment, although they have no communication power. In corporate culture at the technical-description level, employee motivation and aspiration go for a toss. Life becomes the French proverb *metro, boulot, dodo* (commute, work, sleep). Likewise in society, a wealthy man is identified by his wealth figures, nothing else. Rote learning is so high in our education system that a yawning gap exists between what is taught and what the industry and customers require.

Indian movies are made with huge technical advancement, but after two weeks you do not remember the storyline. Parliament continues feverishly to mimic British monarchical governance, which was dictatorial, even though this country is now a democratic polity. In other words, if the content is not powerful, mere technical form does not connect to make a lasting impact.

Is there information overload?

Undoubtedly electronic media and Internet very effectively unearth society's hidden aspects, and without basic information society cannot run today. However, information overload saturates the human brain. TV information is ephemeral, with channels screeching "breaking news" and some TV journalists holding forth like they alone are the nation's conscience. I particularly enjoy newspapers such as the *New York Times*, *Le Monde*, *Financial Times* of London, and *Herald Tribune* that go beyond information and reporting to give readers an analysis of the news, putting it in a context and perspective without any bias.

In business, a descriptor brand such as Coca-Cola needs immense communicative elements to change its perception of being a mere formula. Attempts were made to make Coca-Cola synonymous with words such as thirst, enjoy, and refresh.

The Andrews sisters popularized in song, "Drink rum and Coca-Cola!" But being ingredient-centric, the problem that remains with this kind of brand is that it is very difficult to move with changing trends. By saying that, I cannot ignore that Coca-Cola has for 120 years done incredible innovation in marketing to communicate the brand.

Communication can shake the world

You may consider technical description and information to be part of communication, but they came later. Communication started with visual art before the languages we speak today. That which resides in your memory very pictorially, whether through painting, design, voice, written word, body gesture, or audio visuals stays as unforgettable communication. Politicians have won people's hearts with incredible communication skills. Dazzling examples are Martin Luther King, who fought to equalize Blacks in mainstream American society, to Barack Obama, who became the first Black American president. Hailing from the minority African-American population, they practically had nothing other than communicating power with outstanding intelligence. Mahatma Gandhi shook up the world by changing his attire from a British barrister-at-law to an Indian fakir to represent India's poor. His 1932 arrival in London wearing a loincloth in winter to participate in the Third Round Table Conference with British authorities is a phenomenal communication forever etched in people's minds.

When cinema was nascent, Charles Chaplain left proof that silent communication can be timeless when he auditioned with a comic-gymnastic act on-the-spot, leaving the director spellbound. Historically, dictators have huge communicative power as they play to the masses, always with lies. As Adolf Hitler said, "If you tell a big enough lie and tell it frequently enough, it will be believed." But this is not the communication that is acceptable in any situation.

Now if you look at India, take our famous singers such as Manna Dey, Mohammed Rafi, and Kishore Kumar who have not written but interpreted songs. Technically Dey and Rafi were trained singers but Kishore had no voice training. Weaving his personality into his songs, he connected compassionately with people more than the others. His melodious communicative voice power remains vibrant at the mass level even today.

Need to touch the human chord

To lead people, your communication has to touch a sensitive human chord; education or intellectual capacity is irrelevant here. You either have, or cultivate, this power. To sustain business, only juggling information and technical descriptions is not enough. People do not remember advertising, even when it is often repeated with huge investment, unless the product has some memorable aspect. When its quality is perceptibly different, communication can stroke the spirit. Communicative power boils down to selling the PUB triad. The world has no boring subject; you just need to know how to transform something dull with the real substance of provocation to make it communication effective.

Go on, be a communicator, provoke your audience with curiosity. Information and technical descriptions are necessary facts, but without provoking communication you will go nowhere. X Vram Vrook is my provoking communication headline in this book; you will never find it in any dictionary. Something provoking gets stuck in your mind; you understand its significance, whether serious or frivolous. If it has substance, it draws a picture your imagination will cherish forever. This is communication which can make you a leader.

Country level

Business is created

The power of American marketers to transform religious festivity into business is stark in February 14, St. Valentine's Day. Traditionally lovers in English-speaking countries expressed their love by sending Valentine's cards to each other. The US Greeting Card Association estimates that a billion Valentine's cards are sent annually worldwide. Today commerce flourishes with romance in most countries across Latin America, Europe, the Middle East, and Asia with sales of chocolates and diamond jewelry. Virtual romance floats in cyberspace through the Internet. But fundamentalists oppose Valentine's Day as "cultural pollution from the West" in parts of India and Saudi Arabia where its ban in 2008 created a black market in roses and wrapping paper.

Diwali

India is adapting Westernized ways of celebrating Christmas and Valentine through an organized marketing process, but is it not about time we exported a few of our festivals for the world to enjoy? Why not start with Diwali, the nondogmatic Hindu festival that appears more relevant to most Indians? Give it a character to represent a billion people and market it meaningfully as an international festival. Selling an intangible idea requires tremendous marketing discipline, which is called marketing. Can India market Diwali globally?

Let us play with an example here

First, create the mythological story. Keeping a metaphorical idea that can be relevant to different global societies, design a versatile symbolic expression with activities that have universal appeal beyond religion. Take inspiration from the way Christmas means gifts and Valentine means romantic love. India being a motherland, unlike some 50 countries that describe themselves as fatherland, the representation is women. Buying gold, among other gifts, is a tradition during Diwali. Combine the two, a gold icon can be appropriate. Symbolizing woman from Indian history, exquisite Ajanta Ellora figurines can be interwoven in a modern way and associated with a fruit that is relevant to India yet globally relished. That is the mango. Fifty percent of it is produced in India and the rest in Mexico, Brazil, Equador, Peru, and Haiti, among others, but exported almost everywhere in the world.

Even though it is not mango season during Diwali in the northern hemisphere, it can create a special moment such as the orange-eating culture at Christmas. An exciting activity could be how to get mangoes from somewhere in the world to celebrate Diwali with. In fact this demand will promote the mango culture worldwide and encourage its cultivation for sale during Diwali. So the Diwali symbol could be the golden mango with representation of gifts inside, with a modernized gold Ajanta woman as the personality. This image can be crafted for three-dimensional usage with lights inside for a night-time festival that is visible and prominently placed on the road and at home. It can be replicated and promoted as a brand in various objects from necklaces to watches, spectacles to apparel, and food and beverages to personal care. It has to be very different from everyday life and have some iconic character, which is approachable. Valentine is romantic love; Christmas is charity, gifts, and family; what does Diwali signify that is a universal need? Home coming!

Why is a global festival good for human society?

Everyday life consists of humdrum activities with routine work deteriorating into stress, societal problems, and perhaps a nervous breakdown. People want to be rid of such lows. A highly orchestrated, well-marketed festival can really bring joyfulness into living. It is refreshing to think of Christmas togetherness or dreamy love of Valentine's Day. That can translate to immoderate pleasure. When people crave for enjoyment they are eager to flaunt money and forget life's passive parts. This positive aspect of any festival creates a lot of work and more business.

An international festival from India will create immense goodwill, sharing, and manifestation of our culture. It will provide numerous opportunities for our billion-people country to spread their wings into new business and cultural ventures across the world.

Marketing machine of the monarchy

Marketing, supposedly an American invention, is very much alive and kicking in the US. But its roots certainly lay in undiluted marketing practices polished over centuries by British monarchy.

Sixty years of reign

The UK declared four celebratory days, with holidays for banks, schools, public, and private offices to mark the 60-year reign of Queen Elizabeth II on June 4–5, 2012. Since its inception with Alfred the Great in 849, British royalty has undoubtedly been UK's stellar brand.

Great crisis management

Take how adroitly royalty managed the 1992 fire at Windsor Castle, the world's largest inhabited castle. The fire destroyed the castle's vital historic parts. The question was who will pay the estimated £60 million for restoration? The Queen suggested taxpayers, but Britain's Parliament under Prime Minister John Major refused as it was a private royal home. British monarchy found an out-of-the-box solution in April 1993.

So many people stand outside the huge grilled palace gates to watch the changing of the royal guards. Why not raise money from them by opening up Windsor Castle at £3 per entry, and Buckingham Palace at £8 per admission for the next five years? The repair finally cost £36.5 million; the Queen's personal contribution was £2 million. What is interesting is that the public is still visiting royal residences, only paying double now; £18 a visit to Buckingham Palace. While marketing a selling proposition, we always try to find a corridor that avoids the possibility of getting stuck in adversity. People pay good money to learn such marketing theories at Harvard, INSEAD, Columbia, and London School of Economics (LSE). But without going anywhere, merely by exposing British dynasty loot collected over centuries from various colonies, monarchical marketing found an inventive way to restore Windsor Castle. They simply pumped money from the willing-to-pay public who was not disappointed either.

Famed French furniture in Britain

Aside from booty from colonies, although the British and French never liked each other and had clashed in Waterloo, the British did not hesitate to beautify Windsor Palace with French furniture. Former French President Valéry Giscard d'Estaing commented that he saw more French furniture inside Windsor Palace when he had lunched there with the Queen in 1977 than in France's Versailles Palace.

It is important to know that French royal furniture and décor from the reigns of Francis I, Louis XIV, Louis XVI, and Napoleon have left the grid and benchmark of all time exquisite design sophistication in the world.

Monarchical mela

Visiting royal residences, the monarch's subjects never stop smelling the British Empire where "the sun never sets." This marketing jargon means Great Britain continues to prevail in the cultural imagination of their colonized countries. Through 24 hours, the sun is shining in some or other past or present territory of Britain. Even today Elizabeth II, who is still head of state of 16 nations, knows how to conduct a monarchical mela (festival).

In the 1,000-boat flotilla on River Thames, marking her diamond jubilee, she had invited the 54 Commonwealth members to keep alive "the sun never sets on the British Empire" nostalgia. It is another British monarchical marketing masterstroke, from "looting wealth" to Commonwealth. When you see the Indian flag in the pageant, you do not know whether you should experience pride or humiliation. They have destroyed the backbone of our country's spirit and moral strength by colonizing India for 200 years. Yet we are a part of the Commonwealth!

Encashing royalty with souvenirs

Has monarchy marketing taken a lesson from Walter Disney, who ingeniously converted a smelly rat to become the iconic Mickey Mouse, loved worldwide and selling in both the amusement park and elsewhere? Like selling Disneyland merchandise, souvenir shops outside royal palaces peddle ornamental crockery, Victorian pillboxes, thimbles, Guardsmen's red dress with furry headgear, and aprons saying, "God Save the Queen." Other merchandise "By Appointment to Her Majesty the Queen" includes cigarettes, tea, whiskey, chocolates, and luggage.

Aside from exorbitantly priced limited and special edition keepsakes, you even get imperial Russian mementoes, Faberge eggs, made through traditional 250-year-old methods, hand finished using 22-carat gold, and set with precious stones. Such votives were personal gifts exchanged among Russian, Danish, and British royal families. After all, the last Czar Nicholas II and King George V, grandfather of Elizabeth II, were cousins; their mothers were sisters. Actually countries such as Holland, Belgium, Sweden, Denmark, and Spain still have monarchs, but it is Britain's queen who still rules feudal-style over subjects, not citizens.

Luxury goods from Europe

If you rewind the entire marketing chapter of mass consumption, it gained strength after World War II. There is a clear demarcation between luxury and mass-consumption goods. Unique luxury products, from garments, jewelry, and cutlery to traveling coaches, were created for royalty to flaunt and distinguish their superiority and invoke awe among the masses. European countries such as England and France with long history of kingdoms have preserved their code of luxury goods that command premium prices in the world.

In spite of the US marketing skills, a luxury product can never originate from the US, which has no royal tradition. The difference from traditional monarchy is that without possessing royal blood, you can enjoy their luxurious life if you are rich. What's more is that the nobility today, comprising remnants of the disintegrated Roman and other Western empires, are even selling off royal titles; so for huge sums of money you can become a duke or a countess too.

Scanty antiroyal activity

British monarchy's marketing machine has been so active that according to BBC, 80 percent Britons still want the monarchy. It gained a fillip after Prince William married commoner Kate Middleton. However, antimonarchists exist too. Britain's Republic Party says the royal family is brainwashing common people to stay subjugated and support its upkeep with public funds. "We are citizens, not subjects" is their cry for democracy. "Parasites go home" is another poster decrying royal heritage.

In having a president of India we imitated the British monarchy's titular head system, but will anybody ever buy a souvenir saying "God save the President" when that person changes every five years? If the UK Republics have their way and monarchy is abolished, the UK has to rethink the country's marketing as its biggest brand pull, Her Majesty, would be lost.

British marketing of imperialism

In fact the UK's organized marketing of imperialism is among the best marketing jobs to date. British cultural infusion into their colonies was akin to slow poison that finally consumed their subjects. It was just a handful of British traders who spread the English culture into India. Today nobody faults an Indian who does not speak his/her mother tongue correctly, but if he/she should use improper English, he/she will lose his/her social status. Implementing the British way of life in a colony was the finest marketing action of the British race. Whichever country they went to, they drove the indigenous people to adopt and swear by English culture.

Free trade and commerce are pushing emerging economies to follow the Western marketing model by default. The English language has been the unsurpassed marketing coup by becoming the language of global business. Slavery has migrated from the physical to the colonial to the intellectual level today.

Bigger the better

American marketing has always feted the large, whether in cars or hamburgers, and on getting more value, starting with "More bang for the buck" as they say in advertising parlance. Western business practices have influenced emerging countries. They do not take into account, conform to, or seamlessly mesh with the societal aspects of our billions. The dichotomy is that India and China are now downloading new complexities in the front yard of Americans and Europeans. They are overpowering everyone with issues relating to unemployment, outsourcing, and organized immigration.

Shrinking the big

After their World War II defeat, Japan was disallowed from manufacturing defense weapons. So they set out to conquer world markets with the ingenious weapon of high-quality miniaturization. They copied fundamental Western invention and obsessively created high-quality miniaturized products to win customer hearts across the world.

India needs to think of how to market Indian brands that reflect outstanding quality, functionality, and emotive factor without the constrained perception of cost advantage of being considered low profile, low cost, and low quality. Only by packaging cost, quality, and aspiration at every price point can Indian brands meaningfully surprise global markets and get recognition in digitalized 21st century.

Only Zap-connect disruption can increase profitability

Marketing can be manipulative, but the generation manipulating the markets is clearly the below 30-year-old Zappers.

Three generations

The three generations of 45-plus Retro, the 30 to 45-year-old Compromise, and the widely divergent Zap86 generation have created peculiar socio-eco-political circumstances. The five-year-olds in 1991, when India's economic reforms were introduced, have experienced only the open pockets of their parents because the economy had started booming.

Foreign companies came seeking Indian manpower to solve problems such as Year 2000 (Y2K). So new jobs opened up, salaries saw an upturn, and foreign goods became freely available. This gave everyone ample purchase choice. People who hitherto lived in the closed economy started to spend on unfulfilled urges. More importantly, they indulged their children, whose whims and fancies continue to influence all buying decisions made in every home.

Worldwide phenomenon

From my different work travels around the world, I have realized that the Zap, Compromise (they try to adjust with both sides), and Retro generations are not an exclusive Indian phenomenon. They exist everywhere, albeit with different parameters. My classification of the 19th century being the mechanical era, electronic technology ruling the 20th century, and 21st century being the digital age is doubly endorsed from watching how the Zap generation operates. Like zapping TV channels, Zappers are most comfortable with rapid change in every aspect of life. Their text messaging is phonetic, and giving vowels a miss is an accepted script today. The above 30s may find it jarring, yet their mentality is to co-opt Zapper trends because clearly, discrete numerical form is ruling this digital century that has become totally Zap-driven.

Zappers neglected in India

In India, there is still a huge distance between industries and their attempt to appeal to the Zap generation. Most connect their products and services to Compromise or Retro-generation buyers. They are not sensitive to the fact that the Zap generation has, and will continue to have, a significant influence on their elders. Without this realization and connect to Zappers, Indian brands will become old fashioned and the whole country will be swamped with foreign brands.

Developed countries have the capability to co-opt the trend in advance to drive the world. But the Compromise and Retro generations running business in India either choose to neglect, or do not notice, the attitude and behavioral aspects of the Zap generation. In spite of their children or grandchildren being Zappers, the Retro generation is highly disconnected from them. The pressure from the Zap generation, their way of living and exposure, is so high that neither the Retro nor the Compromise can ignore it.

Disruption through brands

Working in the West for almost four decades from 1970s onward, I, among others, have meticulously used disruption as a weapon in strategizing for brands, industrial products, retails, or corporate-structure design. Industries there welcome the "fresh" perspective as a point of distinction, because these disruptive strategies help their cash registers to ring. In India almost two decades have passed since liberalization brought in gigantic changes to the marketplace.

Indian industrial houses first refused to believe that Indian customers would ever discard their savings mentality. Now that the market has become vibrant and mature, they are in a paralytic situation, wondering how to get back the customers they lost to foreign brands. But I still do not see any attempt to apply the disruptive attitude to retain market share that is escaping to new foreign players. If Indian brands do not ideate about using disruption for profitability and sustainability in the face of incoming foreign brands, they may grow in volume but the bottom line will be ruined.

India needs a poverty-killing machine

We always want to somehow connect to communicate when we engage in any artistic or knowledge-based activity. Six hundred years ago, Leonardo da Vinci secretly "mirror wrote" engineering and other nonreligious ideas because Rome's powerful Catholic Church disapproved such activities. Although his paintings and sculpting brought him fame, Leonardo understood that art pieces which provide future vision can physically only decorate museums or rich people's homes. Art cannot be duplicated to serve livelihood needs of millions of people. So he took to inventing machine after machine to bring incredible functional benefits for improving human life.

Machines for livelihood

To kill India's poverty we need multiple types of blended mechanical + digitally engineered, low-cost, highly efficient, and compact machines for livelihood generation for the population earning ₹3,000–10,000 per month. Such machines require no fundamental invention, just adaptation. Japan, since 1970s, has brought humanized mechanical + electronic-engineering compactness into the market. They incorporated reliability with extreme user friendliness and grand quality in miniature format. That's what all our diligent working-class professionals require but they have no way to get it.

If you travel throughout the country with an engineering eye and bent of mind, you will find poor people struggling for their everyday livelihood. Either they have no machine, or if they do, it is archaic, whereas everything is available in the world today.

Silk yarn is meticulous to make

In South India's famed silk industry, from cocoon to thread making is a very meticulous process. I saw highly skilled men and women working painstakingly and with passion, but in pathetic and constricted conditions, with no machines, no fans, and sitting on the floor. Their gorgeous output of creamy white silk yarn is actually filament carefully unwound from the cocoon as one continuous thread, collected into skeins, reeled, and twisted. You would never believe that the rich, shiny, and twisted yarns sent to silk factories for weaving expensive saris or even to global designers for fashionable haute couture had emanated from this machine-less, hot, and miserable workplace in today's world of advanced technology.

Instruments for goldsmith

Take jewelry, where India's branded market is growing at 40 percent. If you spend time at a goldsmith's workplace, you will realize how workers physically struggle without up-to-date instruments for perfecting their handcrafted art and livelihood. If Switzerland can have sophisticated precision instruments for small-scale watchmaking companies, why cannot India's working class also expect excellent, modern-day machines? Obviously, because their requirement is not on anyone's radar.

Develop a value-led market mindset

Indian businesses are highly driven by the demand-led market, when there is demand, they supply. But to cater to "machines for livelihood," industrialists have to develop a value-led market mindset. There is no stated demand from the millions earning less than or about ₹3,000–10,000 per month, but one has to discover what machines they need. Creating a value-led market for such needs that are hidden in poverty requires huge research, a unique approach, and self-motivation to create worth. Indians have not changed from their age-old high tolerance of poverty.

Modernizing for mechanics

Thousands of automobile, commercial vehicle, and two-wheeler mechanics serve everyone who would not go to bona fide auto-dealers for repair or servicing due to huge costs. They continue to exert physical effort using tools and machines that existed for Fiats and Ambassadors before liberalization. Modernizing equipment will ease their livelihood, and provide business-generation opportunity for such manufacturers. You will find professionals such as technicians, carpenters, plumbers, electricians, masons, MSME workers, fabricators, as well as traders, contractors, small-restaurant owners, mass-market product dealers and distributors, and mom-and-pop store owners all working without efficient, updated machines that could enhance their earnings and deliver better quality to their customers. Neither government nor private industry cares about how they earn utilizing pure wits, high entrepreneurship, and hard work.

Potato chops for extra earnings

On visits to rural India, I find hapless farmers burdened with so much debt that they cannot move anywhere. Micro-finance offers hypnotize them, and they get bogged down without fathoming why they are paying so much interest money. A farmer's 22-year-old son says they cannot make ends meet, so he buys potatoes, boils and mashes them by hand, adds spices and chickpea flour (*besan*) at home, and then runs a few meters, the big vessel on the head, to a corner of the village. Here he has set up a stove and openly fries potato chops. Replenishment happens on foot as they own no means of transport.

They spend ₹300, and generate up to ₹1,000 daily, making a clean ₹700 profit. If this old-fashioned, laborious, and unhygienic preparation job is helped by mechanization, this farmer can standardize his earning, reduce his labor, and increase hygiene.

Industry can help and profit from it

Government appears to have no clue on how to solve liveli-hood generation problems of such farmers despite promises made by politicians during elections. Nor has Indian industry cared in 65 years of independence. Government has set up a National Skill Development Corporation and launched a National Rural Livelihood Mission but whatever may be hap-pening there, those who should benefit are far from benefit-ting from them. So should someone not take interest to invite already-established developed-country industries to bring modernized mechanical + digital machines to increase the earning capacity of India's poor people according to require-ments specific to India?

Aladdin in Thailand

When I was in neighboring Thailand, a street vendor on a motorbike with a sidecar of well-designed workmanship said he had got his Aladdin. The sidecar had arrangements for stocking, cooking, and selling, so he needed no intermedi-ary. He drove to source raw materials and went to different localities at different times for better earnings. He served wearing gloves, a machine cleaned up the cooking plate and also changed the oil without involving his hands. The dustbin had a recycling system. Such practical systems are available for all their street vendors. Why can't we similarly reduce effort, increase comfort in India where large numbers of street vendors physically push their non-mechanized carts, and execute everything by hand?

When America beat all nations in industrial advancement in the last century, they first looked at improving the lot of working-class masses, shifting them gradually from small-home enterprises to becoming first sweat-shop slaves and eventually factory workers. Machines and tools for better earning possibilities were invented even during the Great Depression.

If Indian poverty can be eradicated by adopting the da Vinci engineering code of modernizing tools and machinery, let us make it our single-point action. That will upgrade livelihood prospects for the hardworking working-class, and hoist the pyramid altogether carrying those at the bottom of it too. Simultaneously, everyone will enjoy hygiene and civic improvement.

French inventions for charity

Inventions are definitely needed, so is their acceptance. Remember those employee strikes when Indian banks first tried to computerize? Actually, the very first time people were afraid to use a machine thinking it might replace their jobs was when Frenchman Blaise Pascal invented the mechanical calculator called Pascaline in 1642. To honor his role as a precursor in computer technology, there is even a computer language named Pascal.

Some of the world's most spectacular inventions that we would be lost without in our modern, day-to-day life emanated from France. But were these inventions made for charity or as donations? France has largely not been able to cultivate her inventions for financial gain, while other nations have taken those inventions forward for social and economic advancement.

Unknown inventor running the world

Roland Moreno epitomizes my observation that nonaggressive French inventors donate their inventions to charity for others to exploit. In 1974, Egypt-born Frenchman Moreno invented the computer chip that is used in smart cards. France pioneered the smart-card usage: France Télécom in 1983, French banks in 1992. American Express did not use it until 1999, and British banks and transport systems even later. Just verify in your own pocket how many chips you use: for banking, shopping, commuting, and in your passport and your mobile-phone SIM card, among others. Yet when Moreno died on April 29, 2012, his company Innovatron had only made €150 million from an invention that has touched almost everyone on the planet today.

Without Moreno, where would the world's top billionaires be, such as Carlos Slim Helu who made his US$69 billion from Telmex or Airtel's Sunil Mittal with his US$8 billion? Moreno's chip is making billions of business dollars where France or Moreno have no role to play. Wasn't this invention for charity? It shows how "unsmart" France has become.

Invention without execution makes you a loser

Much before World Wide Web was introduced in 1994, the French enjoyed Minitel, the world's most successful video-tex online service accessible through telephone lines since 1982. French Post launched this online service, handing out millions of terminals free to telephone subscribers. Minitel allowed users to make online purchases, train reservations, check stock prices, search the telephone directory, have a mailbox, and chat in a way similar to what is possible through the Internet. About 25 million of France's total 60-million population had used the Minitel network. But today when you look at the top 10 countries with the highest computer usage, France does not figure in the list.

The ingenious French inventors

Influential French inventions modernizing our life in medicine, communication, computers, transportation, clothing, arts, entertainment, food, physics, chemistry, mathematics, weapons, military, and even sports have come over a few centuries. Blind man Louis Braille invented the Braille system for the blind to read and write. To keep Napoleon's troops well-fed in far-flung places, Nicolas Francois Appert invented canning in 1809. Louis Pasteur invented pasteurization to sterilize food and kill contaminating microorganisms. Undersea explorer Jacques-Yves Cousteau invented the Aqua-Lung in 1943 for supplying oxygen to underwater divers.

Today's standardized metric measurement system was invented by the Paris Academy of Sciences in 1790; oxygen was discovered by Antoine Lavoisier in 1778. Tailor Barthelemy Thimonnier perfected the sewing machine in 1830. American Isaac Merrit Singer turned it into big business. Among women's garments, Herminie Cadolle devised the bra in 1889, Coco Chanel the little black dress in 1920, Louis Réard the bikini in 1946, and Guy Cotton the raincoat in 1960. Father Marcel Audiffren invented refrigeration in 1894 to keep French monastery wines cool. American company GE capitalized on it in 1911, manufacturing refrigeration machines for homes. Individual transportation was another convenience the French gave us. Nicholas Joseph Cugnot physically drove the first self-propelled car in 1769. Édouard Michelin invented inflatable tires in 1895, Louis Renault invented the drum brake in 1902, while French-born Rudolf Diesel invented the diesel engine, and Gustave Trouvé the first electric automobile in 1881.

So where does France stand among auto majors?

France has been overtaken by Japanese, American, German, and Korean companies diving down to the 10th position.

In water transport, the steamboat came from Denis Papin in the 19th century and the first outboard motorboat by Gustave Trouvé. Pierre Michaux and Pierre Lallement developed the bicycle in 1864, but France figures nowhere among the best or biggest manufacturers today; Taiwanese company Giant wins. Frenchman Rinaldo Piaggio invented the scooter in 1884, but world-leader Piaggio is an Italian brand today. Even in air transport, the first flying helicopters were the result of experiments independently conducted by Louis Breguet and Paul Cornu in 1907. Brothers Joseph and Jacques Etienne Montgolfier designed the hot-air balloon and Louis Sebastien Lenormand the parachute in the late 18th century. But France has not retained leadership in these areas.

Extreme right rises as recession weapon

When General Charles de Gaulle became French president after World War II, he believed the French had struggled greatly during German occupation, so he nationalized most industries. Through liberal laws he provided good living conditions with free medical and education facilities for citizens. The people became totally dependent on the state, their only desire was to work less and get greater leisure. The small and medium enterprises (SMEs) in France started vanishing. Selling sophisticated luxury goods to the world's rich has remained a French preserve. But this cannot be a country's backbone. When the government mollycoddles people, the backlash can be nonproductive corruption, as we have seen with India's 100 days of work for poor people. In many cases people work only two hours and not eight hours, sharing the booty with the job-doling official. What's the repercussion? Rural farmers are experiencing exorbitant daily labor charges for eight hours of productive and essential work.

Strength of SMEs in Europe

In Europe's recessionary wave where Greece, Spain, Portugal, and even the UK are suffering, the German economy stands tall on the strength of its SME manufacturing base. German SMEs give financial and political stability, and export globally. SMEs, small and medium-sized businesses (SMBs) and variations of these terms are companies where the number of employees falls below certain limits. The European Union and international organizations such as the World Bank, the United Nations and WTO use the SME abbreviation. Small enterprises outnumber large companies by a wide margin and employ many more people. SMEs are also said to be responsible for driving innovation and competition in many economic sectors.

Whenever a country's economy deteriorates, jobs become scarce, citizens become protesters, and the political fallout is rise of insular extreme right. That happened in France's first round presidential elections on April 22, 2012, when the extreme right party unexpectedly got 19 percent votes among 10 candidates. The more recession grows, so will parochialism. Indian business houses focusing on Europe have to observe this movement. It cannot be permanent, but will experience high social volcanic eruption from time to time.

Typical French inventive characteristics are worth emulating. They include embracing the new, constant effort to differentiate work, being curious, and finding out more. In fact modernity is characterized by the aspiration of freedom, equal rights, and brotherhood that translated in to the 1789 French Revolution's motto of liberty, equality, and fraternity. However, during Nicolas Sarkozy's presidential term 350,000 industrial jobs were lost; the unemployment rate for mainland France in the fourth quarter 2011 was 9.4 percent, close to a

12-year high. This proves that when invention is not put into the execution of industrialization, even an inventive country such as France has to battle an economic crisis, having lost the inventive SME spirit and the AAA Standard & Poor's rating from long years of financial indiscipline. When invention becomes charity the country's economy suffers.

About the future perspective of India's grassroots-level industry

MSMEs will brighten India's future

I have tremendous consideration for Indian MSMEs, the backbone of our country. In value terms this sector is estimated to account for about 45 percent manufacturing output and about 40 percent of total exports. A micro-enterprise has plant and machinery investment below ₹2,500,000 and below ₹1,000,000 in equipment. Respectively, a small enterprise invests up to ₹50,000,000 and ₹20,000,000; while a medium enterprise invests up to ₹100,000,000 in plant and machinery and ₹50,000,000 in equipment. This combined sector is estimated to be nearly four times that of large enterprise, including in labor intensity, and has consistently registered a higher growth rate. I have never worked for any Indian MSME, but I enormously respect their tenacity to perform against severe odds.

In Europe, I have experienced SMEs in different industries. A few CEOs of big enterprises I have worked for had left their CEO jobs after a long tenure and bought SMEs. What I observed is that they would take me on board with them on acquiring the company, although I didn't realize at that time what I would do in such small-size companies of about US$1.5 million. The main thing is their vision for growth, driving the SME's core element to incredibly transform the company in quality, profitability and making it big. Traditionally, all SMEs have excellent craftsmanship in a domain, but lack the scaling factor. When experienced people from big industries enter an SME they look to bring and drive their business process in a simple way to encourage scaling.

In India, the trend I have observed is that senior managers leave big companies and go to angel investors for funds to start a company from scratch in different IT-centric digital domains. Rarely have I seen high caliber professionals enter SMEs to change their business size paradigm. In the history of the Industrial Revolution, North America in particular has industrialized much more in comparison to other countries. You will find that most of today's big companies were micro or small enterprises a hundred years ago.

I believe that bringing the disruptive platform with execution excellence to MSME domains in India is crucial to grow our manufacturing and service base. India's young generation should be encouraged not to discount the avenue of working here or giving it leadership. Rarely do we find MSME owners' children returning to drive their fathers' small enterprises. His/her ambition is to join some big company, gain experience and market value to add to his/her CV. This is the time for India to really take action to boost the MSME sector, starting from making students in professional higher education conscious about and inclined toward MSMEs as the alternate career option for their life. MSMEs will prove their high innovative power in future if this sector is nurtured the way Germany does.

About India's industry perspective

Disruptive platform with execution excellence for Indian industry

The need of the hour for India to change its face is disruptive platform with execution excellence. I see two paths for a solid future:

1. How to transform the demand-let market
The demand-led market is not the defect; it needs ingenuity of vision with adequate capability to transform demand toward leading the market with value. When there is demand that has to be supplied, you don't need to hound your customer about what you want to sell. The category is already known and experienced so it's like having the bonus in your pocket. However, when you want to earn more, instead of competing with everyone to supply some generic requirement, you have to transform the shape of your offer with value. For long-term sustainability of your enterprise, don't believe that squeezing cost is the best solution. Of course, if you can cut the waste with ingenious science and human capability, that is a solution without parallel.

When your customer perceives that you deliver distinctive value that's unbeatable compared to competition, you will know you have exited the demand-led market by providing customer ecstasy. With human initiative and specialized focus it is possible to achieve what you want. It is an avenue wide open for you to change banality and enter the value-led market.

2. Don't ignore the greenfield market
In India, the world's largest heterogeneous society with multiple human behavior, lifestyle, and livelihood generation, there is immense greenfield scope and opportunity for innovation or

invention. You can learn as much you want from the innovative power of developed countries where low, and subsequently costly, manpower has made them resort to mechanization for most of the activities they engage in.

India does not honor/support technical skills. Culturally we have relied on manpower to do as many jobs as possible. On the other hand, the West will not do manual work. This has led them to design a mechanism for different activities, and hence to mass production, quality inspection, standardization, serviceability, inventory management, work force management, and the whole gamut of activities that come with industrialization. As India has never adopted this approach, technical knowledge and skills are not given importance. We get by with *jugaad* which is assembling things together without a predetermined process. Jugaad does not believe in design, testing, validation, and aesthetics.

If you look at the country from top to bottom, left to right, you will find innumerable possibilities to start business. But don't go to solve all possibilities. Take a purposeful decision to select one direction and make it big. To do so you will require a disruptive platform with execution excellence.

The mental stamina of believing in and supporting a business in the greenfield area is huge. It is the most important part, and this is where most Indian professionals fail. It requires deep focus, the strength of will, your superior quality of observation and assessment, some space in the mind to ideate on establishing the new business and believing in it. The individual then has to select a team that will work with the passion, belief, and capability in developing the greenfield business. Your team and you can then ride the infinite V toward success. If you have the entrepreneurship spirit in your body and mind, don't believe in easy earning. Drive the greenfield in a big way to make your existing enterprise transform into a big domain, the way Thomas Edison to Steve Jobs made their indelible mark in society.

Epilogue
Action Surpassmark
Pokes for Your To-Do List

Best Practice to Surpass Practice

Bowler hat, mustache, cane, a disproportionate pair of shoes, a bizarre way of walking, and you have The Tramp, the international superstar of the silent-film era created by Charlie Chaplin. This was his Surpass Practice, unmatched till today.

British-born Charlie Chaplin started his entertainment career at the age of five. He spontaneously replaced his mother suddenly one day when her voice failed on stage. Through a childhood fraught with hardship, poverty, and living in workhouses after his mother was committed to a mental asylum, Charlie emerged "a sort of Adam, from whom we are all descended," says renowned filmmaker, Federico Fellini.

A familiar stage

Chaplin recounted his beginning like this:

> I was news vendor, printer, toymaker, doctor's boy, but during these occupational digressions, I never lost sight of my ultimate

aim to become an actor. So, between jobs I would polish my shoes, brush my clothes, put on a clean collar and make periodic calls at a theatrical agency.

Chaplin's story felt a little familiar in one section, reminding me of my early struggling era in Paris. Even as a sweeper in a lithography print shop where I used to wear workers blues, I'd dress well with a tie from time to time to meet various art-related people in my ambition to become a designer and painter.

The Tramp is Surpassmark

In different comic roles when Chaplin toured British music halls, worked as stage actor and comedian, he followed the best practices of traditional comic theatrical genres, including the Harlequinade developed since the 17th century. At the age of 19, Fred Karno Company took him to the US where he entered films. In 1914, Chaplin created the Tramp persona by accident. To play a comic role he was rummaging through props in Keystone Studio, when he tried on the hat, outsized shoes, tight jacket, cane, and mustache. The bumbling, child-like, good-hearted vagrant developed from there. Chaplin continued to hone and sustain this character as his Surpass Practice through his career.

The Tramp portrayed the human spirit through comic, pathos, and subtlety. This was a Surpass Practice, being totally different from all earlier comic expressions. *TIME* magazine listed Chaplain among 20th Century's 100 Most Important People for bringing laughter to millions: "He more or less invented global recognizability and helped turn an industry into an art." According to film critic Andrew Sarris, "He's arguably the single most important artist … certainly its most extraordinary performer and probably still its most universal icon." Film historian Mark Cousins says Chaplin changed the imagery, sociology, and grammar of cinema. So breaking all previous benchmarks for comic acts, the Tramp became Chaplin's all-time Surpassmark.

Bring in your originality

Surpass embodies excellence. It is defined by words such as excel, outshine, standout. Surpassmark immediately brings in a competitive spirit whereas benchmark is just a catch-up game. Surpassmark is active whereas benchmark is passive. How can you garner expertise by following the existing best, absorbing that very best, and then going beyond to express yourself differently, to surpass everyone in your pathbreaking innovation? Being able to surpass existing best practices by bringing in your own originality on top of them, you will create your "Surpass Practice." I call this the Surpassmark that competitors will vie to have.

Avoid basking in your success

Once you become a benchmark, your enterprise obviously becomes iconic, but it's not a given permanent success status in any industry in the current, ever-changing digital world. An enterprise sometimes unmindfully lives in that glory, in that comfort zone, just like Kodak did. They forgot to create discomfort, to watch market happenings seriously, and fell into the Titanic Syndrome of not being alert, considering success to be infallible. Kodak missed the Surpass Practice here. We're familiar with Philips' invention of the tape recorder sound system in the last century. But it was Sony's marketing ingenuity that created a personal, musical, mobile, electronic device Walkman as the benchmark since 1979. Sony reigned, decade after decade, with this outstanding best practice but failed to surpass its own best practice with renovation. The 21st century saw computer science enter entertainment to change the market rule. Apple redefined customer electronics, making iPod a personal pocket music library, an example of Surpassmark. From the 2001 iPod with iTunes, Apple has evolved through versions to iPod Touch, enhancing customer benefit with inside engineering, not merely aesthetics, thus sustaining its Surpassmark.

Filter your learning

To achieve sustainable profitable growth and establish a Surpass Practice, yours has to be a learning enterprise. Cultivate management and operations to continuously absorb two kinds of best practices:

(1) Your own industry's best practices, to benchmark with the finest existing working process
(2) Best practices of other industries, to extract diverse benchmarks that are bubbling the marketplace, adding external newness, becoming leading trends that create society's new habits

Then filter those best practices and go beyond to create your own Surpass Practice.

When you redefine your own working process and customer delivery, the enterprise has to change to leap forward beyond the best practice. The result will create a Surpass Practice, the real plus with exciting distinction that your enterprise can own. Surpass Practices will increase your enterprise salience, make it outstanding, and attract multiple external and internal stakeholders. Such a seamless process can grow the enterprise harmoniously by absorbing and internalizing all relevant emerging external factors year after year. Most importantly, Surpassmark will become the reference your competitors will covet.

I've heard a lot about best practice, benchmark, and even the concept of next practice, but in my experience, unless that learning transcends to Surpass Practice which can stand for Surpassmark, you remain a me-too. So my proposition to enterprises, irrespective of their industry or size, is to learn best practices but deliver Surpass Practices to become the reference point through Surpassmark.

Benchmark to Surpassmark

Incredible quality of customer understanding will take you to the summit of business. When your product or service better resolves the customer's purpose by increasing tangible benefit with exciting distinction, your customer will pay extra. Only then will your bottom line grow. Surpass Practice applies both at individual and enterprise levels in today's world of banality.

Urge to build capability

To contribute to a company's premium earning, mere cost cutting and standardization will not work. No matter which continent your business is in, China Bazaars are proliferating the world with low-cost products in every domain. Digitization helps in standardizing quality, ease of use, and operating cost reduction. But to really add value in customer delivery and raise business profitability, you must have to create the Surpassmark quality standard. That's done through the voluntary urge of people in your enterprise toward capability building.

Here's a terrific example of an individual's deliberate urge to build capability. Fifty years ago, a young African-American, a minority community in society, had the guts to dream of becoming the greatest in the world. He overstretched himself by running 6 km every day. Having fixed a 4-km fitness schedule his coach reprimanded him for running more. With steely conviction he told his coach the extra kilometers were to fulfill his ambition, so nobody can block his exalted goal. This is the story of Cassius Clay who became Mohammad Ali, the world's No. 1 heavyweight champion (boxing era 1960–1981). He achieved Surpassmark by building his capability, the most important active agent in human life.

Overexposing street smartness

In India, managers tend to hide capability but overexpose good spoken English and educational degrees from so-called high-end MBA and engineering institutes. They'd rather not discuss their own function, but point out defective practice in others. Industry leaders lend an ear to street-smart subordinates who can express themselves, often promoting them over those who have strong capability. This prevalent, unhealthy HR practice rarely takes into consideration the kind of delivery capability customers positively talk about. Unfortunately, this attitude of mistakenly valuing extroverts over real performers results in not building up capability in management and operation levels.

An enterprise aiming for Surpass Practice has to train people to develop competence without complacency to adopt the new. At all levels, people must have a high level of common understanding. I've regretfully experienced the reverse when some clients have advised me to lower training levels explaining mismatch with their people's capability. Tailoring a training process to a lower level of capability actually defeats its very purpose; the enterprise pulls itself down instead of up.

A pertinent example of discounting capability building is India's IT business that's focused on the demand-led market. Global clients need low-cost services, so Indian IT companies just throw in the net to catch fish without much effort. That's probably why IT service has linear growth. There's no capex investment to get an order, just hire more people to get growth and profitability.

Manpower size counts, as do high profitability and share market results. Initially, India's engineering cream from IITs were hired; now basic graduates are adequate, making it evident that the skill level required is not high. No Tier-1 Indian-IT company has tried to make an outstanding difference by creating global Surpassmark, save for one that's galloping up right now.

An outstanding example

In 2010, while on some global research across four continents interacting with top business leaders of billion-plus-dollar companies, I found Cognizant, an American-Indian company, had become a buzz among outsourcing customers and industry advisors. Whether or not they worked with Cognizant, they appreciated that Cognizant had invested to understand a client's future requirement as per its specific industry, helped shape the client's business strategy, and also did so during recession time. They commented that Cognizant's key client-facing personnel were of higher standard and generally younger than other India- IT service providers. This would mean that Cognizant invested in developing people capability too. When I shared this point with Indian IT biggies and predicted Cognizant's quick growth, everybody said it was a smaller company. But that's exactly what happened. In 2013, Cognizant become number two after Tata Consultancy Services (TCS).

Cognizant's ascent just proves that a highly demand-led market such as IT service can be transformed to surpass in value if the process of handling customers and delivering outstanding customer value can become perpetual. This is Cognizant's corporate Surpass Practice leading to exceptional business result among Indian competitors. I'm sure Cognizant will encounter the global biggies to establish that this Surpass Practice can become their Surpassmark worldwide.

Everything boils down to how differently from competitors an enterprise understands customers. There's a scale of four levels: basic, average, superior, and unbeatable, to understand customer requirements. Every enterprise can make the choice. To establish the market reputation of being a high-value business, look at the unbeatable level of delivery. It will automatically impose that your employees have a high level of business understanding and delivery capability. Such capability does not appear on waving a magic wand. The whole enterprise has to first recognize its necessity, accept, and adhere to the change required to live up to the unbeatable platform. Willingness of the workforce is clearly essential for raising the learning curve.

Excellence is a habit

When people reflect on my Surpassmark examples for individuals—of Charlie Chaplin in entertainment or Mohammad Ali in sports—they enjoy their delivery capability. The crux of delivery excellence for an enterprise is such Surpass Practice that establishes Surpassmark.

What is the perceptible code of Surpass Practice? (See Figure E.1.) It's the working process of an enterprise that repeatedly delivers surpass value that's perceived by customers in the competitive environment. That means employees have such a high level of common understanding that they empower themselves to reject delivery that does not meet the Surpassmark. As Greek philosopher and scientist Aristotle, who lived during 384–322 BC, said, "You are what you repeatedly do. Excellence is not an event, it is a habit."

Figure E.1   How Surpass Practice and Surpassmark Can Be Created

Absorbing best practices to create **Surpass Practice** of the enterprise

Varied industries best practices & benchmark

LEARNING ENTERPRISE

Own working process redefined

Invent Surpass practices & own them

It increases the brand's salience to become outstanding

It becomes the industry **Surpassmark**

High attraction for multiple outside and inside stakeholders

This is the **Surpassmark**. The defined **Surpass Practice** of an enterprise becomes like a process & grows the enterprise harmoniously by absorbing all external factors year after year

Invent Surpass practices & own them

Absorbing & internalizing relevant external factors

Source: Author's own.

Postface

After so many years of absence from India, I have discovered there is no language, politics, and culture that connects all Indians across the length and breadth of North, South, East, and West. It is only the jalebi that is identified everywhere and connects everyone without having any complacency. The jalebi has an upside of being popular with everyone, but its downside is equally significant. Especially in North India, it aptly describes a googly, a spanner in the works. Of course, when likened to business, if the ingredients, fermentation, or the cook's craftsmanship is not good, it will have an unappealing taste and shape, just like a business with bad planning or ineffective employees which will not succeed.

The positive part of the jalebi is that its customer touch points, visible points, and eating points have outstanding ecstasy. In the same way, unless all touch points of a selling proposition have ecstasy, it will be a downside in customer connect. Customers will never return. With ecstasy in every bite, customers will zero in like bees to honey. Creating ecstasy is a very delicate operation like correct jalebi-making. It has to be just right in taste and texture, continuously deliver the same experience and be predictable every time. That is how every product and service should be too. If you add unnecessary layer after layer in your selling proposition without going to the crux of its core element, you will never be straightforward. Just like the negative connotation of the jalebi is a strategic poke.